REVELATIONS IN BLUE

JON YOUNGBLOOD

Copyright © 2025 Jon Youngblood

All rights reserved.

No part of this publication may be reproduced, distributed, or transmitted in any form or by any means, including photocopying, recording, or other electronic or mechanical methods, without the prior written permission of the publisher, except as permitted by U.S. copyright law.

The story, all names, characters, and incidents portrayed in this production are fictitious. No identification with actual persons (living or deceased), places, buildings, and products is intended or should be inferred.

Contents

CHAPTER 1   MONDAY, DAY ONE 1

CHAPTER 2   TUESDAY, DAY TWO 39

CHAPTER 3   THE ANTAGONIST 59

CHAPTER 4   WEDNESDAY, DAY THREE 65

CHAPTER 5   THURSDAY, DAY FOUR 79

CHAPTER 6   FRIDAY, DAY FIVE 93

CHAPTER 7   SATURDAY, DAY SIX 102

CHAPTER 8   THE HIATUS, DAY SEVEN 118

CHAPTER 9   WEEK TWO 139

CHAPTER 10 THE LIAISON 158

CHAPTER 11 WEEK THREE 176

CHAPTER 12 THE BROTHERHOOD OF MAN 192

CHAPTER 13 TYRONE'S REGRET 199

CHAPTER 14   THE FIX 203

CHAPTER 15   THE PARENTS 212

CHAPTER 16   THE ALIENS 220

CHAPTER 17   DEATH WITHOUT DIGNITY 236

CHAPTER 18   MAN WITH A GUN 255

CHAPTER 19   NARROWING THE GAP 270

CHAPTER 20   BUSTED 277

CHAPTER 21   THE PLAN 283

CHAPTER 22   THE PRELUDE 293

CHAPTER 23   THE BEGINNING OF THE END 313

CHAPTER 24   THE RENEWAL 323

CHAPTER 25   TAWNYA'S MUSE 331

CHAPTER 26   THE END OF THE BEGINNING 345

CHAPTER 1

MONDAY, DAY ONE

Dan Reynolds' internal alarm went off thirty seconds before his external one. He raised his head slightly to see the time on the digital clock on the nightstand—5:59 a.m. He laid his head back down, shut his eyes, and waited with his usual anticipation for the soulful sounds of Nancy Wilson to emanate from the mini stereo on the shelf at the foot of his bed.

The only thing his father had bequeathed to him that Reynolds truly valued was an extensive collection of jazz, blues, and R&B vinyl LPs, which included every album that Nancy Wilson had ever recorded. Reynolds had transferred these albums to CDs, which he kept loaded in his stereo.

At precisely 6:00 a.m., he heard the almost imperceptible click of the stereo turning on, and moments later, the clear, sweet sounds of Nancy as she began to croon, "You can have him, I don't want him, he's not worth fighting for."

As he rolled over onto his back, he became aware of what had become a regular morning occurrence—a rock-hard erection. As he disentangled his stiff member from the sheets, a thought crossed his mind for perhaps the thousandth time: *If I could ever find a woman who was as beautiful, sensual, and stimulating as Nancy Wilson's voice, maybe I wouldn't wake up every morning with a hard-on—or at least I could put it to good use.*

2 REVELATIONS IN BLUE

As he lay there, reveling in the music, he became aware of another recurring sensation—the urgent need to pee. He fought it for several minutes, then threw back the covers and followed his erect penis to the bathroom where he briefly considered using his teenage tactic of standing back from the toilet and trying to gauge the trajectory of his stream so that it hit the bowl. Then his thirty-two-year-old brain kicked in, and he remembered who had to clean the bathroom. He decided to pee sitting down and gingerly placed the boner inside the bowl as he bent forward at the waist and squatted. It took a while, but he eventually relaxed enough to be able to bleed his bloated bladder. As usual, the erection eroded as his bladder voided.

Reynolds pulled on the cutoff sweatpants and sleeveless sweatshirt hanging on the bathroom hook and headed for the kitchen, where he was greeted by the stimulating aroma of freshly brewed coffee. *Technology is a wonderful thing*, he thought, as he considered how nice it was to be able to set the automatic Grind and Brew coffee maker so that a pot of freshly ground coffee was ready for him as soon as he got out of bed. He filled the oversized stoneware mug he had bought years ago at an "Art in the Park" event in Boise and then nuked it in the microwave for a minute to get it piping hot. As he took a sip of the scalding brew, his mind returned to the sounds of Nancy Wilson still playing in the bedroom, and another thought replayed in his head: *Coffee is like women—best when they're hot and black*.

He took the steaming cup of coffee and went out onto the lanai of his third-story apartment, which overlooked Green Lake two blocks away. The sky had taken on a pinkish glow as the sun peeked over the Cascade Mountains to the east. Once settled into the cushioned chaise longue on the lanai, Reynolds carefully sipped the fiery-hot joe, savoring the slightly bitter taste as it rolled across his tongue and burned its way down his throat.

Then, as if struck by a charging bull, the realization hit him: *Shit, this is it, my first day on the job as a member of Seattle's finest.* His mind went back to the arduous journey he had taken to get to this day, beginning at age seventeen when he had first decided he was going to redeem the family name by becoming the kind of cop his father had never been. It was the summer just before he began his senior year of high school. Then 9/11 occurred, and his priorities changed. He had been instantly consumed with a burning desire to join the military and enter the fight. He began making the rounds of the various military branches' offices to see what they offered and found himself strongly leaning toward the Marines, at least until he walked into the Air Force recruiting office. The recruiter had taken one look at his well-conditioned, 6'4" frame and suggested that he might want to consider applying to be a Special Ops pararescue jumper. It hadn't taken much convincing after the recruiter had described the mission of a "PJ," enshrined in their motto, "That Others May Live." Being able to save the lives of wounded soldiers, sailors, and airmen sounded much more appealing to his humanitarian sensibilities than killing a bunch of people who were, after all, just fighting to remove the infidels from their territory and to uphold their deeply held beliefs—no matter how misguided those beliefs might be.

Then, the recruiter gave him the bad news. To qualify for PJ school, he had to be eighteen- years-old with a high school diploma or GED, plus fifteen college credits. Also, because the training required to become a PJ lasted more than two years and cost upwards of $250,000, it would require a minimum enlistment of six years. However, the more Reynolds researched the training and mission of the PJs, the more driven he was to do it.

He began a rigorous physical training regimen, which raised his already sports-conditioned body to a peak of fitness. He signed up for two voluntary courses the following summer—a seven-day pararescue and survival orientation course and a ten-day advanced course. He also arranged to take two dual-credit courses in the last semester of his senior year, as a start toward the college credits he would need to qualify. He enrolled in Boise State University after graduating high school in May and completed two summer classes before starting full-time in September. He'd been able to finish off the required fifteen credits in a single semester.

Against his mother's wishes, he enlisted in the Air Force in January 2003 and was shipped to basic training at Lackland Air Force Base in San Antonio, Texas. After basic, he was assigned to the weeklong Pararescue Selection Course, which required him to complete the rigorous Physical Ability and Stamina Course. After his acceptance came the additional months of training to prepare him to perform rescue operations in any physical environment—from the battlefield, to the middle of the ocean, to the most remote mountaintop.

After graduating from PJ training at the top of his class in May 2005, Reynolds was assigned to Kadena Air Base in Okinawa for a two-year tour. It was there that he began to practice Aikido, and there that he met Yoshi at his dojo and fell in love for the first time. Then came the surge in 2007 and his first deployment to Iraq, where he came face-to-face with death and dismemberment on almost a daily basis. His initial enlistment expired in December 2008, but he chose to extend for a year to hopefully finish the mission. Then came January 2009 and President Obama's announcement of a buildup in Afghanistan to try to bring that war to a close. He was reassigned to Afghanistan for a year-long deployment. It was during that tour that he began to become disillusioned by the seeming futility of US efforts to defeat the tenacious Taliban and the intransigent Iraqi insurgents. He decided to get out and pursue his initial dream of being a police officer. He was discharged in December 2009 and used his GI Bill to attend Washington State University, where he spent the next four and a half years completing a bachelor's, then a master's degree in criminal justice and criminology, attending school year-round.

Finally, in May 2015, at the age of thirty-one, he loaded his Jeep Wrangler with all his worldly possessions and made the excursion from Pullman, Washington, to Seattle. He lived with his aunt and uncle that summer but spent most of his time backpacking in the Cascades and Olympic Mountains. In September, he applied to the Seattle Police Department. It took him three months to complete the testing process and get hired. He had been number five on the final list out of over a thousand applicants who had initially taken the test, but he still had to wait until they hired twelve other people: Two Black males and a Black female, four Caucasian women and an Asian man from way down on the list, plus the four white guys who were ahead of him.

Next came five and a half months in the Police Academy. They tried to make out that the academy was tough, but after PJ training in the Air Force, for Reynolds, it was a piece of cake. They threw a lot of material at him, but he had always been good at learning and retaining information, and he spent the time necessary to do it. The physical training, self-defense, and weapons training were minimal compared to what he had gone through in the military. He graduated number one in his class but knew that would be meaningless to the old-timers he would soon be working with.

And it was all to get to this day—the day he officially began his career as a sworn officer in the Seattle Police Department. His stomach began to churn slightly, and his heart raced as he considered the prospects of what that career might bring.

Time to start the day, he thought, as he drained the last dregs of the coffee from his cup. He turned off the stereo in the bedroom, inserted his iPod into the receiver in the living room and tuned it to his meditation music, then assumed a lotus position on the floor and began to silently voice his mantra in his head, *Lokah samastah sukhino bhavantu*. After fifteen minutes, his body had calmed, his mind had cleared, and he was ready to begin his morning Hatha yoga routine. As he moved through the various asanas, he focused on relaxing and stretching the long, lean muscles he had spent so many years building and conditioning. Most people would not guess that his 6'4" frame weighed in at 240 pounds. With only ten percent body fat, he did not look that heavy.

As he assumed his final position, the coffee and stretching began to have their usual effect—the need for a bowel movement. He again proceeded to the bathroom, cleansed his colon, and then changed into his running shorts, singlet, and shoes. He felt relaxed and centered as he descended the stairs to the street outside his apartment building. He focused his mind on his breathing as he began his warm-up walk down to Green Lake. After crossing the street to the park, he moved into a slow jog as his feet hit the grass. By the time he reached the asphalt path around the lake, he was beginning to find his running rhythm and synchronize his breathing to his stride. After half a mile, he was running smoothly and almost effortlessly.

He allowed his senses to fully experience the fresh smell of the morning air, the cool breeze coming off the water, and the warmth of the sun, which had long since crested the Cascades. It was three miles around the lake, and he maintained this almost meditative state as he completed two laps in less than forty minutes. He cooled down as he walked back to the apartment and then went through his after-run stretching routine in the front room. Finally, he rewarded himself for his diligence and dedication by pouring himself another cup of coffee and crawling into his recliner to watch the Morning News on MSNBC.

The pangs in his stomach reminded him that it was time for breakfast. He fixed his usual morning repast—a glass of orange juice, two thick slices of his own, home-baked whole wheat bread with flax and oatmeal, and a bowl of the organic cereal he bought at the farmer's market, covered with a mix of fresh blueberries and blackberries. After a third cup of coffee, he hit the shower, shaved, brushed his teeth, and ran a brush over his short, wiry black hair, still styled in the brush cut he had maintained in the military. He stepped back from the bathroom counter and surveyed the image in the mirror—the steely blue eyes, the strong, dimpled chin, the coarse black chest hair, the lean, hard body—and thought, *I'm ready for this. Let's do it.*

He pulled on his padded biking underwear, his baggy mountain biking shorts, and a jersey. Then he packed a pair of black boot socks, a clean white T-shirt, and a pair of boxer briefs, along with a stick of deodorant, into his bicycle rack pack. He paused to think, *what else do I need? Oh shit, my gun and badge.* He went to the bedroom nightstand, where he kept the department-issued 9 mm Glock 19 encased in the leather shoulder holster he had just bought. He slipped on the holster, looked in the mirror, and waited for a visceral reaction. It didn't come. Eight years in the military and three years of combat experience had deadened any fascination with weapons he may ever have had. They were simply tools of the trade, to be used only when the need demanded. He did, however, feel a slight sense of regret that he was going to have to carry this instrument of death whenever he went out in public for the next twenty-five years or so. He got his badge case from the top of the dresser and slipped it into the pocket on the back of his jersey.

Finally, he donned a pair of ankle socks and his biking shoes, pulled on a light, loose-fitting anorak to cover the weapon, strapped on his helmet, pulled on his biking gloves, and took his Trek touring bike down from the stand in the living room. He paused briefly at the door to go through a mental checklist to see if there was anything else he needed. *No. Let's roll.*

Reynolds pushed the Trek out the door and down the hall to the exterior doors, then hefted the crossbar over his shoulder and skipped down the three flights of stairs to the street. It was a beautiful, clear, warm morning—which, he had learned, was a rare event in Seattle in May—and he hoped this was an auspicious omen for his future as a cop. At the bottom of the stairs, he mounted the bike and again headed down toward Green Lake. The traffic was relatively light as he turned onto East Green Lake Way and began skirting around the south end of this beautiful body of water. *Thank*

God for day watch, he thought; *not having roll call until 11:30 a.m. is perfect. Plenty of time to run, work out, eat a leisurely breakfast, and then avoid the peak traffic going into town.*

He negotiated the lesser arterials and back streets until he had to cross the Aurora Bridge to reach the west side of Lake Union. As he cruised down Westlake Avenue, he looked across at the houseboats on the eastern shore and made a silent note to himself: *On my first days off, I'm going to come down here and see about renting one of those. How cool would it be to be able to get up in the morning and go sculling on the "Cut"? I might even have to invest in a sailboat.* Riding his bike always seemed to trigger his imagination, and his spirits soared as he fantasized about living on the water, with direct access to both Lake Washington and the Puget Sound.

In less than thirty minutes he was riding down Fourth Avenue, approaching Cherry Street and the Public Safety Building. He turned onto the sidewalk, climbed the steep ascent toward Fifth Avenue, and swung into the entrance of the subterranean police parking garage. As he rode past the sporadically parked squad cars, his attention was drawn to a red stain smeared on the front fender of an otherwise spotless white patrol car.

"Take your fuckin' hands off me, you motherfuckin' pig bastards!"

The statement was punctuated moments later by the hollow sound of a head striking concrete and a muffled moan. Reynolds glanced up and saw two officers picking a handcuffed man up off the floor.

"Jesus, partner, I was just trying to accommodate the man by taking my hands off him and look what he does—falls right on his Goddamned head. Now he's probably going to yell police brutality," one of the officers said.

"Yeah, you just can't please these assholes anymore," came his partner's reply.

The man kept trying to twist out of their grasp and kick the officers, one of whom kept repeating, "Take it easy, partner, you're going to be home in just a minute." As Reynolds pulled alongside them, the man turned enough so that he could see his face. His long, stringy, graying hair was disheveled and matted with blood that was oozing from gashes on both the side and the back of his head. He was unshaven, and a trickle of blood had run down his face and picked its way through the course stubble on his chin. His clothing was filthy beyond belief, and the front of his old tweed sport coat was stained with vomitus, blood, and spilled wine—the wretched odor of which reached Reynolds twenty feet away. The patrolmen half-pushed, half-dragged the old drunk to the jail elevator.

Reynolds parked his bike in the corner of the garage, wound the cable lock through the wheels and frame, and headed toward the locker room. He walked down the aisle between double tiers of gray metal lockers until he came to number 732, into which he inserted the key he had been issued the previous week.

A sudden chill ran down his spine, and he felt a slight clamminess on his palms and a curious lightness in the pit of his stomach. He opened the locker and stared at the three blue uniforms hanging neatly inside, and the duty belt suspended from the door, weighed down with the tools of his new trade—handcuffs, PR24 nightstick, flashlight, radio holder, Taser, and the empty holster into which he would place his new Glock.

Reynolds had seen his share of death in Iraq and Afghanistan and had been responsible for more than a few dead Taliban and Iraqi insurgents. He had experienced the anguish that came with taking a human life, and he hoped he would never have to fire that weapon in anger, but he also knew that he could do so if necessary. It scared him to think how many of his fellow recruits in the academy had seemed so anxious to "blow some asshole away."

As he gazed at the spotless new uniforms, his mind went back to the incident he had just witnessed in the garage, and it bemused him to think that not once in his anticipation and preparation for this job had he considered the eventuality of having to manhandle a foul-mouthed, foul-smelling drunk, and for the first time he recognized that this might be a regular part of his duties. His concerns had been more along the lines of how to single-handedly take down a stick-up man, or having to go into a dark warehouse in search of a burglar, or taking on several big bikers in a bar fight. Reynolds' skin crawled, and his stomach churned slightly as he considered the prospect of having to stick his hands into the urine-soaked pants of an old wino to remove his personal effects at booking. *So, this is what I have to look forward to*, he thought, *five years of college so I can wrestle old drunks off the street.*

Reality was setting in; he was a cop now. He sat on the bench in front of his locker and thought back again to how long he had waited for this moment. He remembered how proud he had been as a child when his dad would come home from work in his uniform, and his friends would beg him to tell them about all his dad's exploits: "Did your dad ever shoot anyone?" "Has he ever caught a robber?" He had made up lots of stories to impress them and had dreamed about being a cop himself someday. Then he recalled the embarrassment and humiliation he had felt when his dad was suspended for thirty days and demoted from detective back to patrolman after wrecking an unmarked car while driving drunk on duty. It was in all the papers, and Reynolds had caught hell at school for weeks.

He had kind of given up on the idea of being a cop until the final blow came. He remembered the phone call his mother had received from his dad's old partner. He remembered the look on her face when she heard that he had been killed driving home from a bar at two in the morning with some floozy in the car.

Even though his parents had been divorced for several years—the result of his dad's incessant philandering—Reynolds' mom had never gotten over him. She had moved back to Boise to get away, but her life had essentially ended after the divorce. Never an outgoing woman, she became a virtual recluse. Other than going to work, she never left the house except to buy groceries and other necessities. She spent her time reading and watching TV. She had no friends, and Reynolds was her only comfort, support, and joy. She had reveled in his accomplishments as an athlete and in his 3.8 GPA at school, but after his dad's death, she lost interest even in her son. She went into a severe depression and was unable to work. Luckily, she was still the beneficiary on his dad's retirement fund and insurance, and she received a large enough settlement to get by for a while. She hung on until Reynolds graduated from high school and joined the Air Force, then decided to end it all. Tears welled up in his eyes as Reynolds recalled the day during basic training that he'd been called into the first sergeant's office and told that she had been found lying in bed with a bottle of Prozac sitting empty on the nightstand.

But her death was not what had clinched Reynolds' decision to become a cop. It had been the front-page article in the *Seattle Post-Intelligencer* that his dad's partner had sent describing his father as a "dirty cop" with an alcohol problem, who had been disciplined several times for excessive use of force and drinking on the job, and who had also been implicated in a graft scheme involving backroom gambling operations in downtown bars. His dad had spent his last few years on the job walking a beat on First Avenue and had apparently supplemented his income shaking down bar owners. Reynolds had made an immediate decision after reading the article that he would become a cop and redeem the family name in the Seattle Police Department.

This disturbing reminiscence was interrupted by the raucous banter of a group of policemen entering the locker room. Reynolds took a deep breath, stood up, and began to don the neatly pressed uniform of Seattle's finest—navy-blue long-sleeved shirt, Kevlar protective vest, navy-blue pants, and the black leather-and-nylon lightweight combat boots that he had spit-shined to a mirror finish two days earlier, before bringing his uniforms and equipment to the precinct. He hung the basket-weave leather duty belt around his waist, secured the keepers, strapped the Glock in its holster, slid the PR24 into its ring on his belt, squared the eight-point police cap on his head, and walked to the full-length mirror to view the finished product. He had to admit, he looked pretty damned official. The uniform complimented his athletic physique, and at thirty-two years old, he did not look like a rookie right out of the academy. His gaze drifted to the bright and shiny badge on his chest. It didn't feel at all heavy like he was told it would. *Hell, I guess I'm as ready as I'll ever be*, he thought and headed for the assembly room.

As Reynolds entered the large room where roll call was held, his attention was first drawn to the stacks of bulletins on the counter inside the door. He started to take one from each stack—Daily Bulletin, Special Orders, General Orders, Crime Analysis Bulletin. Above the counter, he noticed numerous wooden cubbyholes labeled alphabetically. He reflexively checked the one labeled "R" but found nothing with his name on it.

He surveyed the rest of the room. There was a podium at the front, faced by echelons of small desks. Clipboards hung from hooks along one wall. He wandered over to look at them and found they contained crime reports from the various sectors. Next to them were the inevitable FBI Ten Most Wanted posters, which he perused carefully. He took a desk near the back of the briefing room and read through each of the information sheets. *I should probably save these for future reference*, he thought, so he tucked them away inside the new aluminum attaché case that he had bought to carry his gear and reports. He looked around the room and discovered that he was the only one there, which unnerved him a little until he looked at the clock and found he still had a half-hour until roll call. *Apparently, most of these guys do not follow the advice they gave us in the academy*, he thought, remembering the admonition to get to work in plenty of time to read the crime reports and the latest bulletins. He pulled down the "Robbery" clipboard for the Headquarters precinct, went over to his desk, and began leafing through the police reports.

"You'll be writing a lot of those if you stick around long enough." Reynolds looked up to see a pair of very cool blue eyes staring down at him from a weathered face, capped by one of the few flattop haircuts he'd seen in recent years. The face was perched on a stocky, bear-like, neckless body that appeared solid and strong despite its girth. The face had a look of complete equanimity despite the lines that were etched in the forehead and around the eyes and the venous complexion. Reynold's attention was drawn back to those eyes, which conveyed beyond a doubt that they had seen a lot of life and perhaps their share of death in their time on earth.

"You *Dan* Reynolds?" the man said as he looked at the name tag.

"Yes, *sir*," Reynolds responded, with an emphasis on the "sir" as he reverted to his military mode. A hint of a smile crossed the man's face.

"Don't 'sir' me; I'm just a patrolman like you. Name's Michael Donnelly. I've been assigned as your field training officer, so it looks like we'll be working together for the next six months or so."

Reynolds stood and, resisting the momentary impulse to salute, instead stuck out his right hand. "Glad to meet you, Officer Donnelly."

"Most people just call me 'Mick,'" the patrolman replied, "you might as well too. By the way, you can put your kit there away; I've got everything we'll need in mine. You think you can remember everything you read in those reports?"

Reynolds tried to think of what he had just read, but his mind was blank. "I can't remember a damn thing," he said. "Guess I'm a little amped up over finally getting to work as a police officer."

"Just as well," Donnelly replied, "I can never remember anything by just reading it either, so I usually take notes on the pertinent stuff. Come on down to Crime Analysis, and I'll show you the boards."

Reynolds followed Donnelly down the hall to the Crime Analysis Unit, where he pointed out the pin maps of the city, with each map showing the locations of a specific type of crime.

"This room is your reference library," Donnelly said. "Everything you need to know is hanging on these walls. You just have to dig it out. The officers assigned to this unit do a daily crime summary, which we can pull up on the computer, but it's not in-depth enough for me. So, I usually spend some time in here before shift getting information specific to my sector."

Donnelly went to the burglary map and, after noting where the concentrations of pins were, took down the clipboard of crime reports that was hanging beside it. He took it to a desk and began going through the most recent, making a dot on his own map of his district for each crime and noting any suspect or vehicle descriptions, times of offenses, methods of entry, types of items taken, and any other pertinent information. After he had finished with the residence burglary board, he did the same with the commercial burglary, robbery, sex crimes, auto theft, and larceny boards.

"I understand you've been in the military, Dan?" Donnelly said.

"Seven years," Reynolds responded.

"Well, this job is like fighting a war. As Sun Tzu said in *The Art of War*, 'Know your enemy.' You've got to hit the street armed with as much information as you can to be effective. Too many guys here don't really give a shit; they're just here for the paycheck, the benefits, and a retirement. But if you want to be a good cop, you'll spend a lot of time in this room." Donnelly glanced up at the clock on the wall. "Time for roll call," he said as he headed out the door.

They got back to the assembly room just as a rotund old sergeant with bifocals perched precariously on his nose yelled, "Take a seat." The sergeant was a perfect caricature of an old Irish cop—maybe 5'10", 250 pounds, short-cropped graying hair with a bald spot on top. His jowls and chin hung in folds on his face, which had the ruddy, veiny look of a heavy drinker. His uniform was form-fitted, or perhaps one could say his form fit the uniform. A massive gut put a definite strain on the gold buttons holding his shirt together, and his gun belt was almost lost beneath his girth.

Reynolds started to take a seat next to Donnelly in the front row but was confronted by a gruff-looking old-timer, whose look told him that he was taking his seat. He moved to the back row and found an empty desk.

There was a flurry of comic asides and grab-assing among the officers as they took their seats, which ended when the sergeant yelled the first name: "Williams."

"Yo." came the reply.

"Butler."

"Here."

"Work Two-David-One with Williams. Amundson."

"Here."

"Work Two-David-Two. Gominski."

"Yo."

"Your own."

Reynolds felt a nervous anticipation building as he waited for his name to be called. He hoped to God his voice wouldn't crack or choke up in front of these men on his first day, but then comforted himself with the knowledge that he had been through a thousand roll calls before. He swallowed to wet his throat and breathed deeply. Finally, he heard his name and responded with a strong "Here, Sergeant," again reflexively reverting to his military training.

"Work Two-George-Three with Donnelly. He'll be your FTO," the sergeant replied. After finishing reading the roll call, the sergeant gave out a car and suspect description of a guy who had been knocking over some convenience stores in the area. Then he said, "For the benefit of the new men starting today and especially for you old-timers, we're going to have a little inspection. Fall in at the back of the room." A chorus of grumbling ensued as the officers reluctantly got up from their desks and formed three ranks at the back of the room. "Attention!" the sergeant yelled out. At that, a lieutenant—the shift commander—who had been standing in the back of the room came forward and stood beside the sergeant. "Prepare for inspection!" the sergeant yelled. Reynolds, who had been through this drill innumerable times in the military and police academy, stood fast in the back row. But most of the officers, who obviously did not do this very often, had to look around and take cues from the few who knew what they were doing. Finally, the first rank figured out they needed to take two steps forward and the second rank one step forward.

The sergeant and lieutenant then began a tour down the front rank, eyeing each man in turn. They stopped in front of one man, and the lieutenant ordered, "Let me see your weapon." The officer drew the semi-automatic from its holster, ejected the magazine, locked the slide to the rear, and handed both the pistol and the magazine to the lieutenant, who checked the bore for cleanliness and the ammo to make sure they didn't have mold on them, then handed them back.

They continued until they came to a stop in front of Reynolds. "Let me see your handcuffs," the lieutenant ordered. Reynolds had to think for a moment to remember which side he kept the handcuffs on but then fumbled with his left hand and managed to pull the cuffs from their case on the back of his duty belt. He handed them to the lieutenant, who worked the revolving arm a couple of times and handed them back. "They're too tight," he said. "Put some graphite on them."

"Yes, sir," Reynolds responded in his best military manner, and the two moved on. When they had finished, the sergeant and lieutenant returned to the front of the ranks. "You're looking pretty good, men," the lieutenant said dispassionately. "Keep up the good work." Then he turned on his heel and left the room. "Dismissed!" yelled the sergeant. "Have a safe day."

Donnelly picked up an extra-large attaché case from the bench on the side of the room and, with Reynolds falling in tow, headed for the patrol clerks' office where he checked out a radio and got the keys to their patrol car, noting where it was parked. "Put your case away while I check out a shotgun and AR-15 from Property," Donnelly said. "And don't forget your flashlight; it's probably the most important tool you have in this job. I'll meet you at the car."

When Reynolds got to the car, Donnelly beckoned him back to the trunk, where he was busy checking their equipment. "As long as you're working with me, you'll do this every day," he said as he physically checked the first-aid kit for missing items, checked the fire extinguisher to make sure it was fully charged, and made sure he had two clean blankets and that the respirator was in good condition. Then he pulled the fingerprint kit and checked to make sure it had powder, tape, slide cards, and a serviceable brush. "I carry my own fingerprint kit, so I don't worry too much about this one," he said, "but if you're on your own, be sure and check it. They teach you how to function check those weapons in the academy?"

"Yes, sir," replied Reynolds.

"Then that's going to be your job whenever you're riding, which you will be for a while," Donnelly answered.

Donnelly handed Reynolds the Remington Model 870 shotgun and AR-15 semi-automatic rifle. He took them to the clearing barrel in the corner of the garage. Beginning with the shotgun, he first ejected the three rounds of 00 buckshot and one slug round from the magazine and went through the function check he had been taught in the academy—slide back the forearm and make sure there are no rounds in the chamber, check the bore, check the ejector spring and firing pin, close the receiver, let the hammer fall, put on the safety, and reload the magazine. He then did the much simpler function check on the AR-15.

When he returned to the car, Donnelly was behind the wheel, adjusting the seat and checking his rear-view mirrors. He pulled a clipboard from the huge attaché case he had placed on the floor of the cruiser. On the clipboard was a steno pad turned to a blank page. He filled out the top of the pad with the date, Reynolds' name, the vehicle number, and the beat number, along with a brief description of the weather. Then he took a blank patrol log from the case and filled in the heading information, which somewhat duplicated what he had written on the steno pad.

When he was done, he fired up the engine and pulled slowly out of the dim garage onto the brightly sunlit street. Reynolds noticed that they were about the last car to leave. As if reading his mind, Donnelly said, "Most of these guys get so lax that they just jump in their cars and head for their favorite coffee spot when they hit the street. But the time will come, at some point in your career, when you'll need every item of equipment in this car, and unless you check it every day, that will be just the time when it isn't there or isn't working. So, as long as you're working with me, we go through this procedure every day, all right?"

"You got it," Reynolds replied, reassured by the conscientiousness that he had heard was sorely lacking in many of the older cops. "If you don't mind my asking, how long have you been on the job?"

"Twenty-five years," Donnelly replied matter-of-factly.

"Aren't you eligible for retirement?" Reynolds asked.

"Yeah, but I'm not ready yet. Don't even know what I would do with myself if I did retire. I'm going to give it another five years," Donnelly responded.

"You spend your whole time in Patrol?"

"No, I worked Traffic and then Motors for five years, then came to Patrol. Worked Patrol for another five years, then spent eight years in Special Squad until they got stat-happy. Been back in Patrol ever since."

"Did you ever try to promote to sergeant?" Reynolds asked.

"Nope, never even took the test," Donnelly replied. "I enjoy doing police work too much to spend my time behind a desk doing paperwork."

"What was the issue in the Special Squad," Reynolds asked, "if I'm not prying?"

Reynolds knew the Special Squad was a plainclothes patrol unit that worked more or less independently within the Patrol Division but also assisted the detective units on stakeouts, undercover assignments, and so on. It was said to be the epitome of police work and he had aspirations of working there himself someday.

"Like I said, they got statistic-conscious," Donnelly answered. "Instead of giving us our head to work the good stuff, they had us busting masturbators in the peep shows and homosexuals propositioning guys in park bathrooms, and other trivial bullshit just to keep the arrest count high. Like everything else in this fucking society—it's quantity over quality every time."

Donnelly pulled the vehicle into the city garage and stopped in front of the gas pumps just as the radio dispatcher began an in-service check of the patrol units.

"Listen up to the radio," Donnelly said, "and when he calls Two-George-Three, tell him we're out at the pumps. We need to clean up after the pigs that had this car last shift." He then got out of the car, picked up some window cleaner, and began cleaning the smoky haze off the inside of the windows. "I wish to Christ they'd outlaw fucking cigarettes," he muttered as he finished the glass, emptied the ashtray, and picked up a couple of butts from the floorboards. He then checked the air pressure in the tires and made sure the attendant checked the oil and fluid levels under the hood, including the window cleaner. When the vehicle was gassed, and he was satisfied with its condition, he drove around to the automatic car wash.

"Nothing looks worse than a filthy police car on the street unless it's an overweight cop in a dirty uniform," he said. "This car is more than just transportation, it's another tool of your trade. You might ask a hell of a lot from it someday, so take care of it. Also, people judge the whole Department by the one officer they may deal with, so take the time to make a good impression. It pays off when we have to ask the citizens for a raise."

Finally, they pulled out of the car wash and headed for the Central District, where George sector was located. Donnelly removed the radio mike from its holder and calmly stated, "Two-George-Three clear, two-man."

"Roger, Two-George-Three," came the reply from Dispatch.

"You familiar with the CD?" Donnelly asked.

"No, never been in this part of the city," Reynolds replied, although he recognized the initials "CD" as referring to the Central District, a low-income, predominantly Black residential and business area located between downtown Seattle and Lake Washington.

"There's a map in my case with our district outlined in red. Get it out and study it. Before I let you drive, you'll need to know every street and alley and what hundred block you're in, not only in our district but in the entire sector. You also need to know the location of all the schools, hospitals, and major businesses, so keep your eyes open and make mental notes. Also, when you're riding, you're the 'book man.' That means you do all the report-writing. See that steno pad on the clipboard? I want you to write down in there every piece of pertinent information that comes over the radio—suspect and vehicle descriptions, stolen cars, wants, whatever—okay?"

Reynolds looked over the previous information Donnelly had written in the steno pad and found that it contained a complete history of every day he had worked, including a brief description of every call he had gone on and all the relevant information from that day. He wondered if every cop was that thorough and meticulous but then thought back to roll call that morning. He had observed most of the officers come in, pick up a couple of bulletins from the stack, fold them up without looking at them, and stick them in the sap pocket of their trousers. He decided he may have gotten very lucky in his FTO assignment, a sentiment he expressed to Donnelly.

"I think I may have gotten the lucky draw in getting you as an FTO," Reynolds said.

"No luck to it," Donnelly responded. "Truth be told, the sergeant allows me to pick who I want to work with, and I picked you."

"Why me?"

"I reviewed your file and was impressed with your background and the fact that you are not a wet-behind-the-ears kid. I'm getting too old to be a babysitter," Donnelly responded, then added, "your size was a plus too."

When they reached the district, Donnelly began a slow, seemingly desultory patrol down the side streets and alleys.

"There's been a lot of daytime burglaries in this area lately, so keep your eyes open for anything suspicious. Look for kids on the street who should be in school, check the back doors and windows of houses, keep your window down, and listen up for any unusual noises like glass breaking or dogs barking excessively."

Reynolds noticed that instead of cruising along the major arterials, Donnelly made a point of crossing them. He began to understand why when, as they approached Empire Way from a side street, he observed an old white Thunderbird shoot by the intersection at an excessive rate of speed. Donnelly immediately floored the squad car, made a rolling stop at the intersection, and pulled into the traffic lane behind the T-bird. He gunned the cruiser until he was about a block behind the speeding car, then leveled off to get a pace that he maintained for two blocks. Then he floored the cruiser again until he was about two car lengths behind the car before he flipped on the emergency lights and gave a short blast on the siren.

"You don't want to turn on your emergency equipment until you're right on their ass," Donnelly cautioned. "Just in case they might want to rabbit."

The driver of the T-bird, a Black male in his thirties, looked in the rearview mirror, and Reynolds could easily read the exclamation— "Motherfucker"—on his lips when he saw the cruiser locked on his tail. The driver pulled to the curb and Donnelly pulled in behind him, positioning the front end of the police car so that it extended out into the traffic lane to protect his approach to the car.

Donnelly grabbed the mike from the dash and advised Dispatch, "This is Two-George-Three on a traffic stop in the 3200 block of Empire Way, Washington license Sam Charles Henry 257." Then, in an aside to Reynolds, "Pull up that vehicle license number on the computer and see what you get."

In a matter of moments, information on the vehicle popped up on the computer screen. "No wants or warrants," Reynolds answered. "It's registered to a James Johnson, 1021 East Van Buren, #21, Seattle."

"Write that down in my notebook," Donnelly directed. "Okay, I want you to take a position on the right side of the car, behind the back window, as I approach. Make sure there is no one hiding in the back seat or front passenger seat. Also, watch the driver's hands— that's what kills you."

Both officers exited the vehicle and slowly approached the car, checking the interior as they went. Donnelly positioned himself just behind the driver's-side window and very calmly and politely said, "Good afternoon, Sir. May I see your driver's license, registration, and insurance certificate please?" The driver, who seemed to be preparing for a confrontation, was taken aback by the display of courtesy. He took his driver's license from his wallet, pulled a registration slip and insurance certificate from a holder on the visor, and handed them to Donnelly.

"Do you know why I stopped you today, sir?" Donnelly asked.

The driver hesitated a minute and then replied, "I may have been driving a little fast."

"Sir, I paced you driving 50 in a 35-mph zone. Please wait in your car," Donnelly advised, and then, turning on his heel, walked back to the police car, motioning to Reynolds to maintain his position behind the car.

Donnelly double-checked the name on the computer for wants and warrants. No warrants were outstanding, but he did find that the man's driver's license had long since expired. So, he typed in the information for a citation, printed off three copies, and returned to the driver's-side window. "Mr. Johnson, are you aware that your driver's license expired six months ago?" he asked.

The man seemed a little flustered and stammered, "Yeah, I just haven't had time to get it renewed."

"Sir, I'm citing you today for driving 50 mph in a 35-miles-per-hour zone and for driving with an expired driver's license. Please sign here. It's not an admission of guilt but merely acknowledging your receipt of the citation."

The man muttered under his breath, "Motherfucking pigs," but, recognizing his guilt and the futility of arguing, signed the citation.

"Sir, here is your copy of the citation. All the instructions are on the back. Please take care of it within fourteen days or a warrant will be issued. Have a good day." Donnelly handed the man his documents back, along with his copy of the ticket, and without waiting for a reply, walked back to the cruiser, with Reynolds following close behind. He filled out the back of the citation with the exact circumstances and quoted the driver's admission that he was speeding and was aware his license was expired. "You never know if these things will go to court or how long it will take so be sure and write down all the pertinent information on the back of the ticket," he said. "Put it in the notebook too."

"You're certainly a lot more polite than any cop who has ever given me a ticket," Reynolds said. "But I was expecting a lecture on obeying the traffic laws."

"You'll learn quickly in this job that you can dictate the outcome of just about any situation with your attitude, tone of voice, and demeanor. I know cops who can turn even the most trivial situation into a donnybrook just by the way they handle it. And lecturing people usually just pisses them off; they know what they did wrong. Twenty-five years is a long time, why make it any harder than it has to be? I've found that by being courteous and civil and treating people with a little respect and allowing them to maintain their dignity, I very rarely have to get physical. Just remember, in this job you're going to be dealing with bad people at their baddest and good people at their worst. They aren't dealing with Dan Reynolds, they're dealing with a uniform wearing a badge and a gun. The uniform will do 90 percent of the job for you if you don't screw it up. Just remember to not take anything personally, treat people the way you would like to be treated, and you won't have to be replacing uniforms nearly as often."

Donnelly stuck the citation between two rubber bands on the visor. "Okay, we've got our ticket out of the way for the day. That will keep the sergeant off our back. Let's see if we can do some police work."

They cruised for some time in a silence broken only by the incessant chatter of the radio traffic, which Reynolds struggled to decipher. He took out his Miscellaneous Incident Report Codes, which noted the disposition of calls-for-service, and tried to match up the various types of calls with their dispositions as the other cars cleared with Dispatch.

"You'll know them all by heart within a month, believe me," Donnelly said. "You'll also get to the point where you can pick out your own call sign and clue into the important information almost subconsciously. Right now, it probably all sounds like a bunch of gobbledygook."

"You got that right," Reynolds responded.

"Where you from?" Donnelly asked.

"I was born in Seattle, but I moved with my mother to Boise, Idaho, after my parents divorced when I was in junior high school."

"What made you decide to become a cop?" Donnelly queried.

Reynolds hesitated, then replied, "My dad was a cop."

"Here in Seattle?" Donnelly asked.

"Yeah," Reynolds responded, not really wanting to discuss his father.

"I remember a cop named Reynolds. Got killed in a car wreck," Donnelly said.

"That was my dad," Reynolds said in a quiet monotone.

Donnelly picked up on the reluctance to discuss his father, so he asked innocuously, "You got that 'cop dynasty' thing going in your family?"

"No," Reynolds answered, but, recognizing that Donnelly had probably heard of his father's reputation, added, "I just felt the need to redeem the Reynolds name on the Seattle PD, and I wanted to accomplish everything my father never did, so I tried to educate myself to the point that I could take advantage of every opportunity."

"So, you know all there is to know about being a cop then?" Donnelly responded somewhat sarcastically.

"Right now, I don't feel like I know a damn thing about being a cop," Reynolds answered.

"Well, let me tell you, you don't," Donnelly responded. "But at least you have the right attitude. This isn't the kind of job they can teach you in college; you've got to learn it on the street. Some people never learn it because some things just can't be taught. You've got to have the right instincts and personality—and those you're born with," Donnelly replied.

"You saying my education was a waste of time?" Reynolds asked defensively.

"No, I wouldn't say that. It will sure as hell come in handy if you want to be promoted," Donnelly responded. "But if you want to be a good cop, keep your eyes and ears open, ask questions when you have them, and don't be in too much of a hurry to start throwing people in jail. Take some time to get the feel of that badge. Keep in mind that this is a serious job, and it demands serious people. There is no other job in the world, with the possible exception of the military, in which a person with a high school education can create so much havoc in other people's lives and cause such major long-term consequences—so it deserves to be taken seriously every minute you're in that uniform or acting in a police capacity. There are three classes of people in this world: the citizens, the crooks, and the cops. The cops comprise a thin blue line between the citizens and the crooks, and it's our job to protect the citizens from the crooks. If you aren't here to do that job, then you shouldn't be here at all."

Reynolds was weighing that advice when he became aware of Donnelly reaching for the mike and responding to a call that he had not even heard.

"Two-George-Three, 19th and East Alder," Donnelly intoned into the mike.

"Two-George-Three, investigate a burglary at 1504 Princeton Avenue. The suspects ran out when the resident came home. Described as two young Black males," the Dispatcher directed.

"Two-George-Three received," Donnelly replied. "Write that down in my notebook—the time, type of call, address, and suspect description," he directed Reynolds.

Donnelly headed toward the call but did not seem to be in a particular hurry, which frustrated Reynolds, who was bristling with anticipation at the thought of his first criminal investigation.

"Shouldn't we get there as quickly as possible?" he asked.

"We'll get there soon enough," Donnelly replied. "Just keep your eyes open on the way in. Look for anyone matching that description or vehicles in a hurry."

They took a circuitous route to the call. Three blocks from the address, Reynolds saw two Black males, aged about fourteen, jive-walking down the sidewalk ahead of them. Donnelly saw them also and immediately got on the radio. "Dispatch, can you contact the complainant on this burglary at 1504 Princeton Avenue and see if they have a clothing description or would be able to recognize the suspects?"

Dispatch came back moments later, "Two-George-Three, negative on being able to identify the suspects. The complainant only caught a glimpse of them running down the alley. She thinks they were wearing dark clothes, and one wore a hoody."

"Well, those kids are wearing dark clothes, and the bigger one has a hoody. Let's have a chat with them. Be ready for them to rabbit when we get out. Slowly move around behind them as I talk with them," Donnelly directed.

They pulled to the curb and both officers exited the car simultaneously. "Gentlemen, can we have a word with you?" Donnelly asked in a calm and matter-of-fact tone as Reynolds began to slowly walk around behind the boys.

"Wha'ch you want? We didn't do nothin'," one of the boys responded.

"Shouldn't you young men be in school?" Donnelly asked.

"We gets out early on Monday," the boy replied. "We just on our way home."

"Where do you go to school?" Donnelly asked.

"Washington Middle School," came the reply.

"How come you're walking back toward the school then?" Donnelly asked.

"We had to take a friend home," the other boy said.

Reynolds noted that both boys were acting very calm, cool, and cocky, but he thought he detected a very distinct acrid odor of nervous perspiration.

"I'm going to ask you to have a seat on the curb there," Donnelly said.

"You po-lice can't arrest us," the larger boy said. "We ain't done shit."

"You're not under arrest," Donnelly replied. "I just want to get some information from you."

Reynolds observed both boys glance around at him and then back at Donnelly. They seemed to be weighing their options. Then one boy piped up, "Hell yeah, why not."

"We're going to have to pat you down first," Donnelly advised them. "It's just standard procedure, both for your protection and ours."

The boys, without being further directed, went to the car, placed their hands on the side, and stepped back with their legs spread. They had obviously been through this drill before. Donnelly and Reynolds each frisked one boy and had them sit back on the curb. Donnelly asked both boys if they had any identification on them, and neither did. He then pulled out a book of Field Interview Report forms from his case and began asking each boy, in turn, his name, address, and so on, and filling in the pertinent information on the report form. When he was done, he called Dispatch and requested they contact Washington Middle School to verify the two were students there and whether they were supposed to be in class. The school didn't have a record of either name the boys gave, so they placed the boys in the back of the patrol car and drove to the school, where they contacted the school resource officer. He immediately recognized both boys and accompanied Donnelly, Reynolds, and the boys to the school office, where Donnelly recorded the boys' real names and addresses. Both young men were supposed to be in class, so the resource officer cited them for truancy and contacted the boys' mothers to have them come and get them.

Donnelly and Reynolds then proceeded to the address of the burglary.

"Just for future reference," Donnelly said as they pulled up to the residence, "even-number addresses are on the north and east sides of the street, and odd numbers are on the south and west. Keep that in mind when heading into a heavy call."

Donnelly reached down into his oversized attaché case and pulled out a Victim's Follow-Up Report and a large plastic container. "My fingerprint kit and camera," he responded to Reynolds' quizzical expression. Then he grabbed his notebook and flashlight and got out of the vehicle.

"Should I take the computer?" Reynolds asked.

"No, we'll just get the information and write the report later," Donnelly responded.

Reynolds tucked his machined aluminum D-cell flashlight into his sap pocket and followed Donnelly to the door.

Donnelly took a position on one side of the front door and waited for Reynolds to take the other side before knocking. "Never stand in front of the door on any kind of call," he reminded Reynolds.

The knock was answered with a resounding, "Who's zat?" to which Donnelly replied, "Police."

A rotund Black woman with her hair tied in little piglets and wearing a blushing pink velvet pantsuit, which did nothing to compliment her mammoth proportions, opened the door with a plaintive, "Bout time you po-lice got here."

"Sorry for the delay, ma'am," Donnelly responded. "We stopped two young men a couple of blocks from here that we thought might be possible suspects. It took some time to get them identified. Could you show us where the suspects entered the house? And please don't touch anything you haven't already touched."

"Those Black-assed little bastards broke out the window in my back door again," the woman said as she led the officers to the door. Reynolds looked around at the total disarray in the house as they walked to the back. He wasn't sure how much of it was caused by the burglars and how much was the usual state of affairs. Clothing was strewn over the floor in every room, and dirty dishes were piled high in the sink. Half-empty bottles of stale beer sat on the kitchen table next to ashtrays filled with cigarette butts.

"Any idea who might have done it?" Donnelly asked as he obliquely scanned several pieces of broken windowpane lying on the floor with his flashlight, looking for fingerprints.

"Sheeet, there's so many of them little niggers runnin' around this neighborhood, it could have been any of 'em," she replied. "None of the little bastards go to school hardly."

Donnelly opened the plastic container, removed his small digital camera, and took pictures of the point of entry, then began dusting the inside doorknob for prints. From the doorknob and from two shards of glass he found outside on the ground, he managed to get four partial prints and one fairly full print, which he taped on slides and labeled. He then began a careful room-by-room check of the house, photographing anything that appeared to have been disturbed by the suspects and dusting anything that might have been touched.

The house was a mess. The dresser drawers in the bedroom had been pulled out, and the contents dumped on the floor. Clothes were piled on the floors of the closets. The desk drawers in the anteroom off the living room had been pulled out and thrown around. A jar of peanut butter had been dropped on the kitchen floor and broken, splaying its contents in all directions. Donnelly was able to get a nice print off a piece of the glass container, however.

"Kids sure like to make a mess," Donnelly muttered to no one in particular as he continued with his room-to-room search. When he had finished, he sat the victim down in the front room and got an inventory of what she had found missing so far, which consisted of her big-screen TV and her home entertainment system. Reynolds couldn't help wondering how someone who lived in such a dump could afford a big-screen TV and stereo system but then opined that everyone has their priorities, and they were probably her primary source of entertainment.

Donnelly finished gathering all the information he needed for his report, then got a case number from Dispatch, which he wrote on the Victim Follow-Up Report, and instructed the woman to send it in if she discovered anything else missing or had additional information. He then motioned to Reynolds to follow him and headed out the back door. "They sure as hell didn't pack a big-screen TV very far," he said. "Let's check out the alley and any open garages or sheds."

Reynolds took one side of the alley and Donnelly the other. Three houses down from the victim's, Reynolds found a vacant house with an old, detached garage whose side door was partially open. He took out his flashlight and entered the dark interior. A quick scan with the flashlight revealed a large mound in the corner covered with a black plastic tarp. Sure enough, when he pulled back the tarp, there was the new Sony big-screen, along with a receiver and speakers. He went outside and called Donnelly to come and check it out.

"Better call the dicks," Donnelly said as he got on the radio and requested Dispatch to check with the Burglary detectives to see if they wanted to come investigate the scene.

Dispatch soon came back with the reply, "Two-George-Three, Burglary says to just photograph and fingerprint the articles and put them in Evidence. They have no one available to respond."

"Should have figured as much," Donnelly said. He retrieved his fingerprint kit and camera from the house and photographed and fingerprinted each item, obtaining eight good prints altogether. He and Reynolds then put the items in the back seat of the patrol car before going back to the victim to let her know they had been recovered. As relieved as she was that her property had been found, her disappointment was palpable when Donnelly told her it had to be retained as evidence. As they left the house, Donnelly suggested to the owner that she replace the back door with a solid-core wooden door with a deadbolt lock. "Sheeet, I can't afford no new door," the woman replied. Reynolds had to smile. *She can afford a new Sony big-screen but can't afford a new door*, he thought to himself as they returned to the car.

"She was certainly happy we found the TV," Reynolds observed as they got back in the cruiser.

"She probably had to finance it at an exorbitant rate of interest and is probably still paying for it," Donnelly responded. "But it's probably the only real pleasure she has in life, other than a cheap bottle of wine occasionally, so who are we to judge? Let's go get some coffee and write this report up."

They stopped in front of a rundown little restaurant with a bright pink façade. A large hand-lettered sign across the front window read, "Pinky's Soul Food Café." Donnelly removed the patrol car's laptop computer from its mount, grabbed his notebook, and they headed inside, taking a booth near the back of the long, narrow dining area. Inside, it looked like a typical "Mom and Pop" restaurant, with Formica-topped tables and booths covered in red vinyl. In the corner, an old-time jukebox was playing 1960s soul music. The only other patrons were a couple of old Black gentlemen playing checkers at a front booth. Donnelly immediately began writing up the burglary report. It was several minutes before a sullen young Black girl emerged from the kitchen area and approached the table.

"Ya'll need a menu?" she asked with a distasteful tone.

Donnelly looked over at Reynolds and asked, "You hungry? They got the best soul food in town here." It was 2:30 p.m., and Reynolds hadn't eaten since breakfast.

"Yeah, I could use something to eat."

The young waitress brought over two menus, laid them on the table, and walked away without saying a word.

"She's pleasant," Reynolds commented.

"It ain't cool to be nice to cops at her age," Donnelly responded. "Remember, don't take it personally."

Reynolds looked over the menu. Nothing sounded particularly appetizing. In fact, most of the dishes included body parts of pigs that he didn't think were even edible. As he was contemplating his choices, he heard a bright and cheery "Hey Mick, how you doin', man?"

He looked up to see a small, light-skinned Black man with a totally bald head approaching from the kitchen in the back. "You gonna have some of my ham hocks and beans today? I just made up a big pot," the man asked.

Donnelly glanced at Reynolds, who shrugged an okay. "Hell yeah, Pinky," Donnelly responded. "I think my partner is getting a little hungry. So, how's it going today?"

"Same old shit, man, same old shit," Pinky responded. "Just tryin' to make a little bread so I can give it to Uncle Sam. Anything heavy goin' down?"

"Just these damn daylight burglaries," Donnelly replied. "You know how it goes, as soon as you stop one group of kids, another bunch starts in."

"I hear ya, man," Pinky said. "I've had to put bars on my windows and doors, and they still try breakin' into the place. But I ain't had to deal with no stick-ups since I blew away that little nigger with my shotgun last year."

"Yeah, that's about the only thing they respect," Donnelly replied. "It sure as hell doesn't do any good to run them through the juvenile court system. We arrest them and they're back out on the street before we get the report done."

"Yeah, can't win, man," Pinky said. "But at least you can eat good. Let me go get you some ham hocks."

He disappeared into the kitchen and returned with two heaping plates of ham hocks and beans and a plate piled high with cornbread. Reynolds had to admit it tasted a hell of a lot better than it sounded, and he slicked his plate clean. Donnelly ate while he finished up the police report and managed to finish both the report and the plate of food at about the same time. He slid the computer across the table to Reynolds. "Take a look at that," he said. "From now on, you'll be doing the writing."

Reynolds read through the clear, concise statement of the facts related to the crime and was impressed with the manner in which Donnelly had answered the universal questions of who, what, when, where, and how. He had written lots of reports in the military and had taken police report-writing classes in college and in the academy, but it was nice to see a real example of a well-written report.

Reynolds finished reading the report and slid the computer back to Donnelly, who took a buck from his billfold, laid it on the table, then got up and started for the door. Reynolds stopped at the cash register to pay for their meal, but the young waitress, who was sitting in a corner booth reading a magazine, only looked up at him for an instant and then went back to her reading. "Forget it, kid," Donnelly said as he walked out the door.

"Don't you pay for your meals?" Reynolds asked as they got in the police car.

"Most of the restaurants in the district bounce for the district car," Donnelly said. "Pinky would be offended if you tried to pay for your meal. He just likes us to stop in occasionally. He figures its cheap insurance."

Reynolds wasn't sure he was comfortable with that idea. It had been strongly pointed out in the academy that accepting gratuities was not allowed and could result in dismissal. He definitely did not want to wind up like his old man, so he decided that from now on, he would pay full bore, regardless of what Donnelly did.

They cleared the burglary and were immediately dispatched to take a runaway report. A woman's fourteen-year-old daughter had been gone for two days, but the mother seemed more concerned with the fact that the daughter had taken her leather coat than that she had not come home.

Back in the squad car, Reynolds decided to get Donnelly's take on their stop of the two young Black males earlier and whether it was a legal "stop and frisk" situation. "Hell yeah," Donnelly responded. "According to the *Terry* decision, a police officer is allowed to stop a person without making an arrest if the officer can articulate a reasonable suspicion that the person has either committed or is about to commit a crime. You're also allowed to do a pat-down search of their clothing to make sure they don't have any weapons that could harm you. We were completely justified. Those boys were in the vicinity of a known crime, they matched the victim's description of the suspects, and they were out walking the streets during a time when they should have been in school. To me, that's grounds for reasonable suspicion in anyone's book. Stop and frisk is probably one of the best tools we have as street cops to control crime."

"So why do you think the court in New York declared the NYPD's stop and frisk practices unconstitutional?" Reynolds asked.

"Because they were abusing the law," Donnelly responded. "They made it a primary tool in their little war on crime and getting illegal guns off the street, and were indiscriminately stopping people, primarily males of color, and patting them down. It got totally out of hand, and they finally got shut down. It's why you constantly need to be asking yourself as you do this job, 'Can I justify this action in a court of law?', because you sure as hell are going to have to at some point."

The rest of the day, they chased one routine call after another, including another residential burglary. Reynolds wrote his first actual crime report over a cup of coffee at a drive-in and, on the third try, was finally able to elicit a nod of approval from Donnelly. Reynolds had lost all track of time and was actually surprised when Donnelly turned toward town with the comment, "Let's head for the barn."

It seemed to Reynolds as if he had been in a fantasy land all day—full of new sights, sounds, smells, tastes, and experiences. He was in a state of euphoria as they drove into the police garage. He hadn't felt this alive since he was rappelling out of helicopters to rescue downed pilots in Iraq.

"You turn in the shotgun and AR-15 and meet me in the sergeant's office," Donnelly said. "I'll show you where all these reports and forms go."

After clearing and turning in the weapons, he waited with Donnelly while the sergeant reviewed and signed their reports. They then put the traffic citation, Field Interview Reports, and Incident Reports in their respective receptacles and headed for the locker room.

"What time do you usually get here in the morning?" Reynolds asked.

"I'm usually here by 10:30 a.m.," Donnelly responded. "Along with hitting Crime Analysis, I like to make occasional rounds of the dicks upstairs to see what they're working on and shoot the shit. Say, do you want to stop by the Greeks for a drink?"

"What's the Greeks?" Reynolds asked.

"It's the restaurant and lounge across the street that serves as the designated 'debriefing' area for a lot of cops to go and wind down after work, which usually means getting shit-faced," Donnelly responded. "Every precinct has its own watering hole."

"No thanks," Reynolds replied, "I don't drink, but I'll meet you here at 10:30 tomorrow if that's all right."

"No problem, kid," Donnelly responded. "But I wouldn't advertise that not-drinking thing. A lot of cops don't trust anyone who doesn't drink. See you in the morning."

Reynolds almost reluctantly took off his uniform and changed into his bike clothes. He didn't really want this day to end. His adrenaline was still pumping as he mounted the Trek and rode out of the police garage. Traffic was relatively light, and he was able to ride hard and fast all the way home. The six-mile ride left him calm and relaxed. He fixed a sandwich and a glass of milk, grabbed his copy of *Inside the Criminal Mind*, and kicked back in his recliner until his eyes began to droop. He went to bed a contented man, looking forward to many more days as one of Seattle's finest.

CHAPTER 2

TUESDAY, DAY TWO

At 6:00 a.m. sharp, Nancy came on as usual, this time singing one of Reynold's favorite songs, "Yesterday." He completed his ritualistic, boner-driven, bladder bleeding exercise and poured a cup of freshly brewed coffee. This was an Aikido and strength training day, so he fixed a light breakfast of cereal, toast, and orange juice as he drank his first cup of coffee. After eating, he quickly perused the *Post-Intelligencer* as he sipped a second cup of coffee, taking time to read the letters to the editor, which he always found amusing, if not interesting. Then he donned his biking togs, stuffed his Aikido *gi* and workout clothes in the rack pack of his bike, and headed out the door.

It was only a mile to the Yokota dojo in the University District. Reynolds had begun practicing Aikido while he was stationed in Okinawa. He had been attracted to the discipline because of its name, which means "the way of harmony of the spirit," and its philosophy, which emphasizes neutralizing an attacker without seriously injuring them. He found a sensei who had originally trained under O Sensei himself, Morihei Ueshiba, and who later adopted the *Iwama-ryū* style while training under Morihiro Saito. Reynolds devoted himself to the discipline for two years until he was deployed to Iraq during the surge and then began training again while he attended Washington State University. He obtained a black belt while there and continued his training after moving to Seattle.

His Yokota sensei had also trained in Japan in the *Iwama-ryū* style, and Reynolds had arranged private training sessions with him every Tuesday and Thursday at 7:00 a.m. They began each session with various warm-up exercises called *junbi taiso* and then practiced a number of forms, or *kata*, before engaging in freestyle practice, in which each, in turn, took the role of *uke*, the attacker, or *tori*, the repeller of the attack. This included a variety of weapons-training *kata*, including various forms of weapons-taking and weapons-retention. After an hour and a half of sustained and vigorous Aikido training, Reynolds hit the Nautilus room that his Yokota sensei had set up in a space in the rear of the dojo. Aikido does not emphasize strength training, but his Yokota sensei felt that strength and endurance were important both to maximize one's ability to utilize the physical techniques and to achieve inner peace and confidence. He, therefore, put each of his Aikido *kayas* through an intensive circuit training regimen at the end of each session. Reynolds pre-set each machine to a weight that would cause total muscle fatigue in fifteen to twenty repetitions. The exercises were designed to achieve a total-body workout in less than thirty minutes. He went through each exercise, working one muscle group to exhaustion before immediately moving to the next machine and concentrating on the next muscle group until he had completed two full circuits.

When he finished, he felt totally spent physically, but after twenty minutes of meditation and a shower, he felt relaxed and rejuvenated—both mentally and physically. He pedaled downtown under clear skies and a bright morning sun, arriving at the precinct at 10:15 a.m.—just enough time to change clothes and meet Donnelly for his morning rounds.

As it turned out, Donnelly was in the locker room changing when Reynolds walked in. When they were both suited up, Donnelly took him on a tour of the follow-up units, where they talked to several detectives and supervisors about what was happening in their particular areas of interest. Then, it was back down to the Crime Analysis Unit, where they surveyed the previous day's crimes and suspects and checked the Field Interview Reports that had been turned in. Donnelly took copious notes in his steno pad during the entire process and updated his personal map of his sector with the locations of the most recent criminal activity. Then they headed up to the Records Bureau to run the names of several individuals that the dicks were interested in or who had felony warrants. They got the file numbers of each person and took them to the Identification Section, where Donnelly obtained mug shots from previous arrests. He made up three-by-five cards on each one, with mug shot attached, and added them to his little file box. They managed to get back down to the assembly room just in time for roll call.

"You do this every morning?" Reynolds asked.

"No, just every few days," Donnelly replied. "Like I said, the name of the game is 'know your enemy.' The more you know, the better you can do your job."

The sun was playing hide and seek behind low, scattered clouds as they pulled out of the police garage after roll call. As Donnelly went through his morning routine at the gas pumps, Reynolds filled in the log sheet and started a new page in Donnelly's steno pad.

They cleared with Dispatch and headed for the district. Reynolds' head was full of all the information they had dredged up that morning, and he found himself carefully observing every car, license number, and person he saw on the streets, looking for something that matched. Neither said much as Donnelly drove by several possible addresses for various subjects they had identified that morning, looking for activity or vehicles associated with them.

The silence became a little uncomfortable for Reynolds, and without any real reason other than to make conversation, he asked Donnelly, "So, what are you going to do when you retire?"

"Well, I'm thinking about moving to Alaska or Canada, getting me a piece of property on a lake or river miles from the nearest neighbor, building a little cabin, and spending my time hunting, fishing, drinking good scotch, and reading the collection of books I've accumulated over the years and never took the time to read."

"You like to read, eh?" Reynolds asked.

"Read and watch TV, that's about all I do anymore when I'm not working," Donnelly replied. "I like reading about history, politics, and current events and watching the news shows on TV. I can't afford much else right now, what with paying child support to three women. How about you, Dan? What do you like to do when you're off duty?"

"I like to read and watch the news shows too, but I also get outdoors as often as I can. I do a lot of backpacking and bicycle touring."

"Do you like to hunt and fish?" Donnelly asked.

"You know, I really haven't had any desire to kill birds or animals, particularly big game, since I went hunting with my dad when I was a kid," Reynolds replied. "I remember we were sitting on a hill glassing the valley below when a big, beautiful buck mule deer came wandering up from below. We both opened up on him, and he ran back the way he came. He made it about half a mile before collapsing beside a Forest Service road and dying. As I looked at him lying there, lifeless, with those glassy, vacant eyes, I was ashamed that we'd killed such a beautiful creature. I haven't hunted since. I guess I enjoy watching animals live in their natural surroundings too much to want to see them dead. I like to photograph them, though and I usually take a fishing rod with me backpacking to supplement the dehydrated meals I take."

"Two-George-Three," the radio tersely interrupted.

"Two-George-Three, 29th and South Washington," Donnelly responded.

"Two-George-Three, handle a disturbance at the Blackbird Tavern, 23rd and Walnut."

"Two-George-Three, received," Donnelly replied.

Donnelly kicked up the speed from the 10–15 mph he had been driving through the residential area and headed for the call.

"The Blackbird is a pretty rough place," he advised Reynolds. "When we get there, I want you to stay near the door and be ready to call for help. You never know what you're going to find on a call like this, so keep your head on a swivel and your eyes open going in. I got a disturbance call one time, and it turned out to be a double homicide, but don't start building up a lot of preconceptions in your mind. Just be ready for whatever you find."

Donnelly approached the tavern from the rear and parked half a block away. After informing Dispatch of their arrival, he got out slowly, his heavy machined aluminum flashlight in his left hand, and walked slowly toward the building with Reynolds in tow. Reynolds felt that same old anxiety and anticipation he used to feel when flying into a rescue situation in the military. This was the first police call he had gone on with any hint of danger or excitement. As they walked toward the tavern, he was glad to see that a backup unit had positioned itself in the alley half a block down. Donnelly motioned for Reynolds to stay behind him as he sidled up next to a small window and looked in, surveying the inside of the bar. Not seeing anything unusual, he told Reynolds to take a position at the back door off the alley while he went around to the front.

"I'll double-click the mike on the radio as I go in," Donnelly said. "Then you go in, but stay close to the door."

Reynolds stayed outside until he heard the double-click and then entered the dark interior of the bar. As he looked around, he saw several Black males playing pool at the two tables at the front and a few more sitting at the bar drinking. They all looked up briefly, an expression of disdain and disgust on their faces, and then went back to their business. Reynolds stood just inside the door, scanning everyone in the room as Donnelly began a slow walk around the interior, carefully appraising each patron. He worked his way up to the bar.

"We got a call of a disturbance here, Willie," he advised the bartender. "What's going on?"

"Ain't shit going on here, man," the bartender said. "You sure you got the right place?"

"Yeah, I'm sure," Donnelly replied. He then went over to the restrooms and, after knocking on the door, checked first the women's and then the men's before returning to the bar.

"How come there's blood all over the men's john?" he asked the bartender.

"Don't know, man," the bartender replied curtly, "maybe somebody had a nosebleed."

Donnelly again walked around the bar, checking each patron for any signs of injury. He stopped next to a slightly built older man sipping a beer at the bar.

"How long have you been here, Jackson?" he asked.

"Bout half-hour," the man replied.

"See any disturbances?" Donnelly asked.

"Ain't seen shit," the man replied defiantly.

"Open up the back room, Willie," Donnelly ordered the bartender. "I want to look for a disturbance."

"You got no right looking' in there, man. You got a warrant?"

"I'm wearing my warrant on my right foot, Willie. Now open the door, or I'll kick it down. Whatsamatter, you got more stolen TVs stashed back there?"

"Ain't nothing back there but empty beer kegs, man," Willie said as he begrudgingly opened the door.

Donnelly made a quick check of the room and reappeared. "That raid the squad made on you last month got your attention, eh?"

"I'm clean, man," the bartender replied. "Now if you ain't found no disturbance, whyn't you jus' move on out o' here."

"Sure, Willie," Donnelly said, "we're going, but you better hope no bodies turn up around here, or we'll be back to see you."

As they walked back to the car, Donnelly called Dispatch on the portable and asked if they had the details of the complainant, but, as is often the case, they had refused to give a name.

"What do you think happened?" Reynolds asked Donnelly.

"Oh, it might have been a crank call, but more likely, a couple of guys got in a beef and split before we got there."

"Does that happen often?"

"Too goddamn often," Donnelly replied.

Donnelly cleared the call as "Unable to Locate" as Reynolds filled out the log sheet and made an entry in Donnelly's steno pad. He could feel the adrenaline begin to subside as they drove away, being replaced by a warm, sleepy feeling.

They patrolled the area around the bar for several minutes, looking for an injured person, but without success.

"Man, you could literally feel the hatred as we walked into that bar," Reynolds commented to Donnelly.

"You've got to realize that you're working behind the lines in enemy territory up here, partner," Donnelly replied. "A lot of these fuckers would just as soon cut your throat as look at you, and they would if they thought they could get away with it. This ain't the 'burbs' up here. You're dealing with a whole different culture;

might just as well be a foreign country as to what you're used to. When these folks have a beef, they settle it with guns and knives, not small-claims court. They don't much like or trust white folks, so keep that in mind. Watch your back and their hands, trust no one but a fellow cop, believe nothing they tell you, and you should be all right."

"My sociology professor would say that's our fault. Almost four hundred years of slavery, segregation, and discrimination certainly isn't conducive to teaching them white values or integrating them into white society."

"Spoken like a true liberal, partner," Donnelly sneered. "Sure, they've been repressed and discriminated against, but you've got to remember, you're a cop, not a social worker. You're out here to enforce the law and keep the peace. You haven't got the time or the means to change society or convert any souls. Just do your job to the best of your ability, give people the respect and dignity they deserve, and leave the job in your locker with your uniform when you go home at night. If you start carrying all these people's problems around on your shoulders, you'll either wind up at the end of a dirt road with your gun in your mouth or killing yourself slowly with a bottle of booze."

"Seems to me you take the job pretty seriously," Reynolds said.

"Sure, I take it seriously—but with a little perspective. I do the job the best I know how, but I also realize that I'm only one link in a big chain called the criminal justice system, which is kind of a misnomer because there's often not much justice in it."

Reynolds, given his master's degree in criminal justice, was curious what an old-time cop would view as the major problems in the system. He asked Donnelly directly.

"Basically, I think we've subverted the word 'justice.' The system is full of so many inequities and expediencies that justice only happens by accident," Donnelly responded.

"Are you saying the system is weighted to favor the wrongdoers?" Reynolds asked.

"I'm saying the system is so weighed down with technicalities, protocols, and precedents that the truth of guilt or innocence and appropriate punishment often gets lost in the process."

"How many of the problems with the 'system' rest with police practices, do you think?"

"You know, we definitely have room for improvement in law enforcement, but our problems are minuscule compared to the rest of the system," Donnelly replied. "I would generously estimate that this police department operates at about 50 percent optimum efficiency. By that, I mean that if every cop in this Department performed to their maximum effectiveness, we could double our productivity in terms of arrests and clearing cases. But even at 50 percent efficiency, we inundate the court system and the correctional system, so what would happen if we doubled it?"

"What do you see as the major stumbling blocks to improving police performance?"

"That's easy—cynicism and complacency. Police departments have made major strides in improving professionalism and practices over the last forty years. A lot of that has to do with hiring more people like you with higher educational backgrounds and more idealism. We've dramatically improved the training and developed better procedures, processes, and practices like community policing, but the bottom line is the individual officer and their personal motivation and commitment to doing the job, and I don't know if that has improved much. Don't get me wrong, we have some really good officers who are highly motivated and who do great work, but not enough. Even the good cops get soured on the system after a while. It doesn't take too many years of seeing the courts let criminals walk on minor technicalities or watching prosecutors plea-bargain good felony cases down to petty misdemeanors in order to get a quick conviction to get you wondering if it's all worth it.

"Look around the assembly room at roll call. Most of those guys show up five minutes before. Some are still hungover from closing the Greeks the night before. Look at how many of them are overweight and out of shape. There really isn't much incentive for them to go out and bust their ass. They get paid for longevity, not performance. Stick around six years, and you're maxed out in salary, except for cost-of-living increases. Then, if you're interested in making more money, you either need to promote—which essentially takes you away from police work and into supervision and management—or you start working side jobs. Half of these guys are just here for the paycheck and the retirement. They know that if they show up for work, answer their calls, and write a ticket every day, they can skate through twenty-five years, no problem. In fact, going out and doing real police work can get you in trouble because you step on people's toes and increase your exposure to physical injury and harassment and brutality charges. It's easier to just come to work, maintain a low profile, do the minimum possible to get by, and put in your time."

Reynolds was impressed by the sincerity in Donnelly's voice and the concern written on his face. "So how do you get around that?" he asked.

"In my opinion, we need to provide incentives to keep good cops on the street and functioning in areas where they can be most effective. Instead of the Patrol Division being the dumping ground for everyone who can't make it someplace else, we need to make it an elite division in the Department. We need to raise the standards in terms of professionalism, training, physical fitness, and performance; then we need to provide long-term pay incentives based on those standards.

"Basically, we have three primary career tracks in police work—administration, investigations, and operations. People should be encouraged to pick a path and stick with it. If a cop really wants to do on-the-street police work, they should be able to stay in Patrol or

Detectives and be rewarded for the quality and quantity of work they do. I'd do away with automatic step increases and just do annual merit raises based on fair and objective performance standards."

"But how do you implement quantitative performance standards without inviting manipulation of those standards?" Reynolds replied. "Like you mentioned earlier when the Special Squad started emphasizing the number of arrests over their quality."

"That's where good supervision comes into play," Donnelly replied. "It would be up to sergeants and lieutenants to evaluate the quality of a person's work along with the quantity when writing performance reviews."

"What all would the Operations Division encompass?" Reynolds asked.

"I would include Traffic, Detention, Uniformed Patrol, and Special Squad," Donnelly responded. "I would require every officer coming out of the academy to first be assigned to either Traffic or as a Detention Officer for a minimum of a year. Like us, traffic officers should be assigned to a specific sector as part of a 'team' policing system and be responsible for all traffic functions within that sector, including investigating traffic accidents. Detention Officers should be required to transfer to Traffic for at least a year before being considered for Uniformed Patrol. If they liked either of those assignments, they could stay as long as they wanted and perhaps promote within that section. If not, they could apply to transfer to Uniformed Patrol. Only highly motivated officers would be accepted into Patrol, and they would be required to meet strict standards of job knowledge, physical fitness, and performance."

"What about guys who want to promote?" Reynolds asked.

"Like I said, they can be promoted within their career track. That way, they can use the knowledge and experience they have gained where it will be most effective. If a person didn't want to promote, they could still be rewarded financially and professionally throughout their career."

"So where does that leave the guys who just want to skate through until retirement?" Reynolds asked.

"It leaves them looking for another career," Donnelly responded. "Why should civil service reward mediocrity? The private sector doesn't. That's why everyone ridicules government workers in this country. We've created a civil service system that gives people a right to their job without reasonable standards of performance. Police work is a special job; it demands special people. If a person doesn't have the ability or the desire to do the job well, they should find another line of work."

"Well, I think it could work," Reynolds responded. "I was a pararescue jumper in the Air Force. You had to apply for consideration and then pass an intense physical and mental qualifying exam to get accepted. The training approached that of a Green Beret or Navy Seal, and once you got through it, your level of esprit de corps and commitment was through the roof. Both officers and enlisted had to go through the same training and most stayed in that field their entire career."

"Why'd you get out?" Donnelly asked.

"I became more and more disillusioned with Bush's little wars in Afghanistan and Iraq. I finally concluded that by staying in, I was lending tacit support to—in my view—misguided government policies with no hope of success. The only way a citizen soldier can voice his objections to a war is to refuse to fight, so I got out. Besides, I really wanted to go to college and become a cop... So, have you had any luck selling your ideas to the police union or the administration of the Department?"

"Hell no. The police union just wants to build in more protections to keep marginal officers on the job while giving them better pay and benefits, and the administration is afraid to upset the union. It's just like everything else in this society. As long as the right people are benefiting from the status quo, why do anything to change the system for the good of the whole?"

As Donnelly talked, he was maneuvering to catch up to a red Coupe de Ville. When he was positioned two car lengths behind it, he told Reynolds, "Get on that computer and check wants and warrants on Washington license Adam-George-Henry 985."

Moments later, the computer spit out a report. "We've got a felony Failure to Appear warrant on the registered owner of a 2004 Cadillac two-door with license Adam-George-Henry 985. Warrant is on a Samuel L. Byington, Black male, date of birth 9/12/85. The charge was Aggravated Assault, and it says he may be armed and should be considered dangerous," Reynolds said.

Donnelly contacted Dispatch. "This is Two-George-Three, we're following a red 2004 Cadillac, Washinton license Adam-George-Henry 985, southbound in the 3200 block of Martin Luther King Way. There appears to be a felony Failure to Appear warrant on the registered owner. We're going to make a felony stop."

Donnelly flipped on the overhead lights and gave a brief burst on the siren. Reynolds, who could see the driver's eyes in his rearview mirror, was almost able to read his mind as his eyes darted around, looking for options. Unfortunately for the driver, he was boxed in by traffic and, with a look of resignation, he began pulling to the curb.

"Unlock the shotgun and take a position behind your car door when we get stopped. If he starts to rabbit, we'll let him go. We don't need a chase in this traffic. I'll take the driver. Don't shoot at him if he tries to run—too many houses around."

As the Caddie came to a stop, Donnelly set up a car length behind it, with the nose of the patrol car protruding into the traffic lane. He opened his car door, put the radio on loudspeaker, grabbed the mike, and took a position behind the door with his Glock semi-automatic trained on the driver's-side door.

"Driver," he intoned into the mike in a firm and commanding voice. "Roll down your window, remove the keys from the ignition, and place both hands out of the window with the keys in your hand," Donnelly ordered.

The driver hesitated a moment as he looked in the rearview mirrors and observed the twelve-gauge shotgun and 9-mm leveled at his car. He then turned off the ignition, removed the keys, and did as he was directed.

"Driver. Open the car door using the outside handle and step out of the car," Donnelly commanded.

The driver again complied.

"Place both hands on the top of your head and walk backwards to the rear of your vehicle," Donnelly ordered.

Again, the driver did as he was directed.

"Lie face-down on the pavement with your arms and legs spread."

When the driver was prone on the ground, Donnelly directed Reynolds, "I'll cover him. You put the shotgun away and frisk him,"

Donnelly approached the prone figure and, after briefly checking the inside of the vehicle for other occupants, took a position at his head, while Reynolds covered him from behind. Reynolds, recalling his training from both the military and the academy, did a thorough pat-down search from head to toe, including removing and checking the individual's shoes. He then cuffed his hands behind him and double-locked the cuffs.

"What's your name?" Donnelly asked the man as he lay on the ground.

"Joe Jackson," the man replied.

"You got any identification?" Donnelly asked.

The man didn't reply, so Donnelly said to Reynolds, "Does he have a wallet on him?"

Reynolds had felt a wallet in the man's back pocket when he had searched him, so he reached over and removed it.

"This driver's license says Samuel Byington, and the picture looks just like you," he advised the man after checking the wallet. Again, the man did not reply.

"Mr. Byington, I assume you know why we stopped you," Donnelly said. "You're being arrested for a felony Failure to Appear warrant. Officer Reynolds will read you your rights."

Reynolds took the Miranda Rights card from his shirt pocket, read them verbatim, and then asked, "Do you understand each of these rights I have explained to you?"

Byington responded with a surly, "Yeahhh."

Reynolds helped the suspect to his feet and, with his right hand firmly attached to the subject's upper left arm, escorted him to the back of the car and placed him in the right rear seat, securing him with a seat belt.

"You call for an impound on the vehicle and sit with him while I do an inventory search of the car," Donnelly directed.

Reynolds made the radio call and then took a seat on the driver's side in the back of the car. As he entered the vehicle, he could smell that same strong, acrid odor of nervous sweat that he had noticed yesterday with the kids. The young Black man glared at him insolently but did not say a word. He obviously had been in this situation before. Donnelly finished checking the inside and trunk of the Caddie and returned to the patrol car with a small .32 semi-automatic dangling from his pen by the trigger guard.

"Found this stuffed down in the front seat," he said as he got in. "Were you planning on using this?" he asked the driver.

The man didn't say a word. Donnelly removed the magazine and cranked the slide to make sure there was not a round in the chamber, then placed it in a small plastic bag and secured it in his attaché case.

Meanwhile a backup unit had rolled on the stop and volunteered to wait for the tow truck, so Donnelly proceeded to drive downtown to the jail. When they got to the booking area, Donnelly directed the man to a small room where he had Reynolds remove the cuffs and told the man to remove his clothes. Donnelly went through the strip-search procedure with him as Reynolds, after donning a pair of latex gloves, carefully went through the man's clothing pockets and placed his clothes and belongings in separate plastic bags. They then gave the man a pair of orange coveralls to put on and took him to the counter, where he was booked into jail.

An hour later, after writing the arrest report and individual officer statements, they headed back to their district.

"You hungry?" Donnelly asked.

"I'm starved," Reynolds replied. "Nothing like a little adrenaline rush to give you an appetite."

"I think we've earned a decent meal," Donnelly replied as he pulled into the parking lot of an upscale little restaurant called The Harbor on Lake Washington. Donnelly put them "Out to Eat" with Dispatch, and Reynolds followed him into the simple but elegant ambiance of the lakeside eatery. They stopped briefly at the hostess' stand, where a pleasant young Black woman asked, "You want to eat outside, Mick?"

"Sure, hon', that would be great," Donnelly replied.

The young hostess escorted them back to a corner table on the outdoor patio, away from the other patrons. Donnelly slid into a chair with his back to the wall, and Reynolds took the chair next to him with his back to the lake. The hostess left a couple of menus, and Reynolds began exploring for something that excited his palate.

"And what can I get for Seattle's finest today?" The mature, mellow, and melodious female voice sounded vaguely familiar to Reynolds. He racked his memory briefly, and then it came to him in a flash: *She sounds a lot like Nancy Wilson*, he thought. He had not only listened to Nancy sing almost daily for years; he had gone to see her perform at The Alley jazz club just before she had retired in 2010. The voice was unmistakable. He allowed his glance to drift up from the menu. The first thing that caught his eye were two long, elegant feet ensconced in a pair of simple leather sandals, the toenails painted a deep red with a silver design on each toe. As his gaze rose further, he saw two very taut and muscular calves sitting atop slim ankles. The skin tone was that of lightly creamed coffee and had a distinct sheen to it, indicative of excellent muscle tone. His eyes rose to take in the well-muscled but slender thighs emerging from a pair of khaki Bermuda shorts. A trim and narrow waist blossomed into a full bust, apparent even under the loose-fitting burgundy polo shirt bearing the restaurant's logo. Finally, his eyes reached the face—strong chin; full lips encircling a wide mouth; pronounced, high cheekbones; small, delicate ears; a patrician nose; the head framed with kinky black hair styled in a semi-afro, but more natural. His eyes came to rest on the most distinctive feature of all, two large, hazel-colored eyes that sparkled with life and intelligence—and also, at that moment, a degree of humor.

"I don't think what my partner wants is on the menu," Reynolds vaguely heard Donnelly say, "but I'll have your steak sandwich with the house salad and ranch dressing."

The waitress tried to hide a closed-lip smile and looked directly into Reynolds' eyes. "And how about you, chief?"

Reynolds had forgotten everything that he had seen on the menu but could not disengage his eyes from hers to look at it again. "That sounds good," he managed to stammer, "I'll have the same."

She allowed her eyes to remain locked with his for a moment longer and then turned on her heel. "You've got it," she said as she walked regally away with a slightly exaggerated swaying of the hips. Reynolds could not take his eyes off her, focusing on the long legs topped with a tight and muscular butt. "She must be six feet tall," he said. "She's got the body of Venus Williams and the face of Halle Berry."

"Your tongue's hanging out a bit, partner," Donnelly said. "You look like Michael Jordan driving for a dunk."

"That's a beautiful woman," Reynolds replied.

"Don't get too excited," Donnelly said, "she's probably screwing half the guys on UW's basketball team."

"Does she go to the university?" Reynolds asked.

"Yeah, I think so. I came in here one day and saw her over in the corner taking notes out of a huge textbook."

Reynolds could not get the image of the young woman out of his head, and it seemed an eternity before she returned with their orders. "Here you go, Officer Donnelly," she said as she placed his order in front of him, "and this is for you, chief." After setting the plates on the table in front of them, she stood directly facing Reynolds with her shoulders back, her legs slightly apart, and her hands on her hips. Reynolds could not help looking back into those lovely hazel eyes which met his gaze directly. "Is there anything else I can get you? If not, enjoy your meal," she said. Reynolds allowed his eyes to drift to the name tag on her shirt that he had caught out of his peripheral vision. "Thank you, Tawnya," he replied, "I'm sure we will."

As she turned and walked away, Reynolds became aware that he had a slight erection. *Shit*, he thought to himself, *I hope she didn't notice that.* He looked down and was relieved when he saw that the tablecloth covered his lap. *Man, I'd definitely have a hard-on every morning if I woke up next to that.*

They finished their meal in silence, Reynolds' mind still focused on the young waitress. After polishing off the steak sandwich, Donnelly pushed back from the table and took out a small, fat cigar from his pocket. "You mind if I smoke?" he said.

"I'd rather you didn't," Reynolds replied. Donnelly looked at him with a somewhat disgusted expression and then put the cigar back in his pocket.

"Well, let's get back to work then," he said, leaving a dollar tip behind as he got up from the table. Reynolds didn't know what the cost of the meal was since they hadn't gotten a check, but he took out a twenty-dollar bill, left it on the table, and reluctantly followed Donnelly out the door.

Donnelly, fully satiated from his meal, drove to a four-way stop intersection, pulled to the curb a half-block away, and parked.

"Might as well see if we can get our ticket for the day while we let our dinner settle," he said.

It was less than fifteen minutes before a distracted woman with three kids in the car blew through the stop sign without stopping. Donnelly pulled her over and wrote the citation without hesitation.

After Donnelly returned to the car after getting the ticket signed, Reynolds could not help but comment, "Did you consider possibly giving her a break? She looked like a nice woman who really had her hands full with those kids."

"What if she had blown that stop sign while someone was pulling out in front of her?" Donnelly replied. "She could have injured or killed those kids. Maybe a ticket will get her attention, and she'll concentrate on her driving in the future." Reynolds could not argue with that logic.

The rest of the day was spent responding to routine calls and taking reports. Reynolds was again surprised when he looked at his watch and saw it was time to go home. "Man, this day went fast," he said. "Seems like we just started, and it's quitting time."

"Time flies when you're having fun," Donnelly replied as they pulled into the precinct parking garage.

The bike ride home was particularly enjoyable as Reynolds found himself fantasizing about the beautiful young girl from the restaurant. He considered asking her out and began thinking about what they would do. That exercise consumed his evening as he sat in his recliner, blissfully listening to his Nancy Wilson collection.

CHAPTER 3

THE ANTAGONIST

Tyrone Banks awoke to find himself trapped by a dark arm across his chest and a heavy black leg draped over his thighs. A thick mat of frizzy, bleached-blonde hair tickled the skin on his shoulder. He allowed his eyes to open and scan the interior of the room as he tried to remember where he was. His head felt like it was splitting open, and a vague feeling of anxiety crept over him. He found himself becoming increasingly agitated by the weight on his body and experienced an overpowering need to free himself. He pushed the arm and leg roughly away and got out of bed. Their owner, a twenty-something, slightly overweight girl, grunted as she rolled over and continued sleeping.

Banks sat naked in an armchair he found in the bedroom and again tried to recall where he was and how he got there. Vague memories of the previous evening began to emerge. He recalled going to the Black and Tan nightclub in Chinatown late in the evening. He remembered running into a couple of homeboys and having several double scotches. Then the memory of the three bitches joining them came back—and the blonde one wanting to dance. He was just drunk enough to oblige, and they closed the place up, drinking and dancing. He remembered driving the blonde back to her apartment and doing several lines of coke with her as they listened to hip-hop in the front room. Then he recalled her getting amorous, reaching over and unzipping his pants, and pulling out his cock. She started sucking his dick, and it wasn't long before he picked her up and carried her to the bedroom, tore off her clothes, and fucked the shit out of her. She couldn't seem to get enough, and he remembered screwing at least twice more between lines of coke. It must have been 5:00 in the morning before they had both passed out. He had slept fitfully and recalled having had some really strange dreams.

He looked at his gold-plated, knock-off Rolex. *Shit, its three in the afternoon*, he thought. *I gotta get my ass out of here.*

Banks grabbed a quick shower, slipped on the baggy, oversized jeans and extra-large silk T-shirt he had worn the night before, and found his way out of the strange apartment building. His car was parked in the lot in front of the apartment. As he got in, he pulled out the clip from his front pocket containing his flash money. *Shit*, he thought, *I must have spent over three C-notes last night. I need to get some cash.*

He headed out of Rainier Valley back to his Central District apartment. When he got there, the two prostitutes he ran were also just getting up and about. He rounded them up and took them into his bedroom. "All right, bitches, let's have last night's take," he demanded.

Celise, an eighteen-year-old from California who Banks had found hanging out at the bus station, immediately coughed up $400 from her purse. Katrina, the twenty-five-year-old who Banks had been running for several years, was only able to produce a hundred dollars. "Goddamnit, bitch, is that all the money you made last night?" Banks retorted.

"Sorry, baby," Katrina lamented. "It was just a slow night."

"Bitch, if you're holdin' out on me, I'll kick your motherfuckin' Black ass!" Banks threatened.

"I'm tellin' you, Tyrone. It was a slow night. I stood on that motherfuckin' corner till four this morning and only had two tricks. That's every dime I made."

Banks wasn't in a mood to hear that. He was hungover, on a downer from the coke, and feeling like shit. His right hand shot out, palm open, and caught Katrina flush on the side of her face. Her knees buckled, and she fell backward onto the bed. "Bitch, you get your Black ass out on the street right now, and if you don't have at least five Cs for me tomorrow, don't bother comin' back."

Banks stormed out of the apartment and down to his car. He suddenly felt famished and decided to head downtown to the Kansas City Steakhouse for something to eat. The Steakhouse was an institution on Pike Street and had long been a hangout for the pimps and hustlers from the CD. He still felt like shit when he pulled into the parking garage down the street from the restaurant, but he sucked it up and breezed in the entrance strutting his best cock-of-the-walk stride. He bumped fists and gave the hustler's hug to several brothers he found drinking in the lounge and then wandered over to a table in the corner of the dimly lit bar and sat down. A pretty young barmaid wearing a black leather, low-riding mini-skirt and black spandex tube top came over to take his order.

"Hey, baby," Banks crooned in his coolest hustler's jive, "I needs some steak and eggs—medium-rare and over-easy. And brings me a big mug of coffee with a couple shots of brandy in it. By the way, you lookin' real fine, girl. You wan' come work for me?"

"No thanks, Tyrone," the girl responded. "I'm doin' jus' fine where I'm at. When I suck a cock it's cuz I want to, not cuz I'm afraid of gettin' my ass beat. I'll get your order right out."

Banks laughed as the barmaid walked away, then leaned back in the chair and shut his eyes, trying to will the headache away.

"Hey, bro, what's up?" he heard through the fog in his head. He looked up to see a tall, slender Black man wearing baggy jeans barely hanging from his ass and an oversized Supersonics basketball jersey with a black nylon do-rag covering his shaven head.

"Hey, wha's up, man," Banks replied. "Sit down and take a load off."

The young buck, who everyone called Slick, pulled up the chair next to Banks and leaned toward him as he spoke in a conspiratorial whisper, "You got any shit goin', Ty?"

"Same ol' shit, man," Banks responded. "I got my girls workin' and pushin' a little shit on the side. How 'bout you?"

"A few homeys an' me are workin' on a way to score big taking down grocery stores. We figure we can pull down five to ten Gs each for every hit. You wan' in?"

"Sounds iffy to me, man," Banks responded. "What would you expect me to do?"

"We lookin' for a wheel man, is all," came the reply.

"How soon you lookin' to move, man?" Banks asked.

"Coupla weeks. Whatta you say, you in?" the man responded.

Tyrone considered the proposition. Just driving the car meant that he wouldn't have to go into the store and possibly get recognized on a security camera. Besides, things had been pretty slow with his girls lately, and he could use some extra cash, particularly if he wanted to bring up some of those migrant girls that his cartel connection had turned him onto.

"Hell, yeah. I'm up for some quick cash," Banks said. "When we gettin' together?"

"We meetin' up to Benny Malone's place Friday night to line things out. Show up 'round eight, and keep this under your hat, man. With you, we gots everyone we needs." With that, Slick gave Banks the hustler's handshake and hug and went back to join the group of pimps he had been drinking with. Banks' food came and he wolfed it down, feeling much better as the adrenaline surged through his body at the thought of making a quick five to ten grand. *Shit, I get those extra girls working, I might have to gets me a new Escalade*, he thought.

Tyrone Banks was only twenty-five, but he had lived a full life in his brief years. He was the third child born to a sixteen-year-old mother who went on to have four more kids—all with different fathers. His mother had dropped out of school at thirteen after having her first child. She had lived at home with her mother until after Tyrone was born but then had enough welfare money coming in to get her own place. His mother turned tricks on the side to supplement her part-time job at McDonald's, her food stamps, and her welfare check and she was rarely home. When she was, she was usually asleep or hungover from alcohol or heroin. Tyrone's grandma had been the primary caregiver for him and his siblings, but she had had three kids of her own still at home and did not have the time or energy to provide much supervision.

Consequently, Tyrone was raised on the streets by the other kids in the neighborhood. At ten years old, he was jumped into a gang associated with the Bloods out of California, which his older brothers belonged to, and began muling drugs. By twelve, he was snatching purses and breaking into houses. At fourteen he was stealing cars and robbing convenience stores. He had been in and out of juvenile detention centers a dozen times growing up, but never for long. They would eventually put him on probation and release him back to his mother, who would admonish him to be more careful next time and not get caught, then send him on his way. Unfortunately, at nineteen, he got busted for burglarizing a grocery store and did three years at Monroe Reformatory on a five-year bit. He learned a lot at Monroe and made some good connections. Since then, he had played it smart, setting himself up with a couple of girls who paid his rent, kept food on the table, put high-end clothes on his back, and made his payments on the Escalade. He had a regular clientele of cocaine and heroin users, which allowed him to supply his and his girls' needs and to make a little extra money on the side. And then, occasionally, when an opportunity for a big score came along, he would take a chance on making some quick, easy cash. He had earned a lot of respect on the streets and was known as a guy who could take care of business when it was needed. Two junkies who had tried to welch on their drug debts had found that out the hard way, never being heard from again.

Banks had a very simple outlook on life on the street. *Nobody is going to give you shit, so you need to take what you want. Nobody gives a damn about you but you, so your needs always come first. And the only things that are important in life are looking good, feeling good, and being right*—meaning being respected by your peers. He was a stand-up hustler who could sweet-talk a man out of his last dollar and a woman out of her pants just about every time. He was living large and had everything he needed or wanted in life. He just had to stay on his game and life was good. He left the restaurant and cruised back up to the CD to make sure his girls were on the street. The prospect of a major score had improved his mood considerably.

CHAPTER 4

WEDNESDAY, DAY THREE

A storm had blown in during the night, and Reynolds had to run in the rain this morning. This was the norm in Seattle, and he had actually come to almost enjoy it. The rain created an entirely different mood in the city—a more somber and sober mood, to be sure, but also more tranquil and peaceful. It tended to quiet the left brain and open up the right. On the bike ride into the station, Reynolds allowed himself to drift into a meditative state as he focused intently on the smell of the rain-cleansed air, the beauty of the subdued landscape with the reflections of light and color on the rain-soaked streets, and the muffled sounds of a water-saturated world. He arrived at the precinct feeling very much at peace with his environment.

He met Donnelly in the Crime Analysis Unit, where his partner was poring through the police reports from the previous day. "Isn't most of this information available on our in-car computer?" Reynolds asked.

"Yeah, I suppose," Donnelly replied, "but I'm old-school. I like to dig it out for myself and get as much information that is specific to my district as I can. They do put out a daily crime recap, but oftentimes, it's pretty general. Technology seems like it's taking over police work. I was reading in the paper about a city that had patrol cars equipped with computers and cameras with license plate readers. The officers just drive around all day checking license plate numbers, looking for stolen cars and wanted vehicles."

"That might get a little tedious, but I bet they recover a lot of hot cars," Reynolds replied.

After roll call, they hit their district and began a slow patrol of the side streets.

"Want a tour of the major attractions in this district?" Donnelly asked.

"Sure."

"See that big gray house on the corner? They run a whorehouse and bootleg operation out of there."

Several blocks later, he pointed out a brightly painted Tudor-style house with mirrored glass in the front door and deeply tinted windows all around. "That joint is an after-hours club. They got card games, a roulette wheel, and a craps table going."

Around the corner and down a block, he pointed out a large, two-story white house with the shades drawn on every window. "That white place is a shooting gallery and crack house for the mainliners and crackheads."

"If we know all these places are operating, why don't we shut them down?" Reynolds asked.

"Ain't that easy, kid," Donnelly replied. "I'm sure they taught you about 'probable cause' in that college you went to. You've got to have enough evidence to support getting a warrant before you start kicking in doors and making arrests, and it's not all that easy to get with these kinds of places. They're pretty careful about who they let in these joints, and the people who frequent them aren't likely to make a complaint. Neither are the neighbors, either because they don't think it's wrong or because they're afraid of retaliation. It's tough to find a snitch who'll burn these kinds of places cause most of them hang out there too. It's part of the lifestyle and culture in this part of town, and nobody gets too excited about it. Occasionally, somebody will OD, but we usually find the body lying in some alley blocks away. That's what makes the game interesting. They know we know what they're doing, and we know that they know what we need to make a case against them. We harass them enough to keep them on their toes, but except for the heavy dealers, nobody gets too excited about them."

Reynolds' interest was piqued, and he found himself studying the houses and cars they passed with a whole new appreciation. Donnelly turned into an alley and, after half a block, pulled into the parking lot behind a large wood-frame building. "This place is called Snookers," he said. "A lot of assholes hang out here. We're going to do a walk-through just to see what's shaking, so follow the same drill we used at the Blackbird the other day. You stay near the rear door and be prepared to radio for help if I run into any trouble." He called Dispatch and put them out on a "Shake" at 2419 East Roosevelt.

Before getting out of the squad car, Donnelly jotted down the descriptions and license numbers of the half a dozen cars parked in the lot and then had Reynolds run them through the computer. All of the cars were newer models, mostly Cadillac Escalades and Chevy Yukons, sporting oversized, chrome custom wheels and dark-tinted windows. Two of the cars came back with traffic warrants, and Donnelly noted that in his steno pad. "We'll keep an eye out for these guys and see if we can catch them rolling," he said.

Donnelly made a point of looking in each parked car to see if anyone was inside as he crossed the parking lot. Reynolds felt the adrenaline kick in again as they approached the rear of the pool hall. His heart rate accelerated, his senses sharpened, and he could feel his nut sack draw up tight. He could hear the heavy beat and unintelligible lyrics of rap music blaring from the door as they approached. As they got closer, the so-called music had to compete with the shrill sound of the jive-talking inhabitants, punctuated by the impact of pool balls.

Donnelly and Reynolds stepped inside the rear door. Donnelly moved a few feet away from Reynolds, near the back wall, and surveyed the room. An immediate and ominous silence ensued as twelve Black heads turned simultaneously to see who had invaded their lair. Reynolds glanced nervously around at the gathering and was stunned by the intensity of the hate-filled stares that met his gaze. These guys made the waitress at Pinky's seem almost friendly.

For a long and anxious moment, no one moved. Then Donnelly began a slow and watchful sweep of the room, carefully observing each patron. He stopped next to a tall, slender, extremely dark man sitting at a small table. The man was wearing the ubiquitous black nylon do-rag over a shaven head, a tight-fitting black silk tank top, and baggy black denim pants. His dark skin and clothing contrasted sharply with the heavy gold chain around his neck, the gold watch on his wrist, and the large gold ring with the fake diamond on his finger.

"How's business, Clyde?" Donnelly asked calmly.

"You know, man," came the nervous reply. "Just hangin' in."

"You take care of those parking tickets yet?"

"Yeah, man, I'm clean," Clyde responded.

Donnelly continued around the room, acting nonchalant but carefully scrutinizing each face and mentally comparing it with his recollection of the mug shots he carried in his little file box. He stopped next to a large man who appeared to be studiously ignoring the officers as he sat alone on a bench near the wall, holding a pool cue between his legs.

"What's your name, sir?" Donnelly asked in a civil but businesslike tone. The man did not reply.

Donnelly stepped back slightly and assumed a defensive posture as he said in a more imperative voice, "Sir, I asked you what your name was."

The man turned his head slowly toward Donnelly and, after looking him in the eye for long enough to show that he was not intimidated, said, "You talkin' to me, man?"

Donnelly returned the stare. "Yeah, you got any identification?"

"No, man," the man answered. "I don't carry no I-dentification."

"You got a name?" Donnelly asked again.

"George Washington," came the reply.

"Where do you live?"

"Greenville Apartments."

"You drive?"

"No, man, I walk."

Donnelly knew that he didn't have any grounds to push it any further, so after pointedly looking the man in the eye for several moments, he continued his perambulation around the pool hall. Reynolds observed another small Black man in the corner who was studiously avoiding any eye contact with the officers, but Donnelly only gave him a cursory glance as he walked past and headed back toward the rear door. "Let's go," he said as he started outside.

"What's up with that big dude?" Reynolds asked Donnelly as they got back in the squad car.

"I don't know, haven't seen him around before, but we're going to find out," Donnelly answered.

Donnelly drove two blocks, turned right for a block and a half, then turned into another alley. This time, they turned into the basement parking garage of a large church. It was deserted except for two other cars. Donnelly backed the patrol car into a dark corner opposite the entrance, shut off the ignition, and leaned back in his seat. "Now we wait," he said.

Fifteen minutes went by without a word spoken, then thirty. Finally, a door opened at the side of the garage and a small dark form slipped quickly through and approached the driver's side of the car.

"You took your sweet-ass time getting here," Donnelly barked.

"Shit, Mick, I just can't get up and walk out as soon as you leave. You want to get me killed?" the man said in a high-pitched and whiney voice.

"Fuck no, Dixie. You're my main man, you know that. What's the word?" Donnelly said.

"Don't know, man, who's your partner?" Dixie replied.

"No sweat, Dixie, he's cool. What you got?" Donnelly said.

"Not much shakin', man," Dixie said. "They laid off movin' any shit through the 'Bird' since you put the squad on 'em last time."

"Who was that big dude?" Donnelly asked.

"Name's Robinson. They call him 'Duke.' Don't know his first name. He's up from Portland. Been hanging with Benny Malone. Word's out they might be doing some business together," Dixie answered.

"Keep your ears open, Dixie. Taking down that Malone gang would mean a lot to me."

"Better watch that guy, Mick. He carries a piece, a small automatic in the small of his back, I hear," Dixie responded.

"Thanks for the warning," Donnelly said. "Anything else moving?"

"No, man, things are pretty quiet."

Donnelly reached into his kit on the front floorboards, then got out of the car and walked with the little Black man to the door of the garage, handed him something, and then returned to the car. They waited for several minutes after Donnelly returned, then pulled out onto the street.

"You hungry, kid?" Donnelly asked.

"Starved," Reynolds responded.

"Let's see if we can get on the eating list." Donnelly picked up the mike and intoned, "Two-George-Three."

"Go ahead, Two-George-Three," came the response.

"We'd like to get on your list."

"Go ahead and eat, George-Three."

"We'll be on the portable in about five," Donnelly said.

To Reynolds' delight, they headed toward The Harbor. "By the way, kid," Donnelly said, "what you just saw, forget it. If you ever see that guy around, you don't know him from Adam. He's a good snitch, and they're hard to come by. When you get one, you protect his ass all the way down the line. That means you don't tell anybody—your sergeant, the dicks, nobody. Got that?" Reynolds nodded. "Like I said before, information is the name of the game. A good informant is worth his weight in gold, the best source you can get. You've got to try to cultivate them at every opportunity," Donnelly continued.

As they pulled into the restaurant parking lot, Reynolds began to feel a slight queasiness in the pit of his stomach and a dampness on his palms. He began taking deep breaths to calm the anticipation he felt at possibly seeing the beautiful Tawnya again. He walked tall and nonchalantly as he and Donnelly followed the hostess to a corner table. The hostess brought them coffee and menus as

Reynolds waited anxiously to see who their waitress would be. He was finally rewarded as he saw Tawnya emerge from the kitchen area and walk calmly and coolly toward them. Reynolds found himself thinking of the lyrics from the song "The Girl from Ipanema" as he watched her approach.

She smiled warmly as she greeted them. "Good afternoon, gentlemen. What can I get you today?"

Donnelly ordered fish and chips, and Reynolds, without looking at the menu, said, "I'll take the same, thank you."

As he watched the tall, dark figure glide back toward the kitchen, Reynolds heard Donnelly say, "You look like a cat checking out the canary in the cage."

"Can't help it, man. She's beautiful," Reynolds whispered.

"I take it you're not married," Donnelly said.

"No," Reynolds replied, "I haven't tried it yet—you?"

"I've tried it—three times, as a matter of fact," Donnelly answered.

"But you're not married now?" Reynolds asked.

"No, my last old lady gave up on me about five years ago."

"What is it about police work that breaks up so many marriages?" Reynolds queried, thinking back to the number of cops he'd talked to and heard about that were divorced.

"I don't really know," Donnelly answered. "Maybe it's the hours, never being home on holidays or special occasions, working all hours of the day. Maybe it's the anxiety a lot of cops' wives feel about the job—never knowing if the old man is going to come home in one piece or come home at all. Most cops, who got hitched before they came on the job, married naïve little middle-class women whose only conception of police work is what they see on TV. Very few of them are equipped to understand or share what you really go through on the street, and consequently, a lot of guys shut their wives out as far as the job is concerned. But they have to talk to someone, so they wind up going to the Greeks for a few drinks with the boys after work, or they find some chippy in a bar who's been around cops and knows the ropes. Sooner or later, they either get bored with the old lady or she gets tired of him coming home drunk every night and throws his ass out."

"That sounds like my ol' man," Reynolds said.

"Yeah, I remember your dad," Donnelly replied. "Big, good-looking guy like you before the booze got to him. Had quite the reputation as a lady's man. A real stallion, I heard."

"I swore I would never be like him in any way," Reynolds replied. "He was a big jock in high school, apparently—three-sport letterman in football, basketball, and baseball all the way through school. I was good at sports too but decided to only engage in individual sports, so I did cross-country, wrestled, and ran track. My mother said he was always chasing the wild skirts in school, so I dated the class valedictorian for three years. I decided early on that any relationships that I had with women were going to be built on a foundation of mutual trust, respect, and genuine love and affection."

"Sounds good in theory," Donnelly replied. "How's that working out for you?"

"Not so well, I guess," Reynolds replied. "I haven't had that many relationships. The girl I dated in high school went on to Princeton and became a doctor while I went into the Air Corps. I met a Japanese girl in Okinawa who I really liked, but her parents were adamant they did not want her to marry anyone outside their culture and definitely did not want her leaving the country. We talked about getting married anyway, but in the end, she wasn't willing to defy her parents, and then I got deployed to Iraq and then Afghanistan. I had lots of opportunities at WSU but never found anyone that I was really attracted to. Most of the girls in my classes seemed so young, naïve, and superficial that it was hard to even carry on a conversation with them. And I kept so busy studying and doing my own thing that I never got out and socialized much." Reynolds paused. "How about you, what broke up your marriages?"

Donnelly gave him a sad smile and shrugged. "Well, number one, I always got married for the wrong reasons, mostly selfish, superficial ones instead of what you described—mutual trust, respect, and genuine love and affection. Second, I'm one of those unfortunate cops who started liking the job too much. Couldn't get enough of it. Didn't want to go home at night. I got addicted to the action, and nothing else really mattered. It cost me three pretty good women before I finally got smart and decided to stay single."

"Do you have any kids?" Reynolds asked.

"Two boys and a girl, one from each marriage. Don't see them much anymore. All my wives have remarried and don't really appreciate me coming around too much. So, I just keep paying my $1200-a-month child support and send cards on their birthdays and holidays. Maybe when they get out on their own, we can re-establish a relationship."

"You think it's possible for a cop to stay married?" Reynolds asked as he watched Tawnya taking an order from another table.

"Sure, if you find the right woman and want it bad enough to put the marriage first. I know a lot of good, level-headed cops who live for their families. If you're mature enough to be able to keep the job in perspective and leave it at the station, and secure enough that you don't have to prove your manhood with all the loose pussy you run into on the street, there's no reason you can't be as happily married as anybody else."

"Is it worth it?" Reynolds asked.

"You'll have to make up your own mind about that. You give up a lot being married, especially after you have kids. You probably won't be going backpacking every weekend or working out as much, and you won't be able to sit down and read a book when you want. But there are a lot of times when it's damn nice to come home to the security and sanity of your own home, have your kids run up and throw their arms around you, and have a loving wife who has dinner on the table. Depends on the person, I guess. Personally, I enjoy the solitude and serenity of my little apartment and not having to be responsible for someone else's happiness and dreams. In my experience I've found that women make better anchors than they do sails. Fortunately, on this job, you do run into women who are willing to share their body with you occasionally without making too many demands."

As Reynolds watched Tawnya picking up an order from the kitchen, he envisioned the prospect of her waiting at the door for him when he came home from work and where that might lead.

"Take a word of advice," Donnelly said. "Quit acting like a fawning fool. A broad like Tawnya is not looking for adoration—she gets enough of that every day. She wants someone she can adore. You won't get to first base with that drool running down your chin."

Reynolds felt his face begin to flush, but he got the message. "It probably wouldn't work anyway," he said. "I learned from my experience with Moshi that it is very hard to integrate different cultures, and she probably comes from a very different world than me. I don't think I could make it work with someone who didn't share my values, interests, and tastes, at least to some degree."

"You'll never know if you don't try," Donnelly commented as Tawnya approached with their food.

She sauntered casually and confidently up to the table and placed their orders in front of them. "Anything else I can get you?" she asked, looking coolly at both officers. Reynolds thought he detected a subtle sparkle in her eyes. He met her glance and replied, "No, I think we're good, but thanks." She hesitated a moment and then walked away with that same lovely, swaying stride. *The girl from Ipanema*, Reynolds thought, *tall and tan and cool and lovely*.

To get his mind off Tawnya as he began to eat his meal, Reynolds asked Donnelly another question. "So, what keeps you going in this job, Mick?"

"Pride, I guess. I broke in twenty-five years ago with a bunch of old-timers who advised me to just close my eyes, take what I could get, and wait for my twenty-five. But I couldn't live with myself doing that. Oh, I tried for a while. I was young and single like you when I first came on, and I used to spend my off-duty hours drinking and chasing pussy, and my on-duty hours sobering up so I could do it again the next night. Then I got married the first time and quit running around. Within six months, I was bored shitless. I started to hate coming to work, and then I hated going home. I transferred to night shift and started chippying around, but that didn't help either. Finally, I sat down with a bottle of Jack Daniels one night and took a long, hard look at who I was and where I was going. I decided the reason I wasn't satisfied with the job was because I wasn't putting any effort into it. My self-respect was virtually nil, and it was affecting every aspect of my life. So, I decided to start doing some police work for a change."

"Did it help?" Reynolds asked between bites.

"Well, I guess I carried it to the extreme because it cost me three old ladies, but at least I can live with myself now."

"Was the peace of mind worth it?"

"I think so. You find out that everyone's alone in this world anyway, Dan. When it comes right down to it, the only one you can count on is yourself, *numero uno*. Marriage and I were never too compatible anyway, I'm afraid. All the little dreams most women of our class are raised with—the house in the suburbs, the nice furniture, the china and crystal, the two cars in the garage, 2.3 kids, and a successful old man who comes home from his eight-to-five job in the city with a fat paycheck in hand—seem pretty damn frivolous when you've spent eight hours in the jungle dealing with people who have to fight and steal just to survive. I'm afraid I'm just not cut out for it—marriage, that is." Donnelly wiped his mouth. "Hey, enough of this bullshit, let's get back to work."

Reynolds put a twenty-dollar bill on the table and fell in behind Donnelly as he headed for the door. Suddenly, he heard that melodious voice behind him: "Hey chief, you forgot your check." He turned around with a quizzical look on his face and waited as Tawnya approached him with a large smile on her face and a twinkle in her eye. She placed the folded check in his hand and closed his fingers over it, then turned on a heel and walked away with that slow, swaying saunter. Reynolds opened the folded check, not knowing for sure what to expect. Printed on the otherwise blank check was "Tawnya—360-555-9821." A smile crept across his face as he watched her disappear into the kitchen. He turned and walked out of the restaurant in a buoyant mood, the smile getting bigger as he walked.

"You've got that cat-with-the-canary look again," Donnelly said as Reynolds slid into the front seat of the patrol car. Reynolds didn't say anything, just passed the paper check for Donnelly to read.

"Congratulations, stud," Donnelly said. "I wouldn't advertise it too much around the station if you decide to take her out. We still have a few guys who might not appreciate your taste in women."

"Fuck 'em," Reynolds replied. "I don't need anyone's approval."

"No, but you might need their help someday if you get into some shit."

The rest of the day passed quickly with a string of routine calls for service—a noise complaint, a larceny report, and then a rush-hour fender bender. Reynolds soon found himself straddling his bike and riding out of the station. The trip home went by in a fog as his mind focused on if, when, and how he was going to ask Tawnya out. He decided to call her in the morning before she went to work.

CHAPTER 5

THURSDAY, DAY FOUR

Thursday was an Aikido day. Reynolds was up at his normal 6:00 a.m. and at the dojo by 7:00. He had difficulty maintaining his focus because he was anticipating calling Tawnya when he got back to his apartment. He finally got through his workout, which seemed to take much longer than usual, and rode back to his apartment, where he showered and dressed. Then he found himself sitting on the lanai, drinking coffee and trying to think of what to say when he called. Finally, an approach crossed his mind, and he dialed her number.

"Hi, this is Tawnya," came the cheery response on the other end of the line.

"Hi Tawnya, this is Dan, that cop you gave your phone number to at The Harbor yesterday."

"Well, hello, Dan," she replied, "I'm glad you called."

Reynolds felt heartened by the pleasant and eager sound of her voice, so he plowed ahead with his chosen plan of attack. "I was hoping I could talk you into having breakfast with me on Sunday morning."

There was a brief moment of silence before she responded quizzically, "Breakfast!? You're asking me out to breakfast on our first date?"

"Well, after all, it is the most important meal of the day," he replied with a laugh. "Actually, I always eat Sunday breakfast down at a little diner on Lake Union, and I thought it would give us a chance to talk and get to know each other. We can see where the day goes from there."

"Hmmm," she replied, "well, I have to admit, I've never been asked out to breakfast on a first date, but what the hell, I always enjoy a good breakfast on Sunday morning."

"Great," Reynolds said, "I'll pick you up at 8:00 a.m. sharp. Where do you live?"

"I stay in a residence hall called The Refuge on the corner of 48th and University Drive. It's an all-women dormitory, and you never know what you might run into if you go inside at that time on a Sunday morning, so just park out front, and I'll come down. What kind of car do you drive?"

"I've got a lifted forest-green Jeep Wrangler with big off-road tires. You can't miss it."

"I could have guessed that. Well, okay, I'll see you Sunday then," she replied with a laugh.

"I'm looking forward to it. Have a great day."

"You too, chief," she replied as she hung up the phone.

Reynolds found himself just sitting and smiling as he finished his cup of coffee and contemplated a day with Tawnya. His reverie was broken when he glanced at his watch and saw it was past time to get ready for work. An hour later, he walked into the Crime Analysis Unit, where he found Donnelly perusing police reports.

"You've got a little extra spring in your step this morning, partner," Donnelly said as Reynolds sat down at his table.

"Got a date for our day off Sunday," Reynolds replied.

Donnelly just looked at him for a moment and then shook his head, "Must be nice to be young," he said.

Two hours later, they were out patrolling the back streets of their district when Donnelly pulled to the curb and parked a half-block from a traffic-signal-controlled intersection.

"We might as well see if we can catch our ticket for the day," he said, and they spent the next fifteen minutes watching the signal cycle from green to amber to red and back to green.

"I hate this shit," Donnelly complained. "Sometimes it feels like we're just revenue collectors for the city."

The words were no sooner out of his mouth than a red Buick convertible blew through the red light doing at least 60 mph.

"That's it," Donnelly exclaimed as he pulled into the traffic lane, turned the corner, and accelerated rapidly to catch up with the speeding violator. As before, he got a quick pace on the car and then pulled within twenty-five yards before he flipped on the switches for the emergency lights and siren. As he depressed the horn bar, the siren gave a brief wail, and Reynolds saw a look of instant apprehension on the faces of the four Black teenage occupants of the Buick as they looked simultaneously out the back of the top-down convertible.

"Check the hot sheet for Adam-Nora-Sam 812," Donnelly instructed. Reynolds plugged the license number into the computer and was about to say it wasn't listed when he was thrown violently to his left by a hard right turn.

"They're running!" Donnelly yelled. "Get on the radio and tell them we're in a pursuit and give them our location and direction."

Reynolds looked around to ascertain their location and then keyed the mike, "Two-George-Three is in pursuit. Suspect vehicle is a red Buick convertible, Washington license Adam-Nora-Sam 812. Vehicle is currently eastbound on Jefferson from 25th Avenue, traveling at a high rate of speed. Vehicle is occupied by four Black males."

"All units clear the air, Two-George-Three is in a pursuit," Dispatch replied. "What's your location now, George-Three?"

"Turning northbound on 28th from Jefferson," Reynolds responded as Donnelly wheeled the patrol car through a hard, sliding left turn. Reynolds held onto the shotgun with his left hand and the mike with his right as he scanned right and left for street signs.

"Vehicle is turning westbound on Cherry from 28th," Reynolds announced into the mike.

As they skidded through the turn moments later, Reynolds was surprised to see the Buick stopped dead in the middle of the street, with both doors standing wide open and four young bodies emerging from them.

"Take the driver," Donnelly shouted as he skidded to a stop behind the Buick.

Reynolds bailed out of the patrol car and sprinted after the slender young man who had been driving. He immediately discovered that running in a police uniform with a full duty belt was a lot different than cruising around Green Lake in his running togs. The holstered Glock and his portable radio slapped at his side, and the three-cell flashlight kept banging his leg, but he put that out of his mind as he focused on his breathing and tried to recreate his old 400-meter stride. The suspect had a half-block lead on him initially and was running on the sidewalk parallel to the street, but Reynolds soon began gaining on him as he felt the adrenaline surge through his body. His quarry cut through a yard, jumped a fence, and headed west up the alley, with Reynolds closing ground quickly. Within minutes, that seemed like hours, Reynolds found himself within ten feet of the suspect and knew that he had him.

"I can do this all day!" he shouted at the young man. "You might as well give up."

The kid turned his head to see where Reynolds was and tripped over his own feet, causing him to sprawl face-first onto the dirt alley. Reynolds was on him in a second, placed a knee in his back, and quickly pulled his arms behind him and cuffed him. He had just finished patting him down when he saw Donnelly pulling into the alley ahead of him.

"Great work, partner," Donnelly exclaimed as he got out of the car. "The other three got away, but we'll catch them."

Reynolds picked the kid up off the ground and guided him to the rear of the patrol car, where he did a more thorough pat search before placing him in the rear seat of the patrol vehicle. Donnelly got on the radio. "Dispatch, this is Two-George-Three."

"Go ahead, George-Three," came the reply.

"We have one suspect in custody. Three Black males, approximately fourteen to sixteen years of age, are still at large. They were last seen running on foot southbound from 28th and Cherry. One has on a bright-green hoody and the other two are in dark clothing. Please send an impound to that location."

"Received, Two-George-Three. For your information, Adam-Nora-Sam 812 was just reported stolen. Two-George-One is getting a signed report at this time."

"Two-George-Three, copy," Donnelly responded as he drove back to the location of the stolen vehicle.

Donnelly turned to Reynolds. "Listen up for the radio," he said as he took his fingerprint kit from his case and proceeded to the stolen vehicle, which he began to dust for prints, starting with the interior and exterior door handles, then the side mirrors and the rear-view mirror, and finally the area around the ignition switch. After lifting several prints, he carefully inventoried the contents of the car.

He observed that the vehicle had not been hotwired, and there was no key in the ignition, concluding that the ignition had probably been left unlocked. He noted all this information along with the identifying data from the vehicle registration. By this time, the tow truck had arrived, and while the driver was putting the car on the hook, Donnelly finished writing up the impound report and inventory form, had the tow truck driver sign them, and then instructed him, "Put a hold on that thing for auto theft."

"Well kid, it looks like we've got a couple of hours of paperwork ahead of us," Donnelly said as he slid into the driver's seat. It was two and a half hours later when they walked back to their patrol car after transporting their prisoner to the station, taking a statement from the fourteen-year-old suspect (in which Donnelly had rather easily gotten him to name the other three boys in the car by convincing him that it would be a lot easier on him if he cooperated), booking the fingerprints into Evidence, completing a detailed arrest report, writing their individual officer's statements, and then transporting the suspect to the juvenile detention facility.

"Five hours into the shift, and we've gotten a felony arrest," Donnelly commented as they pulled out of the parking lot of the detention facility and headed back to their district. "Not a bad start to the day. You hungry?"

"Yeah, I've worked up a little appetite. What happens to the kid now?" Reynolds asked.

"Well, by now, he has undoubtedly been released to his mama and is home watching TV, laughing his ass off. He'll be the envy of the neighborhood tomorrow until his buddies figure out that he ratted them out. The worst that will probably happen to him is he'll get placed on probation, even though he's already been handled over a dozen times since the age of eight and has priors for burglary, purse snatching, and petty larceny."

"While you can't excuse the behavior, you do have to feel sorry for kids being raised in this environment. They seem to have two strikes against them from the moment they leave the womb, don't they?" Reynolds opined as they pulled into the local Sonic for lunch.

"Well, there's definitely not a level playing field when you compare kids coming from these neighborhoods to the white kids living on the other side of the Lake," Donnelly responded.

"You'd think in a country as rich as the United States, we could do something about the poverty and social conditions a lot of these kids deal with from day one of their lives," Reynolds replied. "It's no wonder that so many of them get involved in criminal behavior. I wrote a paper in college on the effects of poverty in this country. You know, we have over 40 million people living in poverty, of which over 13 million are children. Many of these kids wake up every morning not knowing where their next meal is coming from, and that's over and above the 30 million kids who live in households that rely on food stamps and other forms of public assistance. Whites may comprise the largest sheer number of people living in poverty, but Blacks and Hispanics are, percentagewise, over two times more likely to live below the poverty line. And when you consider the fact that 35 percent of the kids in this country live in single-parent households where the poverty level is over 30 percent, it's no wonder the US has the highest incarceration rate in the world and ranks so low in education and health care."

"It's a tragic situation, to be sure," Donnelly responded. "And we see the consequences of it every day."

"It's such a pervasive problem," Reynolds continued, "poverty impacts every aspect of a child's development, starting with a lack of prenatal health care and poor maternal nutrition, which leads to low-birth-weight babies with a higher preponderance of congenital conditions, and it only gets worse as they get older. When both parents have to work—often multiple jobs—just to get by, the kids grow up without the nurturing and care they need to develop into well-adjusted adults. They often lack the appropriate kinds of mental stimulation to fully develop their cognitive functioning, which leads to poor school performance and eventually to dropping out of school. They grow up in unsafe neighborhoods where crime and violence are common, which affects both their physical and mental health and leads to antisocial attitudes, beliefs, and behaviors. I've noticed, in just the few days I've been on the job, the change in attitude you see in these kids as they get older. When we pull up in front of a house with young children five and six years old, they run out happily to greet us and show no fear; but then as they get up toward eight or nine, you can see and feel the hostility and anger they begin to exhibit."

"Well, as you said, these kids don't get a lot of appropriate parental supervision," Donnelly responded. "The responsible parents are out working, and the irresponsible ones are out drinking and drugging and living off welfare. The kids wind up being raised by their older siblings or other kids in the neighborhood and, consequently, being indoctrinated into all the negative shit these kids hear about cops and their chances in white society in general. It's tough when the only successful people you see in your neighborhood are the pimps and the drug dealers. But what are you going to do? Johnson's War on Poverty didn't work out all that well."

"Well, actually, we did see a reduction in poverty and an improvement in conditions for minorities in the years right after Johnson's term. A lot of the programs that were put in place are still having a positive effect on poverty, like Head Start and the Jobs Corp. But, as usual, there was a lot of criticism among whites about reverse discrimination and that we were creating a welfare state—which to a degree I guess we were—but I think most objective analysis would support the fact that without those government programs, the poverty level would be much higher than it is."

"Since when is it the government's responsibility to take care of people who aren't willing to take care of themselves?" Donnelly replied. "I don't want my tax dollars going to someone who just wants to sit on their ass."

"You know, I hear that a lot from conservatives, but I never hear them complain about the millions of dollars a year in corporate welfare the government pays to subsidize companies making billions of dollars a year. Then you have companies like Walmart and McDonald's, who pay their employees so little that they can't afford a decent place to live and need food stamps just to eat.

"We both know there isn't any free lunch in the world, but there's no doubt that if we want to eliminate poverty, we are going to have to collectively invest more money in disadvantaged people. Isn't a major tenet of the Christian faith that we are our brothers' keeper? The problem with many conservatives, who mostly profess to being strong Christians, is they have a scarcity mentality. They look at life like a zero-sum game in which there is only so much 'good' to go around, and any 'good' you get means there is just that much less for me. I like Stephen Covey's concept of an 'abundance mentality.' By investing in people, we are going to increase their contribution to society, reduce the need for future welfare programs, and create more 'good' for everyone. But I do agree that we must demand a level of personal responsibility from people in exchange for providing them more opportunities in life."

"So, what is that going to look like in your view?" Donnelly asked.

"Well, I think the ultimate answer to eliminating poverty lies in education, but to effectively utilize education, we have to start at conception and provide every kid what he or she needs in terms of nutrition, medical care, parenting, nurturing, et cetera to reach their full potential. Beyond that, I think we need to adopt a governing philosophy in this country that being a parent is a privilege, not a right. A privilege that must be earned."

"So, what are you going to do, make people get a license to have sex?" Donnelly chuckled.

"No, but I would establish some conditions that must be met in order to keep a child. Let's face it, any imbecile can propagate an offspring, but it takes a high degree of knowledge and commitment to raise a child to be a responsible and productive adult. If I was king for a day, I'd enact a new constitutional amendment—a Children's Bill of Rights. It would stipulate that every child in this country has a right to a suitable home, a stable, nurturing environment, good nutrition, appropriate medical care, and a good education. Every prospective parent would be required to demonstrate that they are or will be able to provide all of these things, as well as meet all of the other physical and cognitive needs of the child. In addition, they should be required to have a basic understanding of child development and parenting skills."

"So, you want the government to decide who can have a child and how it's raised? Sounds like *1984* to me. What are you going to do if they can't meet those conditions? Take away the child?"

"Well, possibly, but first, I think we need to do whatever we can to enable parents to meet those conditions," Reynolds replied as he took a bite of the burger the carhop had just dropped off at the car. "To begin with, I would require a mandatory personal wellness curriculum in our secondary schools that would include comprehensive sex education to help kids avoid premature parenthood, and then classes in parenting, child development, relationship skills, nutrition, meal preparation, et cetera that would prepare young people for the responsibility of having children. If a young pregnant girl has not had these classes, we should provide them to her and the father during her pregnancy.

"Next, I would establish a universal health care system in the country that would ensure that every pregnant mother has access to affordable, accessible prenatal and postnatal health care for her and her baby and continuing care thereafter. I would also have programs for continuing education, job training, affordable childcare, housing, et cetera that would eventually allow parents to meet these conditions and provide an appropriate home for the child. In the meantime, if the parents are actively participating and show a strong commitment to being good parents, I would provide public assistance to meet their financial needs until they can be self-sustaining."

"And if they choose not to participate in these programs, what do you do then?" Donnelly responded. "Resort to involuntary sterilization?"

"Well, one of the few things I have ever agreed with Newt Gingrich on is that we need more orphanages in this country. Actually, not orphanages, but professionally run group homes. I would do away completely with the current foster parent system and establish a network of group homes in every community in the country. These could be government-run or contracted as long as they met strict standards of care. The most important things that any child needs are stability, structure, and nurturing care. All of those could be provided by well-trained, certified house parents in fully supported facilities."

"What do you mean by 'fully supported facilities'?"

"Well, you would need staff to help with cooking, home maintenance, medical care, tutoring, counseling, et cetera," Reynolds responded.

"That sounds like it could get expensive real fast," Donnelly replied.

"I read a book called *To the End of June*, written by a woman named Cris Beam, who has researched this issue extensively," Reynolds replied. "In it, she said something to the effect that we spend over $20 billion a year in this country on a system that nobody—not the foster kids, not the foster or biological parents, not the social workers, not the administrators, and not the courts—think is working. We're spending tens of billions of dollars every year on our foster care system, and to what end? Former foster kids experience higher unemployment, higher levels of poverty, more mental and physical health problems, are less educated, and experience higher levels of incarceration. I've heard that 30 percent of the homeless population went through foster care. Bottom line, we are failing these kids, and it's already costing us a hell of a lot of money.

"Hell, we have the highest incarceration rate in the world and spend $80 billion a year just running our jails and prisons in this country, not to mention the social costs of incarceration, which amount to untold billions of dollars. If we could cut our incarceration rate in half, we could pay for a lot of social programs. It's a shame, but most of these poor foster kids get bounced from one home to the next, so they never have a chance to bond with any adult or achieve any stability in their lives. Then you have thousands of kids a year who age out of the foster system and wind up alone on the street with no support system."

"But most of the research that I've read says that kids are better off if they can be reunited with their biological parents," Donnelly responded.

"I've read that too. In fact, I just read that some conservatives are advocating for a law that limits kids to two weeks in a group home before they are sent back to their parents or adopted out. I think that is ridiculous. I fully support reuniting the child with their parents if the only problems are financial, or housing, or employment. We can provide short-term assistance to deal with those kinds of needs. But when there is severe abuse, or neglect, or drug or alcohol addiction; there is no way you are going to ameliorate those situations in a few weeks, or even months or years. Most kids wind up spending two to three years in foster care even now."

"But are group homes really that much better?" Donnelly replied. "I've heard horror stories about the way some are operated. And if you have a new shift coming on every eight hours, and if staff are leaving all the time--which I'm sure would happen—are the kids really going to get the stability they need and be able to form secure attachments?"

"It could be a problem if you don't have really high standards for the people you hire as house parents and staff," Reynolds answered. "I would like to see a college curriculum dedicated to training highly motivated people for these kinds of positions and then make sure they are paid well enough so that you minimize turnover. I think if you have dedicated, committed folks who are appropriately trained, supervised, and audited, you would be able to retain staff long-term and ensure consistent care for the kids. The most important thing is that kids would have a safe, stable, and nurturing living environment and be around people who genuinely care about them. Kids really can't have too many positive role models in their lives."

"Finding enough people to staff all the group homes you would need would be a real problem," Donnelly said.

"Well, you know that finding jobs for people in the coming age of increased automation, artificial intelligence, and robotics is going to be a major challenge in itself. In fact, I think it is going to be the defining issue of the twenty-first century after climate change. But creating more jobs in social services, such as case managers, social workers, counselors, and group home supervisors, could be a big part of the answer, and we would have a real resource in people who have emerged from poverty and addiction and want to give back to the community that helped them."

Despite his initial reservations, Donnelly looked impressed at Reynold's arguments. "Well, we better get back on the street," he said after a pause. "Good talk. I think you may be wasting your time being a cop. Have you ever thought about running for public office?"

"The thought has crossed my mind," Reynolds responded.

The remainder of the shift went by uneventfully, and Reynolds soon found himself pedaling his bike along Lake Union on his way home. His mind was still racing from his conversation with Donnelly over lunch, and he found himself feeling somewhat embarrassed that he had allowed himself to pontificate at such length with someone he had only known a few days. But he was also stimulated by the opportunity to discuss a subject at length to which he had given a great deal of thought and by Donnelly's enthusiastic—if not entirely supportive—participation. He looked forward to future opportunities for meaningful discussions as he pondered Donnelly's suggestion that he should go into politics. That thought lingered in his mind until he drifted off to sleep that night.

CHAPTER 6

FRIDAY, DAY FIVE

"Two-George-Three in service, two-man," Donnelly intoned into the radio as they cleared the pumps.

Dispatch immediately came back with, "Two-George-Three, handle a two-car accident, no injuries reported, at the intersection of 23rd and East Alder."

"Two-George-Three, responding," Donnelly replied and then turned to Reynolds. "Okay, what did they teach you in the academy about handling a traffic accident?"

"Well, the first thing was to position the patrol car to best protect the scene. Then, check for injuries and render aid to anyone who needs it. Then, locate the point of impact and note the position of the vehicles, pace off those locations to a fixed point, as well as measure skid marks, and then do a quick sketch of the scene. Take photos if you can, and then move the vehicles out of traffic if possible or call for a tow truck if necessary. Try to locate and identify any witnesses to the accident and get their version of what happened. At that point, you sit down with the drivers and write the accident report."

"Pretty good," Donnelly responded. "What do you do if someone is critically injured or there is a fatality?"

"Call for an ambulance for the injured, render first aid, and then secure the scene and call for the Special Detail to investigate."

"Okay, since you're the trained medic, you do an immediate check for injuries when we arrive and, if there aren't any, put the drivers in the back of the patrol car and start getting their personal and vehicle information for the accident report. I'll take photos and measurements and make a sketch of the scene; then, we'll try to get the cars moved."

As they arrived on the scene, Donnelly directed Reynolds to note the time of arrival in his notebook as he pulled the patrol car into a protective position in the roadway and flipped on the emergency lights. "Two-George-Three, arrived," he announced into the mike.

Reynolds quickly emerged from the patrol car and located the drivers, who were standing on the curb. He verified that no one was injured and determined that the two drivers were the only ones in either vehicle. He had each driver get the vehicle registration and insurance certificates from their vehicles and then took them back to the patrol car, where he started filling out the standard accident report. Within minutes, after determining that both vehicles were operable, Donnelly returned to the car and requested both drivers to move their vehicles out of the roadway. He made it a point to get close enough to each driver so that he could smell any alcohol on their breath and observe any physical signs of impairment. When he brought them back to the patrol car, he directed one to have a seat in the car and then took the other driver aside and had him give his version of what happened. He then had that driver wait while he questioned the other driver in the patrol car. Fortunately, one driver readily admitted that he had been distracted and had not seen the light turn red, so the disposition was relatively straightforward. He was issued a summons, both drivers were given copies of each other's personal and vehicle information along with the accident report number, and they were sent on their way. Reynolds cleared the debris out of the road, after which Donnelly cruised to Pinky's

Soul Food, where they finished the report over a large bowl of Jambalaya and sweet iced tea.

As he reviewed the finished document, Donnelly exclaimed, "Damn, I hate doing these things. The fucking insurance companies should have to pay us a stipend for every one we do since they're the ones who benefit from them."

"Why isn't the Traffic Division responsible for investigating traffic accidents?" Reynolds responded.

"Damn good question," Donnelly replied. "I guess the city doesn't want them distracted from writing traffic tickets long enough to investigate accidents. As I've said before, if I had my way, we would have Traffic units assigned to each sector in the city, and they would handle all traffic-related incidents."

Back in the car, they began a slow, random patrol along the back streets and alleys of the district. "Check the windows and doors of the houses for signs of forced entry," Donnelly reminded Reynolds as he drove. After an hour of unproductive activity, Donnelly said, "Fuck it, let's check and see if we have any ladies out today."

As they drove down Yesler from 14th, Reynolds noticed several women—Black, white, and Asian—standing on street corners or walking slowly down the street. They seemed to be repelled by the prowler car like two magnets of like polarity and would turn and walk away when they saw it coming.

"The 'ladies of the evening' are out early today," Donnelly quipped. "You see anything you like? Looks like we have quite a variety today. Hey, there's LaTasha." He pulled to the curb beside a tall, slender, light-skinned Black woman. She wore a blond wig piled high on her head, a low-cut top exposing considerable cleavage, and black hot pants. She turned toward the police car with a look of disgust, which softened when she recognized Donnelly. He motioned her over to the passenger side, and Reynolds had to consciously look away as she bent forward at the waist and placed her elbows on the bottom of the window frame, almost fully exposing her ample bosom.

"Hey, Mick, what's happening," she said.

"Not much, doll," he replied. "How goes it?"

"Same old shit, baby," she responded.

"Let me see your ID and act indignant, so we look official here," Donnelly told her. "Haven't seen you around in a while."

"Been down in Portland for a few weeks," she replied as she handed him her state identity card.

Donnelly pretended to be writing in his notebook as he asked, "Got anything for me?"

"Well, I heard Ricky Bell just got a load of shit from California. They're cuttin' it over at his place on Fir."

"How much?"

"Couple of kilos, I hear. Good shit too."

"Where's he keeping it?" Donnelly asked.

"Apparently, he had it right out on the kitchen table last night, according to one of the girls," she responded.

"Who all's there?"

"Ricky, Tommy Smith, and Tommy's old lady were there last night. Could be a lot of traffic in and out today, though."

"They packin?" Donnelly asked.

"You better believe it," LaTasha responded. "Tommy's old lady even carries a piece in her purse."

"Okay, baby. You're beautiful. Give me a call tonight around 9:00 p.m., and we'll make arrangements to settle up."

Donnelly drove directly to Headquarters, and Reynolds followed him up to the Narcotics Unit.

"Hey, how's it going, Mick?" a tall Black detective said as they entered the small office, crammed with desks and filing cabinets.

"Not bad, Carl. Is Gray in?"

"Yeah, he's in his office. What you got?"

"Come on in and find out."

They walked into the even smaller office of the lieutenant in charge of the downtown Narcotics Unit, which was occupied by a short, balding, slightly built white man with gray hair and piercing brown eyes, sitting behind a large, cluttered desk.

"Hello, Mick," he said. "What can I do for you?"

"More like, what can we do for you?" Donnelly replied. "Got a tip that Ricky Bell just got a delivery of two Ks of high-grade smack."

"Oh, yeah, who's your informant?"

"You know better than that, Lieutenant," Donnelly replied. "She's reliable, I've used her before."

"We got anything on this?" the lieutenant asked the detective.

"News to me," he replied.

"Okay, where's it at, who all's there, and when was it last seen?"

Donnelly explained the setup to him and then Gray turned to the detective. "All right, Carl. Take them over to the prosecutor's office and get started on a warrant. I will get Daniels, Chambers, Andrews and McAllister in to help." He turned to Donnelly, "You guys want to be in on the bust?"

"Damn straight," Donnelly replied.

"Okay, I'll clear it with your patrol commander. We'll meet back here when you get done across the street."

The next two hours were a blur of mounting excitement for Reynolds as they completed the required paperwork at the prosecutor's office, waited in the judge's chambers until he recessed his court and could sign the search warrant, and then returned to the narcotics office. The anxious anticipation continued to mount as they waited in the lieutenant's office while the police helicopter surveyed the suspect's house and videoed the layout. Reynolds listened intently as they planned the approach, then excused himself to use the bathroom just before they headed down to their vehicles. It was decided four detectives would take the front, and Donnelly, Reynolds, and the other two detectives would take the rear. The lead detective in the front would do the "knock and announce" and then double-click the radio mike as a signal to stuff the door. They parked their vehicles a block away, out of sight of the house, and approached on foot, with a detective taking up positions at each corner of the house. Two detectives went to the front door, and Donnelly and Reynolds went to the back.

Finally, the climax came with a loud, "Police, open up. We have a warrant" at the front door, and the two clicks on the mike. Reynolds heard the scurrying sounds of running feet inside and then the crash of a door being torn from its frame. He and Donnelly simultaneously applied their right feet to the back door and Reynolds felt a wave of exhilaration as it tore from its hinges and they burst into the kitchen. Two Black forms were scrambling to scrape up mounds of white powder from the kitchen table. Reynolds heard Donnelly yell, "Police, put your hands on top of your heads." Both immediately threw up their hands, and while Reynolds covered them, Donnelly patted them down and cuffed them. Two detectives led in another suspect, who they had caught trying to flush heroin down the toilet. Two other detectives brought in a female they had caught trying to bail out of a bedroom window.

Within minutes that seemed like hours, the excitement was over, and Reynolds found himself guarding the suspects, three male and one female, while the detectives and Donnelly finished a sweep of the house along with a K9 unit that had been dispatched to the scene. The dog found a fourth male subject hiding in a bedroom closet under a pile of dirty clothes. Patrol units were dispatched to transport the suspects to holding cells downtown while the detectives, Donnelly and Reynolds, began the laborious task of gathering and cataloging evidence. They had to remove the toilet the one suspect had tried to use to flush his dope and drain the trap to salvage its contents. They then divided the house up and began a systematic, thorough search. Several articles were found that came back as stolen on a National Crime Information Center (NCIC) check, including a TV and three handguns. They also found numerous glassine packets containing a white powdery substance in a kitchen drawer, in addition to the loose powder on the kitchen table. Each item had to be photographed where found and fully documented as to where, when, and by whom it was found.

Two hours later, they finally loaded up the evidence at the scene and headed for the station. It was three more hours before Donnelly and Reynolds emerged from the police garage onto the street after finishing writing their reports and officer statements.

"Police work is great, isn't it, kid," Donnelly said to Reynolds. "Five minutes of fun and five hours of paperwork."

Reynolds noted the sarcasm in his voice, but when he nodded his head, it was in total agreement with the first part of his statement—police work was great.

"We've had a productive day," Donnelly said. "Would you like to join me at the Greeks for a celebratory drink?"

Normally, Reynolds avoided bars because he didn't like being around a bunch of loud drunks, but after the day they'd had, he felt the need to vent some of his pent-up emotions. Besides, he was curious about what a bunch of cops talked about during their 'debriefing' sessions, and he also thought it might help solidify his relationship with Donnelly.

"Sure, I'll hang with you for a little while," he responded.

It took a minute for Reynolds' eyes to adjust to the dark inner sanctum of the restaurant's lounge. When they did, he noticed that virtually all the patrons were off-duty cops. He followed Donnelly over to a large, circular table in the center of the lounge, where four men Reynolds didn't recognize were already sitting.

"Hey, Mick," one shouted, "come join us. Who's your friend?"

"This is my new partner, Dan Reynolds," Mick answered. "This is his first week on the street."

"Welcome to the fraternity," the man responded. "You found the right guy to break you in."

"I'm learning that quickly," Dan replied, shaking the hand of each of the men as they introduced themselves.

When the cocktail waitress came to the table to get their order, an officer who had introduced himself as Bill yelled, "Get them whatever they want and put it on my tab. A newbie never pays while I'm around."

Donnelly ordered his usual Glenlivet scotch straight up, and Reynolds, as unobtrusively as possible, ordered a club soda with lime.

"You're drinking *what*?" Bill exclaimed.

"He's a teetotaler," Donnelly answered, "and with good reason—so don't give him any crap."

"He's too damn big for me to give him any shit," Bill said laughingly. "You're still welcome at our table, Dan."

Reynolds spent the next hour listening to the men tell war stories about their exploits in the Department. As the rookie, he knew better than to try and join in the conversation but was fascinated at how much pride the officers seemed to take in their work, which seemed to contradict the complacency Donnelly had attributed to many cops. He learned a lot about Mick Donnelly that night as well, since invariably, he was a player in most of their reminiscences, including the fact that he had once been shot after responding to a domestic disturbance call.

"Just a flesh wound," Donnelly said in response to Reynolds' question about how badly he was hurt. "That's when I learned to never stand in front of a door on a call."

The ride home was especially enjoyable that night. He breathed deeply of the cool evening air as he basked in the feeling of acceptance he had felt from the cops he had met that night. His thoughts then turned to the lovely Tawnya. As he cruised past the houseboats on Lake Union, he saw a couple sitting out on their porch, watching the moon reflect off the water, and thought, *That's going to be us someday.*

CHAPTER 7

SATURDAY, DAY SIX

The day began with a string of 'chippy' calls, as Donnelly called them. First a neighborhood disturbance—a man dumping grass clippings in his neighbor's trash can that almost led to a physical altercation. He agreed to take them out. Then they responded to a dog bite report, then a car blocking a driveway, followed by a petty larceny report (a child's bicycle was missing). They took the opportunity while writing that report to grab a cup of coffee at Pinky's.

They had been back on the air less than five minutes when the silence was punctured by three shrill blasts on the radio and the imperative announcement, "We have a stick-up in progress—816 Capitol at White's Pharmacy—one white male suspect is inside at this time. Units responding?"

"Two-Charlie-Four from 12th and Aloha."

"Two-George-One from 15th and Madison."

"Two-George-Two from Boren and Jackson."

"Two-Charlie-Five from Broadway and Union."

"Two-George-Three will go from 25th and Spruce," Donnelly intoned into the mike.

Radio then commenced making assignments. "Two-Charlie-Four, take the paper. George-Two take the southwest quadrant, George-One the northwest, Charlie-Five the northeast, and George-Three the southeast."

Moments later, the announcement "Two-Charlie-Four, arrived" came over the radio, followed two minutes later by "Charlie-Four to all units. The suspect has left the scene. He was last seen running northbound on Capitol about ten minutes ago. Described as a white male, twenty to twenty-five years old, 5'10" to 6' tall, 150 pounds, slender build, light, pasty complexion, with dark-brown shoulder-length hair tied at the back in a ponytail, Fu Manchu mustache, wearing a light-blue denim long-sleeved shirt and blue jeans, armed with a silver-colored short-barrel revolver. He obtained approximately $150 in currency and a quantity of opioid medications."

Donnelly was speeding toward their assigned area when he began thinking out loud, "I'll bet that's one of the tweakers living in those flophouse apartments down on 14th. If so, he's probably sitting in his living room with a nylon stocking around his arm right now. Let's cruise down that way."

They arrived in a three-block area dominated by old three- and four-story wood-frame apartment buildings. Donnelly pulled to the curb, put them out on the portable, and said, "Let's go knock on some doors." Forty-five minutes and about three-dozen doors later, they stood in front of the manager's apartment in a particularly rundown building. Reynolds had been hesitant to trust his weight to the rotted wooden stairs at the front entrance, and, once inside, he was repelled by the sickly-sweet, musty odor of age, rot, and mildew that permeated the building.

A large, frowsy white female—maybe thirty, maybe fifty—answered their knock on the manager's door. She had long, stringy hair dyed jet black, high, arching eyebrows that had been painted on, and an overabundance of rouge, lipstick, and mascara. A loose-fitting taffeta robe splashed with garish red flowers ill-concealed her bulging body. Her breath reeked of beer; a cigarette hung loosely from her lips—the ash threatening to imminently drop into the cavernous cleavage.

"Are you the manager?" Donnelly asked.

"Yeah, what do you want?" she responded dryly.

Donnelly described the suspect and asked if she had anyone in the building matching that description.

"It sounds like that little shit up in 304. It's like pulling teeth to get the bastard to pay his rent. Just a second, I'll get his lease form," she said as she turned and jiggled and jounced her way to a small file cabinet, returning with a lease application. "Daniel Rensburg," she said, showing the form to Donnelly. Donnelly copied down the pertinent information.

"Have you seen this individual today?" he asked.

"Yeah, I saw him leave about an hour ago."

"What was he wearing?"

"One of those denim work shirts and blue jeans, I think," she replied.

"Do you have a key for his room?" Donnelly asked.

"Sure, I'll get it for you," she responded.

Donnelly pulled out his cell phone, called Dispatch, and asked to have two two-man cars dispatched by phone to the area to take up positions covering the four sides of the building. Radio asked if he wanted a sergeant dispatched, which brought a resounding, "Hell no, I can fuck this up bad enough myself." Then, in an aside to Reynolds, "You have to be careful using the radio. A lot of these assholes have police scanners."

Minutes later, the radio announced, "Two-George-Two to Two-George-Three, in position." That was followed moments later by a similar call from Two-Charlie-Four.

"All right, Dan, we're going to try and take this guy by surprise. Don't let your finger get too heavy on the trigger, but don't hesitate to take him out if you need to. I'll go in first and you follow my lead."

For the third time in three days, Reynolds felt the familiar gut-wrenching, heart-pounding, sweaty-palmed, nut-tightening apprehension of impending combat as he followed Donnelly up three flights of stairs. They crept as quietly as possible on the creaking hall floor to positions on either side of the doorway to Apartment 304. Donnelly listened at the door and could hear the sound of deep, rhythmic breathing coming from inside. He gently tried the doorknob and found it locked. Then he quietly intoned, almost in a whisper, "Police, open up," as he lightly knocked on the door. He then slowly and carefully inserted the key in the lock, twisted, and pushed open the door. He silently counted to three, then dove in a low crouch through the door to the opposite side with his gun drawn. Reynolds waited a couple of seconds and then did the same in the other direction. As he stood up, his eyes focused on the prone body of a young white male sprawled on his back on the bed in the center of the room. A length of rubber tubing lay on the bed next to him beside a used syringe; a bent, blackened tablespoon and an eye dropper were on the nightstand next to the bed; sticking from the waistband of his blue jeans was a silver-plated, .38 caliber snub-nose revolver.

Donnelly holstered his pistol and approached the sleeping suspect while Reynolds trained his weapon on the center of his chest. With a series of quick motions, Donnelly grabbed the suspect's gun, threw it on the floor, flipped the suspect on his stomach, straddled him, pulled his arms back, and cuffed him. All this brought only a muffled grunt and a sleepy, quizzical look from the suspect's half-open eyes.

Donnelly then got on the radio and announced, "This is Two-George-Three. We have the suspect in custody, Code 4. The other units can be clear."

As they pulled out of the station two hours later, Donnelly said, "I think you're my good-luck charm, kid. I haven't had a string of good felony busts like this in months. I am getting a little tired of pounding on that computer, though. Let's splurge a little and head down to The Harbor for dinner."

It was Saturday evening, and the restaurant was packed. The only table available was a small one located right next to the entrance to the kitchen. Tawnya waved and smiled as they walked in, but she was working at a different station and did not have time to come visit. Donnelly and Reynolds both ordered filets in celebration of the highly successful first week of their partnership.

"That guy Rensburg was sure a pathetic-looking mess, wasn't he?" Donnelly remarked. "Damn drugs sure waste a person away."

"Well, over time, they do a number on the brain, for sure," Reynolds responded, "but I don't think the drugs themselves are entirely responsible for the dissipation. It's more the lifestyle that society has forced on the addict that's responsible for that. The drug laws in this country are asinine."

"In what way?" Donnelly responded. "Do you think people should be able to just walk into the local drug store and buy illicit drugs?"

"Well, prior to the Pure Food and Drug Act of 1906 and the Harrison Act in 1914, there weren't any real laws prohibiting or regulating the sale and use of drugs, including narcotics and cocaine, and yes, people were able to buy drugs over the counter in pharmacies, through the mail, and even at food stores. Hell, cocaine was an ingredient in Coca-Cola."

"But addiction was a problem then as well," Donnelly replied.

"Sure, there was addiction, mostly caused by the indiscriminate use of morphine and other opiates as painkillers and in medications, but most people were able to supply their habits cheaply and easily and without breaking the law. Addicts were spread throughout the socioeconomic spectrum—housewives, businessmen, and professionals, including doctors—and most were able to continue to function as responsible members of society. Drugs were easily obtainable, they were inexpensive, and there was no great social stigma attached to their use. A person could be a drug addict and continue to work and remain a reasonably productive, self-respecting citizen. The drugs themselves, particularly the opiates, don't have a significant adverse effect on the human body other than the brain, which changes as it adapts to the drug, leading to tolerance and compulsive use. For the most part, drug use did not cause significantly aberrant behavior as long as a person was able to supply their habit."

"If that was the case," Donnelly interjected, "Why would they ever outlaw them to begin with?"

"The great moralists in this country, as usual, decided they had to protect their poor, weak brethren, and, again, as usual, the only way they could think to do that was by making it illegal. It's funny, though, that they wrote the Harrison Act in the form of a tax bill which also says something about this great land of ours. Anyway, the result is what you see today. The drug trade is the most lucrative criminal activity in existence and is dominated by large criminal enterprises, which have always prospered from human weakness. In the process, we have made criminals out of anyone who uses illicit drugs, creating a drug subculture in which the addict is alienated from society and forced to live in a nether land of shame and degradation. Because drugs are illegal and because they often lead to compulsive use, drug dealers can charge exorbitant prices for them. The addict is forced to deal with criminals to supply his habit and soon learns to identify with them. Because of the cost of drugs, the only way many addicts can supply their habit is by stealing, prostituting themselves, or dealing drugs themselves.

"Meanwhile, since Nixon declared the great 'War on Drugs' in the early 1970s, this country's taxpayers have shelled out millions a year in drug enforcement and related programs. When you consider that about a quarter of drug-related arrests are for possession, use, manufacturing, or drug trafficking, with an additional 20–30 percent for crimes committed in an effort to obtain drugs and alcohol, and that 50–60 percent of crimes are committed while under the influence of drugs, alcohol, or both, I think it's safe to say that 60–70 percent of our prison population is there directly or indirectly because of drugs and alcohol."

"Well, that sounds like a damn good reason to make them illegal," Donnelly responded.

"Well, it certainly led to the prison population explosion of the 1980s and 1990s and is the reason the United States has the highest incarceration rate in the world and why it's spending tens of billions a year in operating prisons, jails, and probation and parole. That does not include law enforcement and court costs or the costs to families to support incarcerated family members, which would add another $200–300 billion to that.

"In the forty years since the War on Drugs began, the US has spent over a trillion dollars on drug control efforts, and what have they got for their money? Demand for drugs is as high as ever. Even our best law enforcement efforts probably interdict less than 15 percent of the drugs coming into the country, and we know from the law of supply and demand that reducing supply just drives up the cost of drugs, which forces addicts to steal more to get their supply. Taking out a major drug dealer only creates an opening in the market for someone else to take his place, and with the enormous sums of money to be made, there is always someone ready to enter the trade. Not to mention that drug enforcement is probably the most dangerous aspect of police work. By any objective measure, one would have to conclude that the War on Drugs has been an abject failure."

"It sounds like this is an issue that you're passionate about," Donnelly responded.

"Well, I told you that my dad was an alcoholic," Reynolds replied. "I hated him for it as a kid when he never showed up for any of my school or sports activities, spent money on booze that could have gone toward making our lives much better, and was abusive to my mother when he was drunk. Then, he died in a car accident while drunk out of his mind, and it solidified my hatred of him. When I started college, I decided I needed to learn more about alcoholism and addiction, so I pursued a minor in addiction studies. I learned that a major factor driving addiction is heredity; some people are just genetically predisposed to addiction. One of my professors said that she knew she was an alcoholic from the first time she took a drink, which is why I have never allowed myself to even try alcohol or any drugs. I never want to end up like my old man.

"I also learned that addiction does not result from individual weakness nor from a lack of character or willpower. Over time, drugs and alcohol rewire the brain, short-circuiting the cognitive decision-making functions and allowing the 'reward center' of the brain to overwhelm any rational thought process."

"So, you're telling me that the individual is not responsible for their addiction?" Donnelly responded. "You've demonstrated yourself that using drugs or alcohol is still a choice—at least when a person first starts to use. And a lot of people recover from addiction, which means they eventually choose to exercise control over their compulsive behavior."

"That's true, but I don't think most non-addicts have any idea how hard it is," Reynolds responded. "They say that the euphoria from using heroin, cocaine, and methamphetamine is hundreds or even thousands of times greater than the normal pleasure we get from eating a good meal or even sex. Even though they say the high is never as good as the first time you use, it still is powerful enough to strongly reinforce the behavior and create an overwhelming compulsion to feel that high again."

"You obviously buy into the 'disease theory' of addiction," Donnelly replied. "So, if it is the drug that alters brain function and leads to addiction, why is it that not everyone who uses drugs or alcohol becomes addicted? In 'Nam, tons of people used marijuana and other drugs, and most of them got off it as soon as they came home. Lots of people use drugs and alcohol recreationally and never get addicted. Hell, I like a drink myself."

"That's true. During the nineteenth century, opiate consumption in the US and England was much more prevalent than it is now, but less than 1 percent of the population became addicted, and those numbers actually were going down before we started passing laws prohibiting use. I think it has a lot to do with what I discussed earlier. People were not stigmatized or ostracized from society back then. I read about a researcher named Alexander, who did an experiment with rats. I'm sure you've seen videos of caged laboratory animals being able to self-administer drugs by pushing a lever, and, over time, they would push that drug lever to the exclusion of food, water, and even sex.

"Alexander wanted to see what effect environment has on this behavior, so he constructed an elaborate 'Rat Park' that provided 200 times more living space than a regular laboratory cage, with half a dozen rats living in an environment which provided copious amounts of food, water, and toys, along with ample space for socializing, mating, and raising litters. He found that his rats were not interested in using morphine. In fact, he brought in rats that had been forced to consume morphine daily for two months and found that, given the opportunity to choose between tap water and morphine-laced water, most of the rats chose the tap water."

"Okay then, problem solved," Donnelly said. "We just take all our street addicts and put them up in luxury apartments with an endless supply of gourmet food and drink, and they will all give up drugs and become model citizens."

"Sarcasm noted," Reynolds replied, "but no. It does, however, indicate that we need to rethink what we are doing now. Look at what Portugal did back around the turn of the century. In the 1980s and '90s, they were experiencing extremely high levels of heroin use among a wide demographic of their population, along with high levels of drug-related crime and HIV infection, mainly among IV drug users. At the time, they were under an authoritarian regime and basically using the same approach to these problems as we have had in the US for years. Then, in 2001, Portugal became the first country to decriminalize the possession and consumption of all illicit drugs. Instead of throwing drug users in jail, they would bring them before a 'dissuasion' committee comprised of a doctor, a lawyer, and a social worker. The committee would discuss treatment options, harm-reduction techniques, and available social services with the drug user in an attempt to get them to change their behavior. In addition, they expanded their harm-reduction efforts and doubled their spending on drug treatment and prevention. Within a few years, Portugal experienced significant decreases in problematic drug use, HIV and hepatitis infection rates, overdose deaths, drug-related crime, and incarceration rates.

"The Netherlands has taken a similar approach. They did not decriminalize drug use and possession but basically have chosen not to investigate or prosecute possession of small amounts of 'soft drugs' for personal use unless there is evidence of other crimes or drug trafficking. They also emphasize and promote harm-reduction strategies."

"So, are you proposing that we legalize all drugs here in the US?" Donnelly replied. "Can you imagine the effect that would have on the number of drug users in the country, particularly kids?"

"Well, actually, Portugal did experience an increase in reported drug users across the spectrum, but they're not sure if that was due to an actual increase in users or just that people were more willing to admit to drug use once the social and legal stigma was gone," Reynolds answered. "There may be an initial increase in people experimenting with drugs, but if we're realistic, anyone who wants to get drugs can do so now. And yes, I do think we should decriminalize the possession and use of all drugs."

"And how would you propose to do that?" Donnelly asked.

"Well, the first goal of decriminalization should be to get the criminal element out of drug distribution by eliminating the profit motive. That means we must have a system for allowing people to obtain drugs lawfully and affordably. I would follow the same model that the legalized marijuana industry is using. Allow private entrepreneurs to produce and distribute recreational drugs under strict federal government regulation for purity and potency and with price controls to minimize the opportunity for a continuing illegal market. That would ensure users would know exactly what they are getting and how potent it is and allow them to support their habit at an affordable cost so they do not have to resort to crime. We could use the same type of dispensary system currently used for marijuana to distribute the product."

"So, are you going to allow just anyone to walk in off the street and buy drugs? What about kids? Can they buy drugs too?" Donnelly queried.

"No, I would make it so anyone who wanted to buy drugs would need to purchase a license at a nominal cost. I would establish a minimum age of twenty-one and require them to produce valid identification to get a license. Just having to go through that process and pay a fee might discourage some casual users from obtaining drugs."

"What's to stop a kid from hanging around outside the dispensary and paying someone to buy drugs for them?" Donnelly asked.

"We would have to police that the same as we do with alcohol and tobacco now. If someone is caught buying drugs for an underage person, they would lose their license to purchase and be liable for criminal prosecution," Reynolds responded.

"So," Donnelly said, "basically, you would send the message to the American people that their government condones and supports the use of drugs. How would that not give anyone permission to become a drug addict? And can you imagine the impact that would have on the economy when people either couldn't work or showed up to their jobs loaded? Drug use already has a major impact on worker productivity in this country."

"You are absolutely right," Reynolds responded. "Drug and alcohol use in this country costs hundreds of billions a year in economic loss right now, including billions in lost productivity. If you add in the criminal justice, treatment, health care, and other social costs, it is over a trillion a year. And that's under the current system. But if we learned anything from prohibition and from the last forty-plus years of the War on Drugs, it should be that you can't legislate morality, and you can't reduce demand for a product that seems to be an inherent human desire, if not need, simply by passing a law. Hell, humans have been using mood-altering substances from the beginning of time, and every society, no matter how primitive, seems to find some way to become intoxicated. We need to quit trying to ride a dead horse and find a better way of influencing human behavior."

"So, what is your plan for that?" Donnelly asked.

"First, we recognize and admit that drug and alcohol use is not a moral issue. Lots of otherwise responsible, moral, and ethical people use drugs and alcohol in moderation without becoming addicted and without becoming a problem for society. You appear to be one of them.

"Second, we recognize that the real issue is compulsive use and addiction, and that should generally be considered a public health problem and not a criminal justice problem. The only time the criminal justice system should get involved is when drug or alcohol use results in or contributes to the commission of an actual crime against persons or property, which could include driving under the influence, assault, homicide, any type of theft, and drug trafficking. Then, the focus should be on investigating, prosecuting, and sanctioning the actual crime. The use of drugs or alcohol should only come into play when deciding on sanctions for the crime, which might include treatment versus long-term incarceration.

"Next, we must recognize that the most effective way to change human behavior is through social stigma and changing attitudes and beliefs, not criminal sanctions. Look at what has occurred with tobacco use in this country over the last several years. As most people began to accept that tobacco use actually caused serious health problems, and as society began sending the message that smoking was not socially acceptable—at least around other people—tobacco use began to significantly decline. Then, when vaping came into vogue and the message went out that this was a safe way to smoke, usage began to increase. Now, we are beginning to apply the same type of social sanctions for vaping, and I expect use will begin to decline again.

"So, if it were up to me, this is what I'd do. I think that the primary responsibility of any society is to educate and inform its citizenry. So first, as we discussed a while back, I would require a mandatory K12 personal wellness curriculum to be developed and implemented in every school in the country. Topics would be introduced on an age-appropriate basis, and the topic of drug and alcohol education would be taught in the early primary school years when young minds are most impressionable. I would not use police officers to teach this class but would bring in health care professionals, treatment specialists, and recovered addicts to educate kids about the real effects of drugs and alcohol, both positive and negative. It should not be a scared-straight program. The material should be presented in a straightforward, objective manner with the message that this is going to be a choice we will all one day need to make, and we need to know the full ramifications of our choice.

"Second, I would pass a federal law requiring mandatory drug testing by all public and private employers. This would include mandatory pre-employment tests, periodic random testing in high-risk positions, and 'reasonable suspicion' tests in all other types of work. The message should be that drug and alcohol use is not condoned in the workplace, but the goal should be to identify problem users and addicts and give them an incentive to get treatment. The loss of a person's job is probably one of the greatest incentives there is; however, termination should be used only after all reasonable attempts to change the behavior have failed.

"Third, we need to adopt and implement harm-reduction strategies on a national level, to include clean-needle programs, accessible safe-injection sites, and widespread distribution of naloxone to users, law enforcement, health care providers, treatment facilities, schools, and safe-injection facilities.

"Fourth, we need to ensure that we have affordable, high-quality treatment services available for everyone who needs or wants them. The best way to do that, I think, is through a universal, single-payer health insurance system that fully covers both physical and mental health treatment, including substance abuse treatment. We would need federal standards governing assessment and treatment based on accepted best practices, and individuals would be assigned to the level of care they need based on the severity of their problem. The costs of treatment could be controlled through the government health insurance system." Reynolds turned toward Donnelly to observe his facial expression and was discouraged by his furrowed brow and downturned mouth.

"Do you really think socialism is the answer to all our problems in this country?" Donnelly responded. "Do you really want a nanny state taking over our lives? What about individual freedom and responsibility?"

"Well, it's a little hypocritical to be decrying socialism in our profession," Reynolds replied. "We work in a taxpayer-funded organization that supplies an essential service to society at large that few individuals could afford to provide for themselves. The same applies to fire protection, public schools, infrastructure spending, et cetera. Health care, to include mental health and substance abuse treatment, should now fall into that category. Few people are seriously advocating for full-blown socialism in which the government takes over all means of production in the country. But more and more, people are realizing that to deal with the real social issues confronting this country, we must collectively take responsibility for each other and help people attain the basic human needs that we all have. In the long run, the country as a whole will benefit, and we can save money in the process."

"Are you sure? It sounds damn expensive to me," Donnelly replied.

"I've read reports that suggest that legalizing drugs would save the federal government over $40 billion a year and states and localities over $25 billion in drug enforcement costs. Research has shown that incarceration costs seven times more than treatment. Plus, it has been estimated that we can generate upwards of $50 billion a year in tax revenues from drug sales. When you consider the savings from law enforcement, court adjudication, and incarceration expenses, the reduction of economic costs from lost productivity, the minimization of the costs—including in human lives—from drug overdoses, and the savings from a single-payer health insurance system, not to mention the reduction or elimination of drug cartels and the human costs they produce, there is no doubt in my mind that the benefits to society would greatly outweigh the financial cost, and the social impact associated with drug use and abuse would be substantially reduced."

Finishing off the last dregs of his after-dinner coffee, Donnelly said, "Well, it sounds good in theory. Now, you just have to convince the majority of the American public and their politicians. Let's get out of here."

Reynolds smiled. "Attitudes are changing quickly in this country. I think we will reach that level of enlightenment sooner than you might think."

To Reynolds' surprise, Donnelly dropped a fifty-dollar bill on the table and said, "I'll catch dinner tonight since you insist on paying." With that, they headed for the door. Reynolds caught Tawnya's eye as they left and mouthed, "See you tomorrow morning." She smiled and waved goodbye as she greeted her next customers.

As he cleared with radio, Donnelly looked at his watch and exclaimed, "Hell, it's time to head for the barn." Reynolds felt mentally and physically satiated from the busy day, the good meal, and, at least for him, the stimulating conversation.

CHAPTER 8

THE HIATUS, DAY SEVEN

Reynolds had a fitful night's sleep and had been awake for an hour when his stereo went off at 6:00 a.m. His mind was filled with the anticipation of spending the morning with Tawnya, and he lay there for a few minutes listening to Nancy Wilson sing "How Glad I Am" and fantasizing that it was Tawnya in the room, singing to him.

A normal spring Sunday prior to this week would have found him camped out by a lake or river, watching the sun rise over a nearby peak while putting a fly on his line and preparing to catch some breakfast. Today brought a whole new level of anticipation.

He finally heard the beeping of his coffee maker, signaling that the pot was brewed. He rolled out of bed and proceeded to the kitchen, stopping briefly to take a pee on the way. He took his cup of coffee out on the lanai and sipped it while listening to Nancy sing and watching the sun come up. Within minutes, he could no longer bear just sitting and waiting, so he got up, showered, shaved, and brushed his teeth, then dressed in his favorite khakis and pulled a V-neck sweater over his naked torso. He slipped a pair of loafers onto his bare feet, ran a brush through his hair, and looked in the mirror. *Presentable*, he thought to himself, *not too dressy and not too casual.*

He went to the kitchen, poured another cup of coffee, and again retreated to the lanai to wait it out until it was time to leave. Finally, 7:30 a.m. rolled around, and he decided he could not wait any longer. As he pulled his Jeep Wrangler to the curb in front of Tawnya's dormitory, he glanced at his watch. It was only 7:45 a.m. Thinking he had a few minutes to wait, he shut his eyes and began doing some deep breathing to quiet his nerves. Within moments, he heard a tapping on the passenger side window and looked up to see Tawnya smiling in at him. He popped open the passenger-side door and gave her his hand to help hoist her into the lifted 4X4. "This thing high enough off the ground?" she asked as she settled into her seat.

"It's only a four-inch lift," he replied as he pulled away from the curb. "Just enough to give me some extra ground clearance on mountain roads and jeep trails."

"You spend a lot of time on mountain roads and jeep trails?" she responded cheerily.

"About every week," he answered. "At least, up to now."

"What's that supposed to mean?" she asked. "You plan on changing your lifestyle?"

"Yeah, I'm considering expanding my areas of interest," he said as he looked her in the eyes and smiled. She returned the smile, and they sat in silence for a few minutes as they gazed out over Lake Union while crossing the University Bridge and continued onto Eastlake Avenue. They pulled into the parking lot of the restaurant and were soon being seated at a window table for two overlooking the water.

"Brandi will be your server," the hostess intoned as she placed two menus on the table in front of them. "Enjoy your meal."

Reynolds waited until the waitress had come and taken their order, then looked again into the bright, hazel eyes across the table. "Tell me about Tawnya," he said.

"Where do you want me to start?" she replied.

"The beginning," he said.

So, she did. It turned out her father, Clarence Fitzgerald (who hated his first name, so always went by Fitz), had been a wide receiver with the Seattle Seahawks for ten years before severely injuring his knee and being forced to retire from playing. Luckily, he had been able to land a job as a scout and had worked another seven years with the Seahawks before he and her mother, Marie, got tired of the rain, and he took a front-office job in Phoenix with the Cardinals. Her mother was white and had been a ballet dancer with the Pacific Northwest Ballet. Her parents had met while both were attending the University of Washington--he on a football scholarship and she on an academic scholarship. Many had thought of them as an unlikely couple. Her father was a product of a large, working-class Black family from Houston, Texas. Her mother was the only child of two white college professors at the University of Washington. Fitz was a gregarious extrovert who loved being around crowds of people; Marie, on the other hand, was a shy introvert who preferred solitude and serenity or the company of a few close friends. Fitz had passed onto Tawnya his athletic genes and outgoing personality, while Marie had imbued her with a taste for the arts and particularly a love of dance. But her parents adored each other, and each was totally supportive of the other's career.

Tawnya Fitzpatrick had been born and raised in Seattle as an only child. Her mother had enrolled her in dance lessons when she was four years old, and she had continued studying ballet and other forms of dance throughout her primary and secondary school years. Her dream had always been to attend the University of Washington and study dance, with the goal of eventually being a principal ballerina for a professional dance company herself. She had achieved the first part of that dream and was scheduled to graduate with a bachelor's degree in June. She had earned an audition with the Pacific Northwest Ballet and was waiting to hear if she had been accepted.

"All in all, I've had a very idyllic life," Tawna continued. "My folks made good money. We had a beautiful home on the bluff overlooking Alki Beach in West Seattle, with a wonderful view of the Puget Sound and the Seattle harbor and skyline. I attended predominantly white schools, but because I was the daughter of the Seahawks star receiver and was good at sports myself, I got along well with all the kids and never felt like I was excluded or looked down on. I hardly thought about the fact that I was Black."

"What kind of sports did you play in school?" Reynolds asked.

"I was the main attacker on the girls' volleyball team all through high school and was a high jumper on the girls' track team," Tawnya replied. "And, of course, I attended a dance academy all the way through my school years," she added before looking Reynolds in the eyes. "And now it's your turn."

Dan gave her a thumbnail sketch of his life, leaving out the bad parts about his father's alcoholism and domestic abuse and his mother's depression and suicide. No use scaring her off before she even got to know him.

The waitress delivered their food, and they slowly consumed it while carrying on an animated conversation about their tastes in music, books, movies, and food, and then graduated to politics. Dan was amazed at how their thinking aligned in so many areas, and, fortunately, Tawnya admitted to being a flaming liberal—which was good because Reynolds knew he could never get romantically involved with a right-wing conservative.

They finished their meal and lingered on for two more cups of coffee as they continued their spirited conversation. Reynolds could not believe how effortless the repartee was between them. As they left the restaurant, Dan suggested they take a walk along the lake for a few minutes to help settle their meal. They walked north along

Fairview Avenue, paralleling the lake, until they reached a small viewing area that overlooked the houseboat compound. Dan expressed his long-held desire to live on a houseboat someday, and Tawnya said she couldn't imagine anything more enjoyable. They spent several minutes discussing the pros and cons of living on the water until Tawnya looked at her watch. "Oh my God," she exclaimed, "it's almost noon. I'm sorry, Dan, because I have really enjoyed this morning, but I have two finals tomorrow and I really need to get back and study for them."

Reynolds was disappointed; he had kind of planned on completing a leisurely stroll around the lake and continuing their conversation. They headed back to the car, and he drove slowly back to her dorm while discussing the classes she was taking and the tests she had in the morning. All too soon, they were parked out front. Reynolds turned off the ignition and turned to look at Tawnya. As their eyes met, he told her, "I've really enjoyed this morning. I hope we can do this again—soon. Maybe next time we can do lunch."

"I would really like that," she replied. "Next time, I will try not to have anything else on my agenda. Will I see you at the restaurant next week?"

"You will if I have anything to say about it," Reynolds replied. "Text me tomorrow and let me know how you did on your tests."

"How about I call you so I can hear your voice?" she asked.

"Even better," Reynolds replied as he added his name and number to her phone contacts.

Tawnya reached over and squeezed his hand before clambering out of the Jeep and heading up the sidewalk to the entrance.

Reynolds could feel his heart pounding in his chest as he drove home. He was too pumped to sit down and relax, so he donned his biking togs and gear and headed down to the Burke-Gilman Trail for a leisurely forty-mile bike ride. It was three hours later when he climbed the stairs to his apartment with the Trek over his shoulder and was able to sink into his recliner and relax with his "Favorites" playlist on the stereo. He didn't feel like cooking, so he ordered a pizza and sat drinking a strawberry lemonade while he waited. Around 5:00 p.m., the phone rang. It was Donnelly.

"Hey Dan," he said, "what do you have going tomorrow? I've got a jury trial in superior court, and I was thinking you might enjoy sitting in and seeing our wonderful court system in action. It's just an aggravated assault case resulting from a domestic violence situation, but you might find it interesting."

"Well, I was hoping to spend some time with Tawnya tomorrow," Dan replied, "but she has finals tests in the morning and afternoon, so, yeah, I'd love to join you. What time do I need to be there?"

"Well, if you want to see the jury selection process, be there at 9:00 a.m. I'm not actually required to be there until 1:00 p.m.," Donnelly replied. "Don't worry about dressing up. Business casual will be fine since you will just be observing. See you in Room 412 at the courthouse."

"I'll go in at 9:00 a.m.," Reynolds responded. "I'd like to see the whole process."

Reynolds got up at his usual 6:00 a.m., got in his morning run, showered, shaved, and had breakfast, then walked into the courtroom at precisely 9:00 a.m. To his surprise, Donnelly was there, seated in the front row of spectator seats. Reynolds sat down beside him and said, "Hey, didn't think you would be here until 1:00 p.m."

"I figured since I dragged you down here early, I might as well join you," Donnelly replied. "I've always been fascinated, as well as majorly frustrated, by our legal proceedings."

The bailiff called the court to order and introduced the judge as he took his place behind the bench. The judge asked both the prosecutor and the defendant's lawyer to introduce themselves and asked if there were any motions or pleas to be heard. Both attorneys indicated that there were no motions or pleas and that they were prepared to go to trial. With that, the judge requested the bailiff to bring in the prospective jurors. He escorted in the pool of twenty potential jurors and seated them in the courtroom. The judge introduced himself and the lawyers for the prosecution and defense and then went on to explain the nature of the trial. He then swore in the pool of jurors and turned the proceedings over to the attorneys for *voir dire*.

After the bailiff had each prospective juror come forward and take a seat at the witness stand, each side's attorney took turns questioning them individually to determine their suitability for the jury. Each side could either challenge a juror's suitability for cause—based on some type of bias in the case—or use one of their peremptory challenges, which did not require a reason.

Even in this relatively non-controversial case, the jury selection process took all morning, and it was 11:30 a.m. before the judge adjourned for lunch, directing all participants to reconvene at 1:00 p.m.

Donnelly and Reynolds wandered down to a quaint little café across from Pioneer Square for lunch, and after being seated, Donnelly asked what Reynolds thought of the jury selection process.

"Well, it seemed pretty straightforward to me," Reynolds replied. "There did seem to be a lot of older people in the jury pool, and it was pretty obvious that the prosecuting attorney was trying to stack the jury with women, while the defense seemed to want more men."

"Sure, it's a domestic violence case, and each side is trying to get people who they think will be most sympathetic to their cause," Donnelly replied. "If this were a major felony case, you can bet they would have hired outside consultants to investigate potential jurors and draft *voir dire* questions. Jury manipulation is now an art if not a science."

"You don't sound too keen on the jury system," Reynolds responded.

"I'm not," Donnelly replied. "Every day, in this county alone, over two hundred people meet in the jury room of the presiding judge's chambers to answer their civic responsibility for jury duty. For two weeks, they come downtown every morning and sit around waiting to be called out on a trial. For ten dollars a day plus lunch and parking expenses, they have to hang out here all day. Hell, that hardly covers their direct costs, let alone any lost wages they may have and the disruption to their lives. These average, everyday citizens are then asked to judge their fellow man in cases that might run the gamut from a DUI charge to serial murder without any expertise whatsoever other than their own accumulated personal experiences and whatever common sense they may or may not have. Too often, their decisions are driven more by their own biases and prejudices, or the theatrics of the attorneys, than by the evidence presented."

"But isn't that supposed to be the rationale for using common citizens as finders of fact?" Reynolds responded. "To allow a jury of your peers drawn from a cross-section of the community to use their collective wisdom to determine guilt or innocence based on the evidence and community values, rather than rely on the judgment of one person?"

"Don't get me wrong," Donnelly replied. "I have no doubt that the vast majority of people selected for jury duty are totally conscientious in their efforts and are fully committed to achieving a fair and impartial verdict. But I also think that most of them are completely unfamiliar with criminal court proceedings, other than the dramatic version they see on TV or in the movies and that they stand in enraptured awe of the whole judicial process and are, therefore, easily manipulated by it. All too often, their decisions are superficial judgments based on the appearance of the defendant and the dramatics of the attorneys rather than on the facts of the case. Then, if you consider the costs involved and the drag jury selection puts on the process, the use of juries, in my humble opinion, is totally unwarranted in this age of backlogged courts."

"I wrote a paper on a famous Idaho murder trial back in the early '80s," Reynolds replied. "A self-styled mountain man named Claude Dallas killed two Fish and Game officers who went to his remote camp to question him about poaching. The defense hired a law firm to run background checks on all the potential jurors, which cost over $25,000 at that time. The jury selection process took three days, the trial itself took almost a month, and then it took a week to arrive at a verdict. I think the total cost of the trial was over $100,000 in 1980s money, not including the cost of attorney fees and the salaries of the judge and court staff. What was really amazing was that a couple of younger female jurors that the defense managed to get on the panel admitted they had voted to acquit on the first-degree murder charges because they were struck by how good-looking, charming, and charismatic Dallas was, even though the evidence of his guilt was overwhelming. The jury ultimately rejected the first-degree murder charges but did find him guilty of voluntary manslaughter and a gun charge, and he was sentenced to thirty years in prison. The reason they gave is that they believed Dallas' claim that he feared for his life after one of the Fish and Game officers said to him, 'We can either do this the easy way or the hard way?' How many times have you said that to a suspect?"

"Many times. Yeah, doesn't surprise me. Think what that trial would cost in today's dollars," Donnelly said. "It's no wonder that prosecutors do backflips to plea-bargain guilty pleas. They plea-bargain 95 percent of cases, and our courts are still backed up for months."

"So, what would you do different?" Reynolds asked.

"I would transition our court system from an adversarial system based on English common law to an inquisitorial system that is often used in Europe," Donnelly replied. "I think professional judges are much better equipped to weigh evidence and determine guilt or innocence than ordinary citizens; but, in serious cases, I would not want to rely on the judgment of only one man. A single judge is fine for municipal and district court cases, but for felony trials in superior court, I would prefer a three-judge panel. And I don't think all judges necessarily should have to be trained lawyers. I would require judges to run for office and would open the elections up to qualified individuals with diversified areas of knowledge—to include the law, psychology, sociology, criminology, economics, et cetera—as well as histories of demonstrated wisdom and fairness. Each three-judge panel would include at least one trained lawyer and the others could be lay people with expertise in other areas. Their decisions should be made by majority rule and become a matter of public record that is broadly reported so that people could cast informed ballots come election time."

"So, exactly how would this inquisitorial system of justice work?" Reynolds asked.

"Well, to start with, I would minimize the use of plea bargaining. Every criminal defendant should be charged with the most serious appropriate offense based on the provable elements of that crime. At arraignment, the defendant would be advised of the charges against them, assigned a public defender if they do not already have an attorney, and be given the opportunity to plead guilty or not guilty. The judge would explain the sanctions the defendant may face based on the crime and the rehabilitative opportunities that may be available, with the goal of incentivizing a guilty plea if the defendant is, in fact, guilty.

"If the defendant were to plead not guilty, the judge would set conditions of release and schedule a preliminary hearing at which the prosecution would be required to present evidence to support the criminal charge in the case. After hearing the evidence, the defendant would have an opportunity to change their plea. If they did not, a trial would be scheduled, either in district court or superior court, depending on whether it was a misdemeanor or serious felony.

"Under the inquisitorial system, the judge—or judges—would become the primary questioners and finders of fact in the process. The role of the attorneys for the prosecution and defense would be limited to calling witnesses, eliciting their basic testimony, and introducing evidence, but without the adversarial relationship. The judges would be free to question witnesses in order to expand on or clarify their testimony and to request additional witnesses, evidence, or information from the attorneys. The rules of evidence would be relaxed to allow for indirect and hearsay evidence, and the judges would decide how much weight each item of evidence deserved. There would be no opening and closing arguments by the respective attorneys, which would hopefully eliminate the flamboyant theatrics of an attorney from becoming a critical factor in the decision. The sole focus of the process would be to bring out the truth and determine guilt or innocence."

"So, if you eliminate plea bargaining and add two judges to every superior court, aren't you going to overwhelm our available courts and greatly increase the cost of the court system?" Reynolds asked.

"I don't think so," Donnelly replied. "Eliminating the jury system and streamlining the court processes should cut the time required for a typical felony trial from two to three days to one day or less. A more structured sentencing system would also expedite the process, so overall, I don't see a great increase in either cost or necessary court facilities. Plus, if we took your suggestion and decriminalized drug possession and use, we could eliminate about half of the criminal prosecutions with which we currently are dealing."

"Hmmm, interesting concept," Reynolds replied. "I'd like to hear more about this structured approach to sentencing you mentioned."

"Another time," Donnelly responded. "Right now, we should get back to court."

Shortly after they returned, the judge entered and reconvened the court. Both the prosecution and defense attorneys were asked to make their opening statements, and then the judge turned the proceedings over to the prosecutor to present her case. Donnelly was the first witness called and spent about an hour on the stand in total, first describing what he had encountered at the scene, recounting what the victim and defendant had said and done in his presence, and presenting the physical evidence he had gathered—including pictures of both the victim and defendant—and then undergoing cross-examination by the defense attorney. When he was excused, the prosecutor called up the doctor who had treated the victim at the emergency room to describe, pursuant to a court order, her injuries and recount what she had told him at the time. Finally, the victim was called to give her side of the story. She was a very reluctant witness, but the prosecutor was able to bring out medical records showing an extensive history of injuries that were suspected to have been from domestic abuse.

Upon completion of her cross-examination, the judge adjourned court for the day. As Donnelly and Reynolds were walking out, the prosecutor advised Donnelly that he probably would not need him again, but to be available if called. As they left the courthouse, Donnelly asked, "What do you say, want to hit up the Greeks for a drink?"

Reynolds looked at his watch. "Hell, it's only four o'clock, and I'm driving today. The Greeks probably isn't full of cops at this hour. I might join you for a while. I'd like to finish our conversation from lunch."

"Hell," Donnelly said, "I made eight hours of overtime today, so I might as well buy you dinner."

"That's not necessary," Reynolds replied, "but dinner does sound good. Save me from having to cook when I get home."

They were escorted to a table in the corner of the restaurant, and each took a chair with his back to a wall. The waitress came and took their drink orders and informed them of the special for the day, moussaka, which both of them went for. Donnelly decided to wash his down with a glass of ouzo, while Reynolds opted for his usual club soda with a lime.

While they waited for their meals to arrive, Reynolds asked, "Okay, what were you referring to when you talked about a structured approach to sentencing earlier?"

"Well, I think nationally standardized sentencing makes sense," Donnelly replied. "If a person commits a first-degree burglary in Washington, for instance, they should get a similar sentence as someone who commits the same crime in New York. The sentence should be determined by the specific crime and the number of prior felony convictions a person has accrued. First offenders should receive a relatively shorter prison sentence, depending on the crime, and a sufficiently long period of parole supervision after release to get them stabilized in the community. Second offenders should get a longer prison sentence and a longer period of time on parole after release. Third-time offenders should be classified as 'habitual offenders' and get an automatic life sentence. They may still be eligible for parole at some point because it has been found that many offenders 'age out' of their criminal behaviors over time, but they should do at least twenty years before being eligible. Under my system, judges would only determine guilt or innocence. Sentencing would be set in stone and offenders would know going in what the consequences of their behavior would be."

"So, you would not take into consideration any extenuating circumstances or individual factors that may have motivated or contributed to the criminal behavior?" Reynolds asked.

"Hell no," Donnelly responded. "Committing a crime is a choice. If you do the crime, then you damn sure better be prepared to do the time. That's the problem with this country; everyone wants to coddle criminals and find ways to excuse or enable their behavior."

"Well, if that's the case, why does a country that touts itself as the 'land of the free and the home of the brave' have the highest incarceration rate in the world?" Reynolds replied. "You do realize that we have over 2 million people behind bars in this country at a cost of over $80 billion a year? It sounds to me like your proposal would just exacerbate that problem."

"Well, at least if they're sitting in prison, they can't be out victimizing innocent people," Donnelly replied.

"That 'get tough on crime' mentality has been around forever," Reynolds responded. "This idea that punishment, retribution, and incapacitation will deter offenders and reduce crime has been especially prevalent over the last fifty years. I think it's because we have traditionally—probably stemming from our Puritan roots—relied on punishment as a means of deterring unwanted behavior. We have the mindset that if the punishment is harsh enough, it will motivate people to change their behavior. So, for any behavior that society deems unacceptable, their go-to approach is to make the behavior illegal and establish an appropriately severe set of sanctions to discourage it."

"And you don't think that is working well?" Donnelly questioned.

"Well, it works reasonably well with well-adjusted, prosocial people," Reynolds replied. "Prosocial people usually have positive norms and values and are willing and able to self-correct if they do something that goes against those values or results in unacceptable consequences. That is not the case with most criminals. I took a course in criminality in school in which we started out discussing what is called the 'criminal continuum.' It expounded the idea that we all lie somewhere on a continuum between being totally prosocial and being totally antisocial. In other words, we are all somewhere between being Mother Teresa and Ted Bundy.

"I also learned that we could classify criminals into basically five distinct categories, each with its own characteristics and contributing factors. Some people are driven to commit crimes because of some extraordinary, isolated circumstance in their life, such as coming home and finding their wife in bed with another man or getting laid off from their job and not being able to pay their bills. Others have a chronic condition such as pedophilia or substance addiction that drives their criminal behavior. These two groups comprise a small percentage of offenders and tend to be at rather low risk of reoffending if you can get a handle on the specific contributing circumstance.

"Then there is another category of offender that is basically cognitively low-functioning or suffers from some type of mental disorder. They are prone to impulsive behavior and are easily manipulated by more sophisticated criminals. Given the proper structure, supervision, and treatment, they are generally rather low risk.

"A larger percentage of offenders are victims of poor environments and negative or under-socialization. They tend to be raised in poverty with poorly educated parents, often a single parent. They never receive the kind of nurturing and structure they need to develop into a well-adjusted adult. They tend to do poorly in school, often dropping out by the ninth or tenth grade. They are not accepted by the 'in crowd' in school, so they gravitate toward a negative peer group that will accept them, which often leads them to engage in inappropriate behaviors such as drug use and petty crime. They typically don't have any viable job skills, so they have a hard time getting or keeping a job. Usually, they have very poor self-esteem and tend to self-sabotage, making them their own worst enemy. These offenders often require long-term, multi-dimensional interventions in order to become productive, law-abiding citizens, but it can be done.

"Then there is the true criminal personality, which comprises about 15 percent of offenders. This group seems to be genetically predisposed to criminality. They begin displaying deviant behavior at an early age and often engage in a wide variety of criminal behaviors because they get off on the risk and reward of crime. They can be highly intelligent and well-educated. They can come from affluent families and prosocial upbringings. They tend to be totally self-centered, with little conscience and no empathy for others. They consider themselves above the law and feel entitled to victimize other people. They consider any attempt to hold them accountable or punish them for their actions as being unfair and vindictive. They assume what they call 'victim stance'—believing they are the ones being victimized. Consequently, they tend to be maladjusting in that punishment tends to reinforce their negative attitudes toward society and just creates the desire to seek revenge and retribution. It makes them worse rather than better, and they tend to be poor candidates for rehabilitation. So, our sentencing guidelines should take into consideration both the type of offender that we're dealing with and their relative amenability to treatment."

"So, what are you going to do?" Donnelly asked. "Require a full psychological evaluation of every criminal we arrest?"

"Well, yes, at least every felony offender. But there are other things we need to consider. There has been a lot of research into what drives criminal behavior. Donald Andrews, who was a Canadian correctional psychologist and criminologist, and James Bonta, a clinical psychologist, wrote a book called *The Psychology of Criminal Conduct*, which identifies the primary factors that are predictive of criminal behavior. Based on their research, they identified what they called the 'big eight' risk factors that lead to criminal behavior. At the top of the list are antisocial attitudes and beliefs that often originate in a family environment of harsh abuse, neglect, negative role models, lack of stability and structure, and poor early discipline and control. The other factors include antisocial associates, a long history of antisocial behavior, an antisocial or psychopathic personality disorder, ongoing family issues, problems at school or work, lack of prosocial leisure activities, and finally, substance abuse. These factors often start to manifest themselves in early childhood through poor school performance, a negative peer group, and constant rule-breaking behavior. Substance abuse usually doesn't come into play until early adolescence and is usually driven by the desire to fit in with a negative peer group or an inherent risk-taking personality. All of these factors can be identified and measured through the use of objective risk and need assessment instruments that identify both the risk factors that drive the negative behavior and the criminogenic needs that should be addressed in treatment.

"In my opinion, if we really want to reduce criminality and violence in this country, we've got to invest in training every professional who encounters a child or family, particularly teachers, to recognize these warning signs and refer them for mandatory assessment and treatment. Many future offenders have been displaying disturbing behavior for years, and if this is recognized and reported, most could be deterred from a future act of violence or crime through appropriate treatment. However, recognizing and assessing a problem does no good unless you have the facilities and resources to treat the problem. We need a substantial investment in family and child case managers and counselors as well as school counselors, behavioral health specialists, specialized treatment programs, and residential facilities to provide that treatment."

"So, what did they teach you about how to deal with these various types of offenders in the criminal justice system?" Donnelly responded.

"Well, as a society, we pretty much learned in the '70s, '80s, and '90s that this 'lock 'em up and throw away the key' mentality doesn't work. They were building prisons as fast as they could and still could not keep up with the exploding prison populations. Keeping people locked up for long periods of time pretty much guaranteed that they would come out as more hardened, sophisticated criminals. The meager programming that was offered to prisoners was intended more to keep them busy and out of trouble than to deal with the factors contributing to their criminality. Recidivism rates were running 60–70 percent, which meant that we basically had a revolving-door system. Most cons who were released were back within three years, either for a new crime or a parole violation. The Crime Act of 1994 impacted crime rates in the country by providing funding for hiring 100,000 new police officers and building new prisons while keeping offenders in longer by incentivizing mandatory minimum sentences and 'three strikes and you're out' policies.

"But you have to ask yourself, at what cost? Fortunately, a number of state correctional departments and the Federal Bureau of Prisons, along with state legislatures and Congress, started asking themselves that question about twenty years ago. They began to figure out that putting resources into effective rehabilitation is much more cost-effective than just locking people up for long periods of time. As I said, there has been a lot of good research into the risk factors that contribute to criminal behavior and the needs areas that can reduce criminal behavior if effectively addressed, and a lot of work has gone into developing risk and needs assessment instruments that can effectively measure a person's risk of reoffending as well as the areas where programming may be effective in reducing that risk. They've also found that mixing low-risk offenders with high-risk offenders increases the risk level of the low-risk offenders; and that treatment is most effective in reducing recidivism when it is targeted to higher-risk offenders who are amenable to change. Pareto's Law comes into play here since over 80 percent of crime is committed by 20 percent of the criminals—so if we can target these high-risk, repeat offenders and structure sentencing and treatment to either keep them in prison or effectively address their crime-producing needs, we may start to see real reductions in crime and recidivism.

"The reason that specialized courts, such as drug courts, have been successful is that they bring together all the players—the offender, the family, the police, prosecutors, judges, probation officers, caseworkers, and counselors—into a cooperative effort to protect society by holding the offender accountable, while also providing strong positive and negative incentives to change the problematic behavior, and programs designed to help the offender do that. If we were to apply this principle when the child is eight years old versus eighteen, perhaps we could make a real difference.

"So, if you ask me what I would do, it would be to basically double down on what is already happening with specialty courts, like drug courts and veterans' courts. There are a few things I would do differently, however. In most cases, courts do not do assessment until after conviction and sentencing, when a felony offender either goes on probation or winds up in the Reception and Diagnostic Unit at a prison. I would do it as part of the pre-sentence investigation process that most felony offenders go through prior to sentencing. I think the federal government should partner with states to establish secure, regional testing facilities in each state staffed by medical doctors, mental health professionals, education specialists, substance abuse specialists, vocational specialists, and psychologists experienced in risk and needs assessment processes. Each offender would undergo an evaluation in each of these areas, and the assessment team would collaborate on developing a comprehensive treatment plan that addresses each of the offender's specific criminogenic needs as well as a timetable for completing the treatment plan. This would be part of the overall pre-sentence investigation, or PSI, report that went to the judges.

"The judges would use the PSI to determine the type and length of sentence based on the risk level of the offender—in terms of risk to re-offend—his/her amenability to treatment, and the length of time needed to complete the treatment plan. Extremely high-risk offenders who were evaluated as psychopathic or high on the antisocial personality disorder scale and who were not considered amenable to treatment or refused treatment would be given maximum sentences for their crimes with no possibility for parole. High-risk offenders considered amenable to treatment and who accepted treatment would be given a minimum sentence long enough to complete their treatment plan, and a long enough tail so they could be monitored on parole for an extended period. They would be assigned to a treatment-oriented facility appropriate for their security classification, preferably a prison-based therapeutic community. Medium- and low-risk offenders would be considered for probation supervision and directed toward appropriate treatment programs in the community as needed. The punitive aspect of sentencing would be a restorative justice model in which offenders would be required to pay appropriate restitution to their victim and/or perform community service. The overarching goal would be to lock up truly dangerous offenders for as long as possible while getting most offenders back out on the street, working and paying taxes as quickly as possible. I think this model, combined with decriminalizing drug possession and use, could reduce our prison population by at least 50 percent." Reynolds exhaled deeply as he said, "I do get carried away at times, don't I."

"You've obviously put a lot of thought and study into this," Donnelly responded. "I can see that I may need to do a little research myself. So, what are you going to do if an offender commits a new crime after investing so much into them for all this treatment?"

"Let me know if you need some books on the subject. I've got several at home," Reynolds replied. "As to your question, I think you need to look at reoffending much like you do relapsing in substance abuse treatment. Changing behavior is difficult, and depending on the circumstances, you may want to reinforce the treatment and give them a second chance. If it looks like you're being conned, and the offender is not committed to rehabilitation, then you would need to look at revoking their probation or parole and sending them back to prison. There has to be accountability for their behavior."

They finished their meal and Donnelly insisted on buying. Reynolds thanked him again, put a twenty-dollar tip on the table, and excused himself. He was anxious to get home and wait for Tawnya's call to see how she did on her tests. Donnelly retired to the bar while Reynolds went across the street to retrieve his vehicle. Reynolds felt stimulated by his conversation with Donnelly and hoped his reasoning would have an impact on his partner's thinking.

CHAPTER 9

WEEK TWO

Reynolds' second week of being a street cop started relatively routinely—too routinely for his taste. He and Donnelly spent the first three days chasing mundane radio calls and writing reports, or, more accurately, Donnelly drank coffee and watched him write reports. The only positive aspect was that by Thursday, Donnelly was signing off on his reports with only an affirmative nod of the head. Reynolds was learning that police work, much like being in a combat zone in the military, can consist of long periods of relative boredom punctuated by short spurts of intense exhilaration and activity.

The highlight of those first three days began with Donnelly asking Reynolds if he wanted to attend the monthly meeting of the Micro Community Policing group that represented George sector. The group was comprised of local community leaders and volunteers, but anyone who wished could attend and address the group. Donnelly, along with the George sector sergeant, another Black patrol officer, and a Black detective, represented the Seattle PD.

"It would be a chance for you to see another side of this community and meet some really good folks who are trying to make it better," Donnelly explained.

"Hell yeah, I'd love to go," Reynolds responded. "Where and when do they meet?"

"Ironically, they meet at the same church where you and I met Dixie," Donnelly replied. "The meeting is tomorrow night and starts at 7:00 p.m., but we are allowed to attend on-duty, which means you get paid for your time."

"I'd be happy to go on my own time," Reynolds replied, "but so much the better."

Donnelly and Reynolds arrived at the meeting about fifteen minutes early, and Donnelly took Reynolds around and introduced him to several of the regular members of the group, which included the local city councilman, a county commissioner, the principals of the local schools, some of the prominent local businessmen, and the pastors of the churches in the district. The city councilman chaired the meeting and brought it to order right at 7:00 p.m. One of the pastors offered a prayer for the group, and they went through the normal process of reading and approving the minutes of the last meeting. Donnelly, Reynolds, and the patrol sergeant were the only white people in attendance.

There were several residents of the area who had signed up to speak, and each brought up current issues they were having in their local neighborhoods. For those that were crime-related, Donnelly, the Black officers, and the sergeant took turns responding with what the police department was doing to address the problems, and discussed further actions that could be taken. Often, these included cooperative efforts between the community members and the police. Reynolds was impressed with the civility and congeniality of the meeting, the articulateness of the presenters and responders, and the level of care and concern each attendee had for the community at large.

As they drove back to the precinct after the meeting, Reynolds said to Donnelly, "There truly is another side to this community that we don't get to see often enough. I'm glad you invited me. I guess I shouldn't be surprised, given the number of well-educated, accomplished Black people, both male and female, that we see in the public sphere today, but it was certainly refreshing to see so many in our own local community."

"Yeah, most of the folks in these communities are hard-working, God-fearing, salt-of-the-earth people just like you find in any other neighborhood. I apologize if I gave you the wrong impression last week when I said we worked in a war zone. There is a distinct Black culture, and most aspects of it are very positive and uplifting. Unfortunately, there is also a portion that is dirty, disparaging, and dangerous. Our job is to not conflate the two and start stereotyping people based on the dark side that we deal with most of the time."

"Well, tonight was certainly a wake-up call not to do that," Reynolds responded.

. . . .

Reynolds still awoke every morning full of anticipation for what the day might bring, but by the end of each shift, he would look forward to getting home and awaiting Tawnya's phone call. She had begun calling him every evening as she drove home from work, and those calls had become the highlight of his day. Tawnya always wanted to know the details of everything he had done that day at work and seemed fascinated by the situations and people that he dealt with. She had been studying hard to finish her coursework at school, and between school and work had very little time to spare. It was evident she was more than ready to graduate and move on with her life. Much to Reynolds' delight, Tawnya had rearranged her schedule at work the next week so that her days off coincided with his.

Reynolds was actually happy with the Patrol Division's work schedule. They worked six days on with two days off so that their days off rotated around the week. Then, when their days off fell on Thursday and Friday, they automatically got Saturday and Sunday as well, which meant a four-day weekend every four weeks. For Reynolds, that meant being able to get out in the backcountry during the week, when most people were at work, which would allow him to go to some of the more popular places without the large crowds. The only issue now was whether Tawnya would be able to get off as well, which apparently would not be a problem—at least at her current job.

Friday started off with more of the same. First came a larceny call for a stolen bicycle, then a runaway report on a fourteen-year-old girl, and then a traffic accident. They had just cleared after completing the accident report when Dispatch called again.

"Two-George-Three, we have a report of a possible domestic disturbance at 2102 East Alabaster, Apartment 3A. Neighbor reports loud screaming and sounds of a fight coming from the apartment upstairs. Complainant is in Apartment 2A."

"Two-George-Three, copy," Donnelly responded, "We're en route."

Donnelly hit the accelerator and within two minutes they pulled up in front of the apartment building. It was an older, three-story unit with exterior stairs connecting the walkways in front of the apartments. Reynolds noted that the 'A' apartments were at the far west end of the building, so they took the stairs in the middle of the building and approached slowly, listening for sounds of a disturbance. When they reached the window of the apartment, Donnelly motioned for Reynolds to stay behind him while he carefully peeked inside. Not seeing anyone, he quickly ran past the window, then motioned for Reynolds to follow. They took up positions on either side of the door, and Donnelly knocked loudly while shouting, "Seattle Police." Reynolds heard a muffled cry from inside the apartment, but no one came to the door, so Donnelly knocked again and yelled, "Seattle Police. Open up, or we will have to break down the door."

After a moment, they heard heavy footsteps approaching the door. It swung open, and a bedraggled Black man stepped into the doorway. He was about six feet tall with a slender build, except for the protruding abdomen hanging over his belt. He was wearing a dirty white wife-beater undershirt and filthy khaki pants, both of which had splatters of blood all over the front. He had a week's worth of stubble on his face and reeked of alcohol.

"Whatch you po-lice doing here?" he mumbled drunkenly, slurring his words.

"We had a call of a disturbance at this address, sir," Donnelly responded. "Have you had problems here today?"

"Fuck no, I ain't had no problems. What you cops bothering me for?" the man replied.

Reynolds noticed that the man had his right arm behind his back as he stood wobbling in the doorway. He motioned to Donnelly to step back.

"I'm sorry, sir, but we are going to have to check your apartment to make sure no one is hurt here. May we come in?" Donnelly said.

"You ain't coming in my house without a warrant," the man replied. With that, he brought his right hand around, and Reynolds saw that he was holding a knife with the blade pointed up.

Instantaneously, Reynolds grabbed the man's right wrist with both hands, then immediately pulled the man towards him while turning his body and taking him to the ground, face down. He bent the man's hand inward for pain compliance and told him to drop the knife, which he did. Reynolds maintained his wrist lock while Donnelly grabbed the knife, then Donnelly cuffed the man's arms behind his back. Reynolds patted him down and then lifted him to his feet. Donnelly did a quick visual sweep of the interior of the apartment and, seeing no one, they half-carried, half-shoved the man to a chair at the kitchen table and sat him down.

"Is there anyone else here?" Donnelly asked the man.

"My wife's in the bedroom," he grudgingly replied.

While Reynolds watched the man, Donnelly—with his hand on his gun—slowly approached the bedroom door and did a visual sweep of the room. Sitting on the bed, he saw a heavy, middle-aged Black woman wearing a low-cut sundress with one large, udder-like breast exposed There was a slash across the upper half of the breast, and blood was flowing, but not spurting, from another slash on the front of her neck.

Donnelly did a quick check of the closets and attached bathroom and then went to the woman's side on the bed. As he approached, he could see that her right eye was swollen and starting to turn black and blue. He checked her and found that she had another slash on her upper left arm. Donnelly immediately called for a Fire Department Medic One emergency response unit and yelled for Reynolds to get the first-aid kit out of the car while he watched the suspect.

Reynolds had applied pressure bandages to the woman's cuts and checked her for other injuries by the time the Medic One unit arrived. They decided to transport her to Harborview Medical Center for further treatment. The woman was also drunk and barely lucid, but she was able to provide them her name and date of birth and acknowledge that the man in the apartment was her husband, also giving them his name and date of birth.

After the Medic One unit had left to take the woman to the hospital, Donnelly and Reynolds did a quick sweep of the house for any plain-view evidence of this or other crimes and then transported the suspect to the city jail. On the way, Donnelly called the Crimes against Persons Unit, advised them of the situation, and asked if they wanted to send someone to take the woman's statement. They did not have anyone available and requested that Donnelly and Reynolds do it.

After trying unsuccessfully to get a statement from the suspect, they booked him into jail for "suspicion of aggravated assault" and "suspicion of domestic violence" and then drove to Harborview, where they found the woman still waiting in the emergency room for further treatment. Apparently, the hospital staff had found the cuts were superficial, and there were no apparent serious injuries, so she was waiting to get some stitches and x-rays.

The woman, who was now somewhat sober and able to communicate, was reluctant to make a statement. In fact, she requested the officers release her husband from jail, stating he did not mean to hurt her. After Donnelly explained to her that her husband would be charged with felony assault on both her and them, regardless of whether she made a statement, she agreed to tell them what happened. Apparently, a neighbor who had been drinking with the two of them had groped her butt, and her husband, after throwing the man out of their apartment, commenced to hit her and cut her with the knife because he thought she had led the man on, and was sleeping with him. He had told her he was going to cut off her tits so that no man would want her.

After finishing her statement and taking pictures of her injuries, Donnelly and Reynolds went back to the precinct to finish their report and individual statements. It was two hours past the end of their shift when they finally headed to the locker room to change and go home. Reynolds saw that he had missed a call from Tawnya but did not want to disturb her if she had already gone to bed. Instead, he sent her a text letting her know that he was fine and just getting off work and that he would call her in the morning. It was a long bike ride home, and he was disappointed that he had not heard that magical voice today.

Reynolds awoke as the sun was beginning to rise over the Cascade Mountains to the east. It looked like it was going to be a clear day, and he basked in the first warm rays of the sun as he sipped his scalding-hot coffee on the lanai. His thoughts instantly went to Tawnya, and he envisioned her in his mind as he listened to Nancy

Wilson croon "The More I See You" from the bedroom. He allowed himself to be fully absorbed in the song as he again imagined that it was Tawnya singing to him. When it finished, he forced himself to snap out of his reverie and began his day with his normal Saturday routine—meditation, yoga and then a run. He was brimming with energy as he settled into his running rhythm, and the miles slipped quickly and easily under his feet.

He met Donnelly in the Crime Analysis Unit, where he immediately sat down to begin perusing crime reports. He intuitively felt eyes upon him and looked up to see Donnelly staring at him. "That was some move you made on that dipshit yesterday," Donnelly said. "But it may have been a little ill-advised. We're not out there to be heroes. Have you ever heard the expression 'Don't bring a knife to a gunfight'? Well, it also applies to bringing bare hands to a knife fight. That's what you have the Taser and that Glock for."

"I thought about that on my ride home last night," Reynolds replied. "Did I tell you that I have been studying Aikido since I was stationed in Okinawa and am still practicing it a couple days a week? Well, ironically, the sensei at my dojo suggested this week that we work on *tanto-dori* techniques. That's how to respond to a knife attack. He also told me that it is better to run or find a weapon than take on a knife attack barehanded. But you saw that asshole yesterday. He was completely wasted and so wobbly he could barely stand in that doorway. I figured his reactions would be so slow that I could have him on the ground before he knew what had hit him. Besides, I have been practicing that maneuver all week."

"Fortunately, it worked out well this time, Dan, but that may not always be the case. It's not worth getting hurt or dying over some drunk wife-beater. Better to step back, pull your Taser or gun, and try to talk the asshole down than take the chance of getting seriously hurt," Donnelly replied.

"You're probably right," Reynolds responded, "but we've all seen the horror stories over the years of cops using their guns in questionable situations. I've always considered lethal force to be the absolute last resort; that's why I started studying Aikido in the first place. As drunk and scared as that dude was, he may have forced our hand and made us shoot him. It would undoubtedly have been ruled a righteous shoot, but I really don't want to ever have to go in front of a coroner's inquest if I can avoid it."

"I hear you," Donnelly replied. "Like I said, it was a helluva move, but in the future, if we find ourselves in a similar situation, back off and try to talk him down. Then, if he won't surrender the knife, you take your Taser, and I'll back you up with my gun. If the Taser doesn't stop him, the Glock will, okay?"

Reynolds nodded in the affirmative. "You got it," he replied.

The shift started out relatively slowly. After patrolling through their district for about an hour, Donnelly cruised down to 14th and Yesler to see if LaTasha was working. She was not out on the street. "Probably parked somewhere in some dude's car with his cock in her mouth," Donnelly speculated. "Let's check out Snookers just for shits and giggles."

They pulled into the dirt parking area behind the pool room and followed the same drill they had used previously. Donnelly did a walk-through of the joint while Reynolds stood just inside the rear door, providing overwatch. Reynolds saw the guy that Dixie had identified as Duke Robinson sitting at a table in the back with three other nefarious-looking dudes. He noticed that Donnelly had seen them as well because he stopped and nonchalantly watched a pool game while obliquely studying their faces. Donnelly completed his walk-through, and after briefly chatting with the bartender, they returned to their squad car, where Donnelly pulled out his little file box containing mug shots. As he leafed through the three-by-five-inch cards with the mug shots attached, he pulled out three.

"Does this look like those dudes who were sitting with Duke?" he asked Reynolds.

"Sure as hell," Reynolds responded as he read the names on the cards—Benny Malone, Tyrone Banks, and Laquin "Slick" Jackson.

"Looks like we need to have another talk with Dixie," Donnelly replied.

Dixie had not been in Snookers, so Donnelly took a chance and headed over to The Blackbird. Sure enough, they found Dixie sitting at the bar, sipping a beer. Donnelly did his usual meander through the bar, checked with the bartender to see how things were going, and then led the way back to the patrol car. A half-hour later, they were sitting in a dark corner of the underground parking garage they had used before. Fifteen minutes after that, they saw the slight figure of Dixie coming down the stairs from the ground level.

"Hey man, what's shaking?" Donnelly asked as Dixie slid into the back seat.

"Nuttin' much that I've heard about," Dixie replied.

"We just saw that dude Duke Robinson sitting in Snookers with Benny Malone, Tyrone Banks, and Slick Jackson. That's a badass combination. Heard anything about what they're up to?" Donnelly asked.

"Yeah, I've seen 'em together a couple of times in there," Dixie said. "Word is that they're planning some kind of score, but no one seems to know what it is."

"Well, keep your ear to the ground and let me know if you hear anything," Donnelly replied.

"I'll try, man," Dixie said, "but like you said, they's some bad motherfuckers. I ain't lookin' to get myself wasted for a little taste."

"I'll make it worth your while, Dixie," Donnelly responded. "Just contact me in the usual way if you hear something."

Dixie nodded his head and bumped fists with Donnelly as he slid out of the car and disappeared up the stairs. After twenty minutes, Donnelly emerged from the parking garage and headed to the drive-in for coffee. As they sipped their hot brews, Donnelly called the Crimes against Persons Unit of the Investigations Division, where he contacted the duty officer. He briefly described what they had seen and what Dixie had told them and asked the detective if he had heard any intelligence on what the four may be up to. He said he hadn't, but that he would run it up the flagpole at their meeting on Monday morning and see if anyone had any information. He asked Donnelly to write an information report and send it up to them.

Back out on patrol, they cruised around some of the business establishments in their district. As they approached the corner of 23rd and Jefferson, they observed five Black teenage males hanging outside a drug store on the corner. "There's trouble," Donnelly said as he pulled to the curb a half-block away and parked. The boys immediately saw the police cruiser and went inside the store.

"What do you think they're up to?" Reynolds asked.

"I don't know," Donnelly replied, "but I'm sure it's no good. It's Saturday, and these kids have nothing to do but hang out and think of ways to entertain themselves, which usually means something illegal."

"It's a damn shame that the school system doesn't have some kind of organized activities for kids after school and on weekends," Reynolds proffered. "Does the Police Officers' Guild have programs for kids?"

"Well, the Department does sponsor what it calls the Seattle Police Activity League," Donnelly responded. "They have several officers who coach sports teams and participate in other activities with the kids. It might be something you'd be interested in."

"Year, I'm going to have to look into that," Reynolds responded. "I might be able to start an Aikido class."

"I'm sure they'd love to have you on board," Donnelly replied as he pulled back out into traffic and cruised by the drug store, where they observed the kids sipping sodas at the fountain.

The rest of the shift went by uneventfully. They had a couple of calls for service to take a larceny report and settle a neighborhood dispute over a man letting his dog shit on his neighbor's lawn. Before he knew it, they were pulling into the police parking garage, and soon after, Reynolds was pedaling his bicycle around Lake Union on his way home, anxiously awaiting a call from Tawnya.

Sunday was another beautiful day. Reynolds was up at 6:00 a.m. as usual, but since Sunday was his day of rest and recuperation from his exercise regimen, he leisurely sipped coffee on the lanai until he started to feel some hunger pangs. He showered, got dressed, and drove the Jeep down to his usual diner on Lake Union. He sat on the patio outside and ordered breakfast, then perused the *Sunday Post-Intelligencer* while he ate and finished his coffee.

It was still early when he left the restaurant, so he put the top down and cruised slowly around the lake, along the cut to Lake Washington, and eventually taking Madison Avenue into the city to the precinct.

On the way to the patrol car after checking out the keys and their other equipment, Donnelly asked, "You been studying that map of our sector that I gave you?"

"Yeah, I think I've gotten pretty familiar with it," Reynolds replied.

"Okay, take these—you're driving today," Donnelly said as he chucked the keys to Reynolds.

"Shit o'dear," Reynolds replied. "To what do I owe this honor?"

"Well, truth to tell, I stayed a little too long at the Greeks last night, and I'm feeling a little washed out today," Donnelly responded. "Besides, I think you've earned it."

They finished their usual routine at the gas pumps and headed for the Central District, where they began a slow, leisurely tour of the side streets. It was a beautiful Sunday morning, and the last day of their workweek, so neither of them was feeling particularly ambitious. As they cruised down 21st Avenue, they passed in front of a large African Methodist Episcopal (AME) church. The doors were standing open and they could hear through the open windows of their vehicle the loud, exuberant sounds of gospel music emanating from inside. Reynolds pulled to the curb and parked, and both he and Donnelly put back their heads, closed their eyes and reveled in the glorious sounds coming from the church.

After several minutes, Donnelly asked, "You religious, Dan?"

Reynolds thought for a moment how he should answer. He suspected that Donnelly was probably a religious person, and he did not want to offend him or get into an argument over religion, but he decided to just be honest.

"Actually, I'm a religious skeptic," he said. "I've never been able to rationally and intellectually accept the premise that there is a supreme being out there in the ether who is capable of creating the entire universe and everything in it, yet allows so much evil and injustice to exist among the highest form of life that he created on earth."

"So, you're an atheist?" Donnelly responded.

"No. If I had to put a label on it, I would call myself an agnostic," Reynolds replied. "I don't deny the existence of God because it's impossible to prove a negative. I'm just highly skeptical. How about you?"

"I was raised Catholic, but I don't actively practice the religion. But I haven't denounced it either. I still believe in a personal God and that the Bible is inspired by His divine word."

"I've tried to read the Bible several times," Reynolds said, "but I get bogged down in all the obvious contradictions and unbelievable claims. Certainly, there's a great deal of wisdom in there, but to my mind, it's the wisdom of man, not some supreme being. To me, the Bible is just a compilation of writings by ancient men who reflected the ignorance and superstitions of their time. It's based on oral tradition that was passed down for centuries in the guise of Christian history."

"What do you mean by that?" Donnelly asked.

"Well, take the creation story in Genesis, for example," Reynolds replied. "Most theologians accept the premise that Genesis was written by a priest or priests in the sixth century BCE, but it has been pretty well established that Genesis is based on a Babylonian creation myth called Enuma Elish, which is estimated to have originated five centuries before. Then you have the Epic of Gilgamesh, who was an ancient Mesopotamian mythical hero, which was written during the second millennium BCE. It depicts a story of an ancient flood that killed most of the world's people, which is probably the basis for Noah's ark.

"But what's most compelling for me is the assertion that God is the creator of the entire universe and everything in it, and that all this occurred around 3700 BCE—when the best scientific estimates say the universe is at least 14 billion years old and may be twice that old if you date it back to the Big Bang. I remember watching a television special about Barbara Morgan and her space shuttle mission back in 2007. She had pictures of the Milky Way galaxy, a minuscule part of which is our own solar system. It's estimated that the Milky Way alone has 200–400 billion stars. Her last slide depicted a plethora of other galaxies. Scientists estimate there are billions of galaxies in the universe, each containing multiple billions of stars. We can only imagine how many planets are out there orbiting those stars that may be capable of sustaining intelligent life, but it must be in the millions.

"So, the biblical idea that the earth is the center of the universe, and all the celestial bodies revolve around it, is just ancient myth, but to think that it was the inspired word of the actual creator is a little hard to swallow. And if one supreme being created all this, how likely is it that He would select one small planet as His 'special creation' and populate it with an almost infinite variety of flora and fauna governed over by his ultimate creation, 'man'? Then he apparently chose one small, ancient nomadic tribe to which to reveal His presence, and then only to a select few individuals, who, for the most part, were uneducated and powerless.

"I'm sorry, but the whole premise of not only Christianity, but all the world's major religions, defies credulity in my mind, and it's scary to me that over 80 percent of Americans believe in a personal God and over 50 percent believe the Bible's account of creation. If so many people can believe the claims of Abraham, Moses, Jesus, and Muhammad, it is no wonder they can also buy into the propaganda of Hitler, Stalin, or Donald Trump. To me, it demonstrates a remarkable lack of critical thinking."

"So, what about Jesus?" Donnelly replied. "Where does he fit into the picture?"

"Well, I believe there probably was a historical figure named Jesus," Reynolds responded, "but apparently, he was a practicing Jew his entire life who really had no intention of creating a new world religion. He very well may have been an itinerant preacher with a devoted following who expressed some views that were contrary to accepted Jewish belief and wound up pissing off both the Jewish and secular authorities and getting himself crucified."

"How about his rising from the dead and being seen ascending into heaven?" Donnelly asked. "You obviously don't believe that either."

"No, I think if he actually was placed in a tomb guarded by Roman soldiers," Reynolds replied, "then some of his disciples probably bribed the guards and took the body somewhere else for burial and then perpetrated the myth that they saw him rise from the dead."

"So, you're saying that the vast majority of people around the world who believe in Christianity or some form of a god are wrong?" Donnelly asked.

"Well, consider the history of religion going back to ancient man. It appears that even the early hominids had spiritual leaders. It probably started with the designated 'fire carrier' in prehistoric times and progressed through the shamans and holy men in early primitive tribes, to the priests in ancient polytheistic cultures, to the religious leaders we have today. It seems to me that human beings—ever since they first developed a brain capable of abstract thought—have had an inherent need to establish some type of control over their lives and to explain the mysterious physical phenomena they encountered. It also appears that even going back to the Neanderthals, early man was aware of his own mortality and feared death. In response, he developed the concept of an afterlife, which is evidenced by the fact that even the Neanderthals would bury an individual's personal belongings with them so they could be used in the afterlife, at least according to some articles I have read.

"Then, to explain the otherwise unexplainable events that impacted their lives, such as vicious storms, drought, illness, et cetera, they developed the concept of a 'supreme presence' that caused these events to happen, and the idea that they could influence these gods' actions by worshipping them and making sacrifices to them. In virtually every culture and society since then, there have been self-professed holy men who've come forward and proclaimed that they understand the gods' wishes and what needs to be done to placate them. Some of these holy men were undoubtedly true believers who just wanted to help their fellow tribesmen, but many were motivated by a need for power, control, and greed, and perhaps all of this came into play in many cases.

"At first, humans began worshipping physical objects, such as monolithic rock structures, idols in the form of carved figures, celestial objects like the sun, or other phenomena such as lightning and thunder. They created a god in their mind for every event that impacted their lives, including death, and various rituals that were meant to appease these gods and curry favor.

"Then the ancient Hebrews came up with the idea of a single God who was the creator of the universe and everybody and everything in it and developed the framework of a religion around that belief. Christianity and Islam are merely offshoots of that basic belief. They began indoctrinating their children in these beliefs from the time they were first able to comprehend what they were being told. The beliefs were reinforced by the addition of the 'fear factor.' If you angered the God or gods, you would be condemned to a cruel fate in this life and beyond.

"We now know, as we've come to understand the human psyche, that beliefs, once formed, are extremely difficult to change and that we tend to only accept information that confirms our beliefs and reject information that refutes them. Consequently, these beliefs get reinforced and passed down from generation to generation—and, again, since it's impossible to prove a negative, no one can present irrefutable evidence that contradicts these beliefs. The only means of conclusively affirming these beliefs would be the Supreme Being coming forth to unambiguously announce His presence and His expectations to the world at large, which hasn't happened. Hence, the perpetuation and proliferation of religious belief based merely on the faith that what we have been told is true."

"But you can't deny that churches and religious people do a lot of good in the world," Donnelly responded. "For many people, the church is the center of their lives and provides a sense of community and belonging."

"That's undoubtedly true," Reynolds replied, "but churches and religious people also inspire a lot of the hate and bigotry that exists around the world and are responsible for many of the atrocities that have occurred in our history—the enmity between Muslims and Jews, for instance, or between Catholics and Protestants, and the discrimination against Blacks and gay and lesbian people. Look at the atrocities committed against Muslims during the Crusades.

"We don't need churches to teach morality and values or to provide charity or a sense of community. Humans are social animals; they naturally form groups, and intelligent, beneficent people can and do organize to provide charitable services and help other people. People can teach their own children good values and morals, and these can be reinforced in our public schools. We really don't need religious institutions to do that for us. Frankly, I think religion has done a lot more harm than good over the course of history."

"Well, I'm still going to hang onto my faith," Donnelly responded.

"Thank you for proving my point," Reynolds replied. "Just know I think you have every right to do that as long as you don't try to force your beliefs on others."

As if by divine intervention, at that moment Dispatch came on the radio and assigned them to a residential burglary call. They spent the rest of the day chasing calls, and Reynolds was relieved when they pulled into the parking garage at the end of shift. He was greatly looking forward to a couple of days off and his planned 'luncheon' with Tawnya tomorrow. He was anxious to get home and call her to make sure she was prepared for what he had in mind.

As luck would have it, Tawnya called just as he entered his apartment. She expressed how much she was looking forward to their date.

"Me too," Reynolds said. "I'll be picking you up at 8:00 a.m."

"8:00 a.m.!?" Tawnya exclaimed. "I thought we were going to lunch."

"We are," Reynolds replied, "but we're going to have to hike aways to get to our luncheon destination. Do you have some sturdy shoes and a rain jacket?"

"I do," Tawnya answered. "I told you that I belong to the Mountaineers' Club and go hiking with them whenever I get a chance."

"You did, now that I think about it," Reynolds responded. "Then you know exactly what you need for a short-day hike. I'll bring some trail snacks and lunch. You just bring your beautiful self and an appetite. Actually, we'll probably work up the appetite hiking in. See you tomorrow."

"Can't wait," Tawnya responded. "See you in the morning."

CHAPTER 10

THE LIAISON

Reynolds arrived in front of Tawnya's residence hall at precisely 8:00 a.m. She was waiting at the entrance and literally ran to his Jeep to greet him. Reynolds observed that she was very appropriately dressed in zip-off hiking pants, a polyester top, a fleece jacket, and low-cut hiking boots. She was carrying a small daypack with two bottles of water in the side pockets.

"What you got in the daypack?" he queried.

"The ten essentials," she responded. "I always go prepared, though I don't have a map because I don't know where we're going."

"I do, and I've got the map and compass. Jump in. How are you?"

"I'm great," she replied. "It looks like it's going to be a beautiful day."

"It's a little cool right now but the weather report says it will be in the seventies this afternoon and completely clear."

Reynolds asked how her week had gone, even though they had talked just about every evening, and they spent the drive up in easy, casual banter. It turns out Tawnya had received a written offer to join the Pacific Northwest Ballet and was scheduled to start rehearsals at the end of May. She was going to continue to work part-time at The Harbor until she graduated and was fully established with the company. The Harbor had told her they would work with her on her schedule, so she should be able to pick her own hours and days off. Reynolds hoped that was an implication that she could plan her days off around his, which brought a smile to his face.

They headed north toward Monroe, then got onto Highway 2 and drove east toward Steven's Pass. About twenty-five miles from the pass, Reynolds pulled off the highway onto a dirt Forest Service road. About two miles down that road, he again turned off onto a two-track Jeep trail. They made their way slowly up the steep, rutted trail for about a mile until it terminated at the base of a steep ridge.

Reynolds pulled into a small clearing and parked. "End of the road," he exclaimed, "we gotta walk from here."

They donned their daypacks, and Tawnya noticed that Dan's was quite large and appeared to be stuffed to the brim.

"You planning on staying a week?" she queried. "That pack is huge."

"Just the necessities," he replied laughingly. "Like you said, you always need to be prepared for any eventuality."

They started up an unmaintained trail, which soon turned into a very steep, switch-backing slog.

"How far is it?" Tawnya asked.

"Only a couple of miles," Dan replied. "Use the rest step when you need to, and don't overextend yourself. We're not in any hurry."

Dan fell into his habitual rhythmic, short stride that allowed him to maintain a steady pace without becoming anaerobic. He adjusted his pace to match Tawnya's but was pleasantly surprised at how effortlessly she seemed to be negotiating the trail.

In less than an hour, they emerged from the tree line and almost immediately crested the ridge. Dan slipped off his pack and sat down on a large boulder, then made room for Tawnya to sit next to him. He took out a water bottle and offered her a drink, but she had already pulled hers from her pack.

Tawnya looked around and saw that they were at the top of a large bowl, at the base of which was a small lake.

"That's our destination," Dan said. "What do you think?"

"It's beautiful," she exclaimed. "It looks very peaceful and private."

Dan thought he heard a level of emotion in Tawnya's voice but could not discern if it was a note of concern or anticipation. "It is," Dan said. "I've come here a dozen times and have never seen another soul. It's on the topo map, but it doesn't show a trail into it, so I don't think people think it's accessible."

When their breathing had calmed, Reynolds stood up, shouldered his pack, and then helped Tawnya with hers. They headed off down the steep trail to the lake. Within fifteen minutes, they reached the water's edge. Dan led her around to a small clearing that was covered with green grass and wildflowers. He put down his pack and pulled out an olive-drab wool blanket left over from the military, which he spread on the grass. He also had two sitting pads with attached back rests, which he placed on the blanket. He made a sweeping gesture with his hand. "Your throne awaits, your Majesty." Tawnya took her seat and breathed deeply as she looked out over the water to the rocky cliffs beyond.

Dan proceeded to partially empty the contents of his pack, which consisted of a small, white gas camp stove, a fuel bottle, some long wooden matches, a folding camp saw, and a small nylon bag containing a sealed package of salmon fillets and another of large prawns. He laid the still partially frozen packages on the nylon bag, then grabbed the camp saw and headed for a wooded area behind them. Minutes later, he emerged from the trees with an armload of firewood and some kindling. Tawnya looked around and saw there was a primitive fire pit on a bare patch of dirt next to the lake. Reynolds went to it and carefully built a small pyramid of firewood over a pile of kindling, poured a little white gas on it to ensure it would burn, and then lit a fire.

"What's the matter?" Tawnya yelled. "I thought you were supposed to rub two sticks together to start a fire."

"Only when you have to," Reynolds replied with a laugh. "I'd rather be talking to you than going through all that hassle."

With that, he came over and took two plastic glasses from his pack and poured the yellow contents of one of his water bottles into each.

"Lemonade, your Majesty?" he questioned as he handed her a glass.

"Why thank you, kind sir," she replied. "I don't mind if I do."

Reynolds took the seat beside her, and they both gazed out at the lake for several moments. As they sat there quietly, Tawnya, almost surreptitiously, reached over, took Dan's hand, and squeezed. "This is beautiful," she said again. They sat with hands entwined until Dan had to jump up and put more wood on the fire. "Need to get some good coals going," he said.

While he waited for the fire to burn down, he pulled out a small aluminum cook pot and a water filter from his pack and went to the lake to fill the pot. He then fired up his little camp stove and put the pot of water on to boil. When it had reached a full boil, he emptied a pack of wild rice into the pot, turned down the flame, and covered it to let the rice cook.

Dan soon had a nice bed of white-hot coals. He took a metal grill from his pack and balanced it on four rocks he had placed around the fire pit. He had already wrapped the salmon and prawns in aluminum foil with lemon, butter, and garlic, so all he had to do was put them on the grill over the coals. Within minutes, they were ready to eat. He took out two plastic plates and dished them up with salmon, prawns, and wild rice, then took a plate to Tawnya.

"Your lunch is served, madam," he said as he handed her the plate. They sat and ate voraciously until the plates were slicked clean. They obviously had worked up an appetite.

"That was delicious," Tawnya said as she loosened the straps on the back of her sitting pad and leaned back in a semi-reclining position.

"Not bad, if I do say so myself," Dan replied.

They talked at length about their respective love of nature and being outdoors. The sun was directly overhead, and it was beginning to get very warm.

"Want to go for a little walk?" Dan asked.

Tawnya nodded her head affirmatively, and so they began a slow meander around the lake. When they reached the outlet of the lake on the opposite side, Dan guided her to a huge boulder half-in and half-out of the water. The top of the boulder was flat and inclined down toward the lake. Dan helped Tawnya climb atop the rock, then quickly followed. They made their way down to the water's edge of the boulder, then both took off their boots and socks and sat down, letting their bare feet dangle in the frigid water. This time, Dan gently took Tawna's hand in his as they sat, enjoying the warm sun on their backs and the cold water on their feet.

After a while, Tawnya suddenly exclaimed, "I'm hot!" She jumped up and quickly stripped off her shorts and top. Wearing only thong panties and a sports bra, she jumped into the lake. Dan laughed as she let out a screech upon hitting the ice-cold water. "What the hell," he said as he also took off his hiking shorts and shirt and jumped in behind her, wearing only his polyester boxer-briefs. In a matter of seconds, they had both taken all the cold they could stand, and Dan helped Tawnya back up onto the rock, quickly following behind her. They stretched out on the warm rock, lying on their backs next to each other, using their clothing as a pillow. As they basked in the warm rays of the sun, Dan reached again for Tawnya's hand.

"So, you want to be a prima ballerina?" he asked.

"Ever since I was a little girl," Tawnya replied. "Dancing on stage has always been my sanctuary. Probably like being in the mountains is yours. When I'm out there, the music seems to infuse my body, and I feel like I'm a hawk, soaring on the thermal currents one moment and then stooping to earth in rapid descent the next. It's the only place where I feel truly free and at peace."

"Do you think you would like the lifestyle that goes along with it?' Dan asked.

"Yes, that was always part of the dream," Tawnya replied. "My junior year of college, I studied abroad in Paris and had the opportunity to dance with the Paris Opera Ballet. I met some truly inspiring dancers and choreographers and thoroughly enjoyed not only performing with them, but the stimulating conversations we would have when we got together at a local bistro or brasserie after a performance. At the time, I couldn't imagine a more satisfying existence than being a lead dancer in an international dance company, centering my life around the culture and lifestyle of the arts, and hanging out with brilliant and talented people every day."

"Do you still feel that way?" Dan asked, with a slight feeling of trepidation at the answer he might receive.

"Some days, those feelings are as strong as ever," Tawnya responded. "Then there are days when I think that I might like to take the same route as my mother, just dancing for a local dance company while being a wife and mother. She would take me with her to her dance rehearsals from the time I was an infant and prop me up in my car seat to watch the dancers. Later, as I got older, the other members of the troupe basically adopted me and would take turns watching me while my mother went through her dance routines and floor work. Later still, they would let me join them as they practiced their ballet movements. I learned a lot from them and never felt closer to my mom than when we were at the dance studio."

"How old are you?" Dan asked, "or is that a question I shouldn't ask?"

"I just turned twenty-four," Tawnya replied.

"Well, you're still young, and there is no reason that you can't achieve all your dreams," Dan replied. "And, by the way, I can't wait to see you dance."

"We're having our final recital of the year at school a week from Friday, the night before my graduation," Tawnya said. "My folks are coming up from Phoenix and I'd love for you to meet them and come see my graduation as well. Would you like me to get you a ticket?"

"I'd be thrilled to see you dance," Dan answered, "and it would be an honor to attend your graduation and meet your parents. Let me see if I can get the days off. I'm sure it won't be a problem."

They lay on the rock for over an hour, absorbed in desultory conversation, until Dan said, "Probably better pack up and head back."

After getting dressed and hiking back to their little campsite, Dan doused the fire pit with water, then they repacked their rucks and headed back up the trail. Since most of the way back was downhill, it only took them forty-five minutes to arrive back at their vehicle. Both feeling pleasantly fatigued and at peace with the world, they were rather quiet on the drive back to Seattle. For Dan's part, he really did not want to say goodbye to Tawnya, so he finally asked,

"Hey, how about we go back to my place and hang out and maybe order a pizza later?"

"That sounds great," Tawnya answered, "but can you drop me by my place so I can take a quick shower and get a change of clothes?"

"No problem," Dan replied. "Tell you what, I'll drop you off and then run home and shower myself, then come back and pick you up."

"Perfect," she answered.

Dan had never showered and dressed as quickly as he did that day. Forty-five minutes later, he was pulling in front of Tawnya's dormitory and, again, she was standing in the door waiting for him. They decided to do a Papa Murphy's pizza and picked one up on the way back to Dan's.

"Would you like to get some wine or beer to go with the pizza?" Dan asked.

"Not for me, thanks. I don't drink. But you can certainly get some for yourself," Tawnya immediately replied.

Dan smiled inwardly. "That's okay, I don't drink either. I do have some strawberry lemonade in the fridge and some iced tea."

"Either would be great with me," Tawnya responded.

Once in the apartment, Dan deposited Tawnya on his love seat, pulled up his "Favorites" playlist on his iPod, then placed it in its designated slot on the stereo receiver in the living room. The playlist had a generous helping of songs by his favorite artists—Nancy Wilson, Dinah Washington, Etta James, and Aretha Franklin—along with a spattering of Billie Holiday, Diana Krall, Norah Jones, Sarah Vaughan, Nina Simone, Melody Gardot, and other jazz and soul singers including Smokey Robinson and Marvin Gaye, as well as groups like The Temptations and The Platters. As the music began to emanate from the speakers, Dan went to the kitchen and turned on his oven to preheat, then poured two glasses of iced tea. He added a wedge of lemon to each, then returned to the living room, tea in hand, and sat down next to Tawnya on the love seat.

After several minutes of casual conversation, Dan heard the buzzer go off on the oven and got up to put the pizza in. He returned to the living room, where he and Tawnya resumed their conversation until the pizza was done. Dan suggested they eat on the lanai and watch the sun go down to which Tawnya immediately replied, "Perfect."

They continued their conversation—mainly about personal likes and dislikes—on the lanai as they ate the pizza and watched the sun slowly slip below the horizon. At length, Tawnya asked, "Just out of curiosity, why *did* you choose not to drink alcohol?"

Dan hesitated to answer at first, not sure if he felt comfortable discussing his father's alcoholism and the chaos and heartache it had caused in the family, but after seeing Tawnya's earnest expression and apparent interest, he decided to tell her the whole story. He expressed that his real concern was that alcoholism was hereditary, and he was afraid that he might also have the gene that led to compulsive drinking. When he finished, he said, "Alright, your turn. Why don't you drink?"

Tawnya was also somewhat reluctant to tell her story, which still caused her deep embarrassment, but for some reason, she seemed to feel a comfort level with Dan that she had not experienced with many other people.

"Well, when I was sixteen, a couple of girlfriends and I decided to go to a 'kegger' that a bunch of the high school football players were throwing at a large campground up in the mountains. Long story short, I drank way too much beer and was getting pretty drunk when one of the players, who I had a crush on, got out a bottle of tequila and asked if I wanted to do some shots. I was drunk enough that I said, 'Hell yeah,' and we proceeded to drink several shots each. At some point, I blacked out and really don't remember what happened next, but apparently, this boy and I took a walk around the lake to a secluded area. The next thing I remember was waking up lying in some short grass, completely naked. My clothes were strewn all around, and I was alone. I got dressed and started stumbling back toward the campground when I ran into my girlfriends, who were looking for me. I knew subconsciously that I had been sexually violated, but I was too embarrassed to tell my girlfriends or anyone else. I've basically kept it a secret all these years."

"That must have been extremely traumatic for you," Dan responded, wondering about the long-term effects it may have had on her psychologically.

"I wouldn't say traumatic," Tawnya replied, "but deeply concerning. I wasn't a virgin at the time, and I really enjoy sex, so it may have been consensual. What really bothered me was that I couldn't remember what happened, so I made a vow to myself that I would never again drink alcohol or ingest anything else that might cause me to lose control of any situation. If I'm going to have sex, I want to be able to decide when, how, and with whom."

Dan was immediately thankful that he had not tried to make a move on Tawnya as they lay almost naked on that rock by the lake. He made a mental commitment that he would not initiate any sexual advances toward Tawnya, even though he felt strongly attracted to her physically.

As darkness conquered the fading light, they returned to the living room, where Dan turned on his electric fireplace. "Just for a little atmosphere," he said as he returned to the love seat.

They sat in silence with their feet up on the ottoman for several minutes, both content to just relax and listen to the music after a rather strenuous day. Dan had his head back, and his eyes closed when he felt Tawnya grasp his left hand and lift his arm up and over her shoulder. She snuggled in next to him with her head on his shoulder as they continued listening to the soft sounds of the music.

"It appears that you have a predilection for female singers—particularly Black female singers," she said.

Reynolds thought about that for a moment and then replied, "I suppose that's true. I think Black singers, for the most part, tend to have deep, rich voices that seem more authentic and heartfelt."

"I've also noticed that you seem to prefer love songs," she added. "Do you suppose that's indicative of some deep, unmet need?"

Dan was somewhat taken aback by that statement but had to admit to himself that he had experienced an emptiness inside for many years. His mother and Moshi were the only people from whom he had received what he considered real, unconditional love and since neither was in his life any longer, he realized he had felt isolated and alone for a long time.

"I didn't know you were studying psychology at school as well," he replied.

"Just an observation," she responded. "Did it hit home?"

"As much as I hate to admit it," he said, "you may be right."

"Well, from now on, when you're listening to these women sing, imagine that it is me singing to you," Tawnya murmured softly as she snuggled in closer. Dan did not say so but acknowledged to himself that he had been doing just that since the day they had met.

At that moment, as if driven by some quirk of fate, one of Reynolds' favorite songs emanated from the stereo, Etta James' rendition of "At Last."

"At last, my love has come along / My lonely days are over, and life is like a song," the song began. Dan turned his head to look at Tawnya, who, coincidentally, was looking back at him. Their eyes met and locked on to each other. Tawnya's sparkling hazel eyes seemed to exude warmth and affection. "You're so beautiful," Dan whispered softly as he gently brushed the side of her face with the back of his fingers and then slowly stroked her left arm. Tawnya smiled as she returned his gaze, then very slowly began moving her face toward his. Dan reciprocated, and in moments, their lips met. They began a kiss, at first softly and gently, then more intensely, until their tongues were exploring each other's mouths. Dan remembered his commitment not to initiate any sexual advances, so he just shut his mind and allowed himself to soak in the moment as he reveled in her kiss, her face cupped in his hand.

Suddenly, Tawnya, in a quick, catlike move, swung her leg over Dan's lap and straddled his loins. She continued the deep and passionate kiss as she began caressing his chest and arms. After several moments, she disengaged from the kiss and sat back, looking deeply into Dan's eyes. Then she reached down and quickly pulled Dan's V-neck sweater over his head, revealing his bare chest. As she ran her hands through the coarse chest hair and caressed his nipples, she bent forward and began kissing his neck and shoulders and mouth.

After several minutes, she again leaned back, reached down, and pulled her sleeveless top over her head. She sat there for a moment, allowing Dan to fully absorb what was happening, and then undid the front clasp of her bra and let it fall, revealing her ample and beautifully shaped bosom—the nipples hard and erect. Dan took several moments to just admire their beauty, then, cupping each breast in hand, began to kiss and fondle them, working his way in from the edges until he took the rigid nipples into his mouth and began gently sucking and kissing each one.

Tawnya had a rapturous look on her face as she again leaned back, then scooted back to sit on Dan's lower thighs. She reached down again and, this time, began unbuttoning and unzipping the fly of his shorts. She stood in front of Dan as he rose up and allowed her to pull his shorts and underwear off. She tossed them aside, knelt between his legs, took his now fully erect member in both hands and began softly stroking it. "Pretty impressive for a white boy," she murmured with a warm smile on her face. "I guess that's one more thing I can thank my father for," Dan replied.

Tawnya leaned forward and began kissing and licking the head of his penis. Dan sat back and reveled in the exquisite sensation as she then took the head of his penis in her mouth and began sucking it, at first slowly and gently and then with increased intensity. Dan's mind flashed back to Moshi, his girlfriend in Okinawa, and to her encouraging Dan to practice Tantra and Kundalini yoga with her, as well as Bindu Samrakshana (the conservation of semen), in order to improve their sexual performance. Even though it had been some time since he had been with a woman, Dan was able to avoid premature ejaculation as he cleared his mind and focused on his breathing and the pleasurable sensation of Tawnya's mouth on his cock.

Tawnya disengaged from his penis and again stood in front of Dan. She was wearing a pair of cotton workout shorts with an elastic waistband that enabled her to slide the shorts and her panties down over her hips and step out of them, giving them a kick with one foot as she did so. Dan leaned forward and kissed the slight swell of her belly and then began working his way down to her vagina. He reached up with one hand and began rubbing the lips of her vulva, which he discovered were dripping moisture. He allowed his middle finger to penetrate her vagina and slowly massaged the inside, then ran his finger around the circumference of her erect clitoris. She moaned with pleasure as he placed his hands on her butt cheeks and gently pulled her down to him. Tawnya took his cock in her hand and guided it inside her as she again straddled Dan's loins. She began a slow grind as she slid up and down on Dan's rock-hard member. Tawnya glanced down and noticed a slight smirk on Dan's face.

"What's up with the smirk?" she asked with a note of concern in her voice.

"I just had a thought flash through my mind of a joke one of the recruits told in the academy," Dan replied. "He asked what the difference was between a good girl and a nice girl."

"And what was the answer?" Tawnya asked.

"A good girl will put it in for you," Dan replied.

"And what would you prefer?" Tawnya replied with a laugh. "A good girl or a nice girl?"

"Give me a good girl every time," Dan responded as he took in her beautiful body. He reached up and began caressing her breasts and nipples while reveling in the sensation of his organ inside her incredibly tight vagina. Dan shut his eyes and lost all consciousness of time until he felt Tawnya's grinding and thrusting begin to intensify. Her low moaning grew to loud gasps as she began yelling, "Oh my God, yes, yes, yes!" She continued to thrust harder and faster until her body began to spasm, and she let out a loud cry—"I'm coming, I'm coming."

As her body stiffened, Dan felt his own body begin to convulse as he shot his wad deep inside her. The climax lasted several moments for each of them but eventually subsided, and Tawnya slumped in a limp mass onto Dan's chest. She pressed herself against him as she threw her arms around his neck and lay her head on his shoulder.

Dan put his feet back up on the ottoman as he held her close to him, with his now flaccid penis still inside her pussy. They lay without moving, listening to the music for perhaps a half-hour. Then Dan began gently rubbing her back and buttocks. She responded by raising her head and gently kissing him.

Within minutes Dan felt his organ begin to engorge. With his hands on Tawnya's buttocks and her arms around his neck, he rocked forward and stood up, then carried her into his bedroom and lay her gently down on her back at the foot of the bed. As she looked up at him longingly and expectantly, he took her long, elegant feet in his hands and began slowly massaging the soles. He then began gradually working his way up her legs, alternately kissing and massaging first her ankles, then her calves, and then her inner thighs. Eventually, he reached her vagina, which he began kissing and licking. After a time, he thrust his tongue inside her, then moved up to begin gently licking and sucking on her clitoris. As he heard Tawyna's breathing become heavy, he felt her hands on his shoulders, gently tugging him. "I want you inside me," she groaned.

Dan continued his kissing and licking as he slowly moved up to her abdomen, then her breasts, then her neck, and finally, he got to her lips. They kissed deeply as Tawnya reached down and guided his cock once again inside of her. This time it was Dan's turn to do the thrusting and grinding, and he began very slowly. Soon, however, Tawnya began pressing herself against him and grinding her hips. The intensity of Dan's thrusting increased gradually until they both exploded again in a magnificent climax. As their bodies relaxed, Dan—still on top of her—gently kissed Tawnya's face and mouth. "That was wonderful," she whispered in his ear. "You're wonderful," he whispered in reply.

He rolled off Tawnya and put his arms around her as she threw her leg over him. They lay entwined together in blissful contentment for many minutes until Dan heard the murmur of gentle snoring in his ear. He looked at Tawnya and saw that she was asleep, so he carefully disengaged himself, got up, turned off the stereo and the lights, and crawled into bed beside her. He did not want to wake her to pull down the covers, so he just covered them with the Afghan that he kept at the foot of the bed. Tawnya did not fully awaken but did roll onto her side with her back to Dan and then snuggled into him, her butt firmly rooted against his belly. Dan suddenly realized how much he had missed spooning with a woman he truly cared about. He soon fell into a deep and blissful sleep.

Dan had forgotten to turn off the alarm on his stereo, so at precisely 6:00 a.m., Nancy Wilson began serenading them. Tawnya awoke, stretched, and then rolled over to face Dan. She put her arms around him and kissed him deeply. "Good morning, sunshine," she said.

"It's a great morning," he replied as he pulled her to him and returned her kiss.

Although Dan had not awakened with a hard-on, he soon felt one coming on. He decided he better get up and pee before acting on his immediate impulse to ravage Tawnya. Tawnya followed him into the bathroom and, once he was done, sat down on the toilet and relieved herself while Dan washed his hands. Surprising himself, Dan was not at all taken aback by this level of familiarity. They made their way back to the bedroom, jumped into bed, and again made deep, passionate love.

When they had finished, Dan went to the kitchen and returned with two mugs of fresh, steaming coffee. He raised the head of his adjustable bed and crawled in beside Tawnya. "Is this a running day for you?" she asked as they sipped their coffee.

"No, I normally do Aikido on Tuesdays, but I'm going to take a break from it today. How about you? Is there anything you have to do or would like to do?" he responded.

"Well, I was kind of planning to do some apartment hunting today. Now that I'm about to graduate, I have to be out of the residence hall by the middle of June," she replied, "but I think I might skip that as well."

"I know of a nice apartment that might be available," Dan responded. "That is, if you're willing to share."

Tawnya looked at him quizzically. "Are you suggesting what I think you're suggesting?" she asked. "You want me to move in with you after only one night together?"

"Baby, I've never felt as happy and contented and at peace with the world as I did waking up next to you this morning," Dan responded. "I was consumed with the thought that I never want to wake up without you next to me ever again. It seems like I've known you my entire life and that we were meant to be together. Besides, think about how much money you could save by living with me."

Tawnya did not say anything for several seconds, then a huge smile crossed her face, and she threw her arms around Dan and pulled him to her. Within minutes, they were again thrusting against each other in violent lovemaking.

When they had finished and recovered their breath, Dan asked if Tawnya wanted to take a shower. She nodded in the affirmative. "With me?" Dan again queried. "Of course," Tawnya responded. They got up and strode to the bathroom hand in hand, then took a long, leisurely, hot shower, taking turns to thoroughly wash each other's body. Once out of the shower and dressed, they again filled their coffee mugs and headed for the lanai.

"Let's grab breakfast at the Egg and I," Dan suggested, "and then we can start moving your things out of the dorm."

Tawnya did not have a lot of personal belongings other than her clothes, which were plentiful. It took two trips to load them all into the back of the Jeep and Tawnya's Honda and move them to Dan's apartment, which, fortunately, had a large walk-in closet that Dan's clothes did not make a dent in filling.

It was late afternoon before they finished finding a place for her special ornaments, pictures, and books and putting away all her clothes. They were both famished by that point, so they drove to the nearest Texas Roadhouse and had a steak dinner. Back at the apartment, they slipped into some comfortable loungewear, took up their respective positions on the bed, and tuned into a movie on the TV. They were not too far into the action before they had both stripped off their clothes and were again making passionate love. After achieving yet another mutual orgasm, they were finally able to finish the movie, after which they fell asleep in each other's arms. It was only 9:00 p.m.

CHAPTER 11

WEEK THREE

Dan's eyes popped open, only to discover that it was still dark outside. He glanced at the digital clock on his nightstand and saw it was only 5:00 a.m. He felt the urge to pee, so he carefully disengaged from Tawnya's arms and went to the bathroom, noting on the way that he had awakened without a full-blown erection.

After relieving himself, he returned to bed and rolled onto his right side, with his back to Tawnya. She snorted a little and then immediately snuggled against him, with one arm around his chest. Dan thought she had gone back to sleep until he felt her hand fondling and stroking his cock. *This girl is insatiable*, Dan thought to himself and smiled in gratitude. He took a deep breath and let himself fully experience the pleasurable sensation. Within minutes he was again fully erect. He rolled over to face Tawnya. "Are you having fun, my dear?" he asked.

"Just getting to know my new best friend," she replied. With that, Tawnya slipped down under the covers, and the next sensation Dan had was of her taking his member into her mouth and sucking. After several exquisite minutes, she emerged from the covers, pushed Dan onto his back, and mounted him, guiding his swollen organ into her pussy. They took their time, and it was a half-hour later before they each exploded in a rush of liquid discharge.

They lay spent in each other's arms until 6:00 a.m. sharp when Nancy Wilson's sultry voice again penetrated the silence in the room. "Is it a running day?" Tawnya asked.

"We don't have to if you'd rather not," Dan responded.

"No, I don't want to be the reason you disrupt your life," she said. "Besides, it's good for us."

They got up, dressed in their running togs, and proceeded to get coffee before coming to rest on the lanai. After finishing their coffee, they completed a yoga routine before heading out the door to the lake. After two laps of the lake and walking back to the apartment, they had a light breakfast of oatmeal and toast, then showered together and dressed for the day.

Tawnya had classes to attend and some work in the library to complete, so they went out the door together—Dan with his bike over his shoulder and Tawnya to her car. Before parting, Dan took Tawnya in his arms and kissed her deeply. "See you tonight?" he said in a questioning manner.

"You better believe it," she responded. "I'll be waiting at the door."

After exchanging his biking togs for his police uniform, Reynolds proceeded to the Crime Analysis Unit, where he found Donnelly poring over a clipboard of police reports. Reynolds took down the robbery clipboard and took a seat across the table from his partner. He began reading through the reports and taking notes until he felt someone staring at him. He looked up to see Donnelly gazing intently. After several seconds, Donnelly asked, "Alright, what happened? You're positively glowing this morning."

"It was a great couple of days off," Reynolds replied.

"Bullshit! You got laid, didn't you?" Donnelly responded.

"A gentleman never tells," Reynolds replied and continued looking through the reports.

He soon came to one that immediately grabbed his attention. "Hey, did you see this robbery report where four Black dudes wearing ski masks and packing assault rifles took down a Safeway store in Rainier Valley two nights ago?" he asked Donnelly.

"No, I haven't got that far yet, but I did hear a news report on it," Donnelly responded.

"I wonder if that might be our friends from the Blackbird the other day," Reynolds opined.

"Don't know, but we might want to have a chat with Dixie later," Donnelly replied.

No sooner had they cleared with radio that they were in service when the dispatcher announced, "Two-George-Three, we have a report of a woman screaming from the second floor of a building at 1921 East Monroe."

"Two-George-Three, responding Code 3," Donnelly said as he kicked the squad car up to ten miles over the speed limit and turned on the emergency lights and siren. Within minutes, they pulled up in front of an old two-story, wood-frame building that apparently, at one time, had housed a Mom and Pop grocery store on the bottom level and appeared to have an apartment on the second level. Seconds later, they heard a woman scream from a broken second-floor window. "Help me! Someone please help me!"

Donnelly and Reynolds quickly ran to the outside wooden stairway leading to the only exterior entrance into the apartment. They were surprised to find that the door had a hasp with a locked padlock on the outside, as well as a locked crossbar across it. Without hesitation, they each simultaneously applied a foot to the wooden lower panel of the door, sending it crashing into the apartment. With weapons drawn, they took turns crawling through the opening and began a shakedown of the apartment. Reynolds proceeded to a back bedroom from which the screaming had seemed to come. He stood on one side of the doorway and listened for a moment. He again heard a woman call out, "Help me," from inside the bedroom. He quickly sprang through the doorway in a crouch, gun drawn. He scanned the room quickly and saw a blonde woman standing next to the broken bedroom window, the frame of which was also secured with a hasp and padlock. He did a quick sweep of the room to ensure there was no one else there, and by this time, Donnelly had joined him.

They assured the woman that they were there to help her and that everything was going to be alright, then escorted her to the kitchen, where they sat her down at the table and asked her what was going on. Reluctantly at first, in a heavy accent, she related to them her incredible story.

She said she was from Vienna, Austria, and had been living and working there as a waitress in a restaurant. Approximately a year previously, an American man had come into her restaurant for lunch and struck up a conversation with her. He had asked her to have dinner with him that evening and, over dinner, had told her that he was a high-level executive with the Boeing Company and was in Vienna on business. She was not immediately impressed, given that he was middle-aged and pudgy with a bald head, but as he had described to her his beautiful home on Mercer Island next to Lake Washington and his luxurious lifestyle, she had begun to become more interested. After dinner, he had asked if she would like to come back to his hotel room for a nightcap. She had agreed, and he took her to a high-end hotel in the heart of Vienna. They had several drinks in his room, and she wound up spending the night with him.

In the morning, over breakfast in the room, he had told her that he had to leave the next day to return to the States. He had conveyed how attracted he was to her and asked if she would come with him. He had promised to marry her before they left Vienna and vowed to provide her with a life of luxury. She was an attractive woman, but she was approaching thirty-five and did not see any better prospects on the horizon in Vienna, so she had agreed.

They had been married that day in a courthouse, and she had spent the rest of the day packing what she wanted to take with her, disposing of the rest of her belongings.

When they had arrived in Seattle, instead of taking her to a beautiful home on the lake, they had gone to this shabby little walk-up apartment over what she later found out had once been his parents' corner grocery store. He had immediately gone about putting padlocks on all the exterior windows and doors. He really did have a job at Boeing, but it was as a low-level worker on the assembly line. He left for work at 4:00 a.m. every weekday and would lock her into the apartment when he left. They ate all their meals in the apartment, and he only allowed her to leave to accompany him on occasional visits to his aging parents. He did all the grocery shopping and anything else that needed to be done outside the apartment. She had become a virtual sex slave. She said that when she awoke this morning, she realized that she had finally reached her breaking point and decided she had to escape, whatever it took.

Donnelly took a written statement from the woman, and then asked Dispatch to check the local women's shelter to see if they had any vacancies. Fortunately, they did, so Donnelly and Reynolds stood by while the woman packed a suitcase and then transported her to the shelter. They both shook their heads in disbelief as they drove away. "I need a cup of coffee after that," Donnelly said as he drove down to Pinky's. As they drank their coffee, Donnelly again tried to probe Reynolds about his activities over their days off, but Reynolds chose to keep that information secret for the time being.

After coffee, Donnelly suggested they do a shake at Snookers to see if Dixie was there. As luck would have it, he was sitting at the bar when they arrived. After a quick sweep of the pool joint, they slowly made their way back to the underground parking garage and waited for the informant. It took a half-hour before he finally showed up.

"Know anything about a stick-up at the Safeway in Rainier Valley a couple of days ago?" Donnelly asked.

"Like I told you before," Dixie responded, "they's been rumors for weeks that Benny Malone and his crew were planning a score, but I ain't heard nothing 'bout the grocery store robbery."

"Well, keep your ear to the ground," Donnelly said. "We'll make it worth your while if you come up with any good information."

Dixie nodded his head and then disappeared into the gloom of the underground garage.

"Tomorrow morning, we'll check in with the dicks in Robbery to see if they got any info on this case," Donnelly said as they drove out of the garage.

The rest of the day was filled with routine calls, and before Reynolds knew it, he was pedaling his ass home as fast as he could. The anticipation of the pleasure that awaited him filled him with energy. As she had said, Tawnya was waiting at the door for him when he arrived—completely naked—and they immediately fell into a tight embrace and passionate kiss. After they had finished making love, Tawnya asked if Dan had had anything to eat.

"Yeah, we grabbed a bite at the Burger King around six o'clock," Dan responded. It turned out that Tawnya had finished off the leftover pizza for dinner, so they retired to the living room and tuned into a Netflix movie. Halfway through, Reynolds stood up and reached out his hand to Tawyna. "I'm bored," he said. "I need a little excitement." She willingly let him lead her into the bedroom, and they were soon naked in bed in the throes of passion again.

As they lay in the afterglow of sexual fulfillment, Dan said, "I think we need to adjust our daily routine somewhat."

"How so?" Tawnya responded.

"I think we need to set the alarm for a half-hour earlier in order to accommodate our morning extracurricular activities," Dan replied.

"Maybe we need to make it an hour," Tawnya responded, chuckling.

"An hour it is," Dan replied. And so, from the next day forward, they would awaken at 5:00 a.m., engage in an hour of leisurely lovemaking, then rise and start their day. In the evening, when Dan got home, they would strip naked, curl up on the bed, and start to watch TV, only to be short-circuited by their intense desire to again merge into one being. Dan had never been happier in his life.

The next morning, Reynolds and Donnelly made the rounds of the detective division and ended up in the Robbery/Homicide Unit. Donnelly asked if they had any leads on the Rainier Valley Safeway robbery and was told they did not but that there had been another robbery of a grocery store on Capitol Hill the previous evening. Again, it was four Black males wearing face masks and armed with assault rifles. Donnelly filled the lieutenant in on what they had learned from Dixie about Benny Malone and the other individuals they had seen with him at the Blackbird. The lieutenant thanked them for the information and told them to stay in touch.

Back out on the street, they began slowly patrolling the business areas in their district. They patrolled in silence for a half-hour until, as they drove past Rainier Middle School, out of the blue, Reynolds interrupted their reverie by asking, "What do you think of our education system in this country?"

"I think it's pretty fragmented and inequitable," Donnelly responded. "There are some really good schools and some really bad schools, with a lot of mediocre ones in between. Which one you get pretty much depends on how much money you have. What brought that up?"

"I just started thinking about these kids hanging out on the corner by the school and wondering what their prospects in life really are. The chances are pretty good that many of them will drop out of school by the tenth grade, and even then, will probably only be functioning at a sixth- or seventh-grade level academically. The most likely prospects for their future are a menial, low-wage job without benefits or prison. Either way they will end up a fiscal liability for society."

"I suppose you have a grand scheme to save our education system as well," Donnelly said with a smile.

"I've got a grand scheme to fix all society's problems," Reynolds replied laughingly. "The curse of spending six years in college."

"Let's hear it."

"Well, as I see it, there are only two ways to mitigate the poverty and income inequality that plague this country—education and entrepreneurship. The first makes the second possible.

"Since the founding of our country, we have held onto the concept that education is best administered and funded at the local level. Consequently, there are 295 school districts in the State of Washington and thousands more across the country, each with its own superintendent, assistant superintendents, and numerous administrative staff. Each of these school districts also has a separate, elected school board made up of laymen from the community, and between the superintendent and the school board, they exert autonomy over what schools in their district teach and how they teach it. That results in the fragmentation that you mentioned.

"On top of that, schools get most of their funding through local property taxes; hence, local taxpayers, through local bond elections, for the most part determine what schools will be built and what resources the schools will have. That results in the inequality that you mentioned. Per-pupil annual spending varies tremendously from state to state. Even within individual states, funding varies dramatically based on property values in each school district.

"To me, our system is an anachronism. Local control may have made sense back in the horse-and-buggy days when most kids stayed close to home after completing school and worked on farms or in local industries. That is not the case today. Whether we like it or not, we live in a global economy. Our kids are competing against kids from all over the world for the good jobs of the future. Yet, we are one of the only major countries in the world without a nationalized education system and defined national goals for education.

"Most kids today, particularly those in rural areas, cannot continue to live locally after school because there are no jobs for them. The smart kids leave to go to college elsewhere and never come back. Most of the rest migrate to the big cities so they can find jobs. This situation will only get worse as automation, robotics, and artificial intelligence completely change the nature of work in this country and the rest of the world."

"Okay, so far, I agree. So, what's your plan?" Donnelly said.

"Well, first, I would nationalize our education system. The US Department of Education should be the governing force for all public primary, secondary, and post-secondary education in the country. It should establish national education goals based on the needs of the country as a whole and the types of career opportunities that will be available to kids now and in the foreseeable future. The overarching goal should be to provide as equal an opportunity as possible for every child to reach their full potential as a person and become a responsible and productive member of society.

"To accomplish that, I think we should eliminate all local school districts and break up each state into five to seven regions, each with its own deputy superintendent who would work under a state superintendent of public instruction. The primary responsibilities of the deputy superintendents would be to act as a conduit of information between the state superintendent and the individual schools in the region and to conduct audits of each school's performance. Each region would be designed to incorporate a similar demographic in terms of urban or rural residents. The state superintendents would report to the secretary of education at the federal level. Operational control of schools would be delegated to the principal of each individual school.

"Further, schools should no longer be funded through property taxes. All school expenditures, including the construction of new schools, should be funded jointly through state and federal income taxes. To the greatest degree possible, per-pupil spending should be equalized nationally and only adjusted to account for differences in the cost of living in different areas. National standards would be developed for school facilities and resources, and every school would be required to meet those standards or be upgraded or replaced."

"You mean, without local taxpayers having any say whether a new school is built in their area?" Donnelly asked.

"Oh, they would have a say in terms of recommending a location or making suggestions on design features, but not in whether outdated, dilapidated school buildings are replaced. Besides, the cost would not be coming solely from their pockets but would be distributed nationwide."

"So, how about *what* and *how* schools teach? Do you want the federal government telling parents and kids what they will take in school?" Donnelly queried. "And what about private and parochial schools? Who's going to govern them?"

"Well, as I see it, the US Department of Education should be the driver and the facilitator behind developing appropriate school curricula for public schools throughout the country based on proven best practices and national need, but innovation should be encouraged at both the national and local level.

"The federal agency could bring together state superintendents, educators, academicians, and business leaders from all over the country in order to collaboratively determine what essential knowledge and skills our kids will need to succeed in today's and tomorrow's economy and also to predict what career opportunities will be available to them. They can use that information to develop recommended school curricula that will meet the country's and the individual's needs going forward. Again, the goal should be to enable every student, based on their individual interests and abilities, the opportunity to maximize their potential and be an effectively functioning and productive member of society. As far as private and parochial schools go, I think they should be able to determine their own curricula but should not receive any government funding. If people want to send their kids to private or parochial schools, they should foot the entire bill. Taxpayer money should only be used to support public education."

"So, how do you see that playing out at the level of the individual child?" Donnelly asked.

"Well, first, we need to recognize that a child's long-term success in school and in life depends a great deal on their early developmental years. We need systems in place that ensure every child, to the degree possible, receives the physical and mental health care, the nutrition, and the appropriate structure, stability, and nurturing as an infant and toddler that they will need in order to maximize their ability to learn. As I've said before, that would best be accomplished through a universal health care system that every citizen has access to, regardless of their financial circumstances, and social support systems that meet every child's social, physical, emotional, and psychological needs.

"Second, we need a universal pre-K program in our public schools that provides every child with the foundation they need to be successful in school and in life. Every child should progress through pre-K, kindergarten, and primary school through the eighth grade. The emphasis during these years should be on academics—essentially reading, writing, and arithmetic. Progress in school should be competency-based, meaning each child would have to meet a level of competency in each of their subjects in order to pass onto the next grade level. High-achieving students should have advanced-placement classes available to them so that they are not held back in their learning; low-functioning students should be assigned tutors and given the extra help they need to progress.

"Again, as I've said before, in addition to academics, each child should have to take a K12 personal wellness curriculum. These classes would educate kids, on an age-appropriate basis, in areas that affect their personal and social development and health. It might start out in kindergarten, discussing appropriate touching and dealing with strangers, then progress to proper nutrition, the importance of exercise and physical activity, drug and alcohol education, social skills, and finally, in secondary school, to civics, comprehensive sex education, parenting skills, child development, and relationship skills, along with budgeting and financial management. In short, this curriculum would be designed to give kids the knowledge they will need to effectively manage their lives and be responsible, independent, and effective adults."

"So, every child gets a basic academic education. What happens when they get into secondary and post-secondary schools?" Donnelly responded.

"Well, starting in the sixth or seventh grade, we would begin conducting proficiency tests with each student, as well as aptitude testing to determine their strengths and weaknesses, and personality tests to see what kinds of work and social environments are most suitable for them," Reynolds answered. "Have you ever taken a Myers-Briggs personality test?"

"No, never heard of it," Donnelly responded. "What does it tell you?"

"Well, it gives you very good insight into the type of person you are and what kinds of work would be most conducive to your long-term success," Reynolds replied.

"So, who's going to do all this testing? Our teachers are overwhelmed as it is, and a lot of schools have only one school counselor, if that," Donnelly retorted.

"Unfortunately, that's all too true, which means we are going to have to invest sufficient resources to train and hire enough guidance counselors and behavioral health counselors so that each child has ready access to a personal counselor throughout their school years."

"Where's the money for that going to come from?" Donnelly asked.

"Well, as you probably know, thousands—if not millions—of jobs are going unfilled in this country because businesses can't find qualified people to fill them. This situation is going to be exacerbated in the future with the escalating use of automation and robotics, which will replace many jobs currently done by people while creating thousands of new jobs that will require specialized knowledge and skills. One field that will not be replaced by a robot will be social services, such as counselors, social workers, and case managers, and I think this is an area that we really need to encourage appropriate students to pursue. In terms of who is going to pay for it—obviously taxpayers, for the most part, but we need to think of it as a long-term investment in the future of the country and as a means to greatly reduce poverty, hunger, crime, and incarceration, along with their associated costs to society.

"One of the sources of those taxes will be businesses, large and small, since they will be a primary beneficiary of this system. In addition to that tax revenue, we need to not only solicit their input into what knowledge and skills they require—both present and future—but actively engage them in providing qualified instructors to teach that knowledge and those skills in both our secondary and post-secondary schools. The long-term return on our investment will come from a vastly increased number of people productively employed and paying taxes, and a greatly reduced number receiving social services or being incarcerated or otherwise cared for at society's expense."

"Okay, so you've done all this testing and evaluation—what happens next?" Donnelly asked.

"The guidance counselor brings in the child and their parents and fully explains the results of the tests and what they mean in terms of the kinds of work or career in which there appears to be a viable future for the child, and in which the child would most likely be successful. The parents and child would be given time to discuss and select a career path that best fits the child's interests and abilities. They would again sit down with the counselor and discuss the school options and curriculum that would best suit the child's career goals."

"Okay, so what happens if the classes or training aren't available at the child's local school? Donnelly asked.

"Well, this is where school choice and remote learning come into play. Within our public school system, we would need to provide specialized schools such as STEM academies and technical education schools that provide the instruction the child needs. Obviously, these would be located in metropolitan areas for the most part. If a child were unable to attend these schools in person, which I think we should facilitate through residential housing facilities if possible, we would need to provide remote learning capability so they could access the classes from their local school."

"My question, again, is who is going to pay for all of this?" Donnelly asked.

"Again, taxpayers would cover the costs of each child's education as long as they are pursuing the agreed-upon career path. That would include technical and vocational education as well as undergraduate and postgraduate work in college—if the child chose to go to college. However, we would probably want to look at cost-sharing with the parents on a sliding fee scale based on their income or wealth."

"What happens if the child changes their mind at some point in the program or after they actually enter the career field?" Donnelly asked. "And how about kids that want to be an artist or writer or some other artistic field with low chances of financial success?"

"We need artists and writers and musicians and dancers in society, and as long as they demonstrate the aptitude and ability, I think they should be allowed to pursue those goals. If they can't make it or change their minds at some point, then they should be allowed to pursue another option as long as they have the ability and it is a viable career choice, but that should obviously be limited. We can only afford so much as a society."

Donnelly shook his head and chuckled, "Yeah, you may have made the wrong choice in being a cop. I really think you should consider politics. I just hope that in this future utopian society of yours, they still need an old cop like me."

They had been sitting at a four-way-stop intersection during this conversation. Donnelly put the gear shift in drive and pulled out into traffic as he said, "We better move on and do some work."

The rest of the day was relatively routine. They managed to get their traffic citation when a car ran a stop sign in front of them. They investigated a non-injury traffic accident that happened during rush hour and then responded to a residential burglary call that occurred while the home's occupants were at work. Before they knew it, they were pulling into the parking garage at the end of the shift.

Reynolds quickly changed clothes and mounted his bicycle for the ride home. He couldn't wait to be in Tawnya's arms. Again, when he opened the door, she was standing just inside, completely naked. "I saw you coming," she said. He tore off his bike clothes, picked her up, and carried her to the bedroom. The next hour was spent in exquisite lovemaking. This evening cemented a precedent and tradition that they would repeat just about every day that Dan worked. It filled each waking hour with a sense of excitement and anticipation that kept him smiling inside all day long.

CHAPTER 12

THE BROTHERHOOD OF MAN

Friday dawned overcast and cool. Reynolds arrived a little late to his rendezvous with Donnelly at the Crime Analysis Unit due to a stubborn erection as he and Tawnya showered that morning, which required a second session of lovemaking before he left for work.

They completed their due diligence there, sat through roll call, and were soon heading out to their district.

"Kind of a gloomy day," Reynolds observed as they began patrolling the side streets and alleys. Within minutes, they were dispatched to a three-car accident at the intersection of Martin Luther King Jr. Way and South Jackson. Unfortunately, the driver of one vehicle, who had apparently run a red light, suffered a deep gash on his forehead from slamming into the steering wheel. Reynolds treated and bandaged the wound but thought it would probably require stitches, so they called Medic 1 to respond, and the driver was transported to Harborview Medical Center's emergency room. His vehicle was inoperable and had to be towed. They completed their on-scene investigation, then stopped by the hospital to give the driver a copy of the other drivers' information and a traffic summons for running the light, after which they headed to the local Burger King, where they finished writing the report.

They had no sooner cleared from the accident than Dispatch called again. "Two-George-Three, can you handle a domestic disturbance in Charlie-Four's district, 2109 Chesterville Avenue? They're tied up."

"Two-George-Three, copy," Donnelly responded.

They arrived at the little side-by-side duplex apartment, took their positions beside the front doorway, and knocked. "Seattle Police," Donnelly announced.

The door opened to a spectacle that almost caused Reynolds to break out laughing. Standing in the doorway was a white male, probably in his mid-to late twenties, wearing a pair of crimson polyester bell-bottomed pants straight out of the '70s. His shirt was satin with a bright, red-and-yellow floral pattern on a green background, unbuttoned to just above the waist. He had on a wide white belt and white leather shoes. His clean-shaven face was framed by peroxide-blonde, fully permed hair, which amplified his rouged cheeks and mascaraed and lined eyes. He stood in the doorway with a hipshot stance, his right hand firmly planted on his right cheek, which displayed the dark-red nail polish on his fingernails.

"Thank God you're here," he exclaimed effetely as he bent a limp left wrist in their direction. "I want that man out of here."

Reynolds looked past the clownish caricature in front of him to a rather conservatively dressed young man sitting on the couch in the living room.

"May we come in and discuss what the situation is here?" Donnelly asked.

The male at the door stepped aside and allowed the officers inside, then immediately began pacing around the living room with a conspicuous swish, again stating emphatically, "I want that man out of my house—now."

"May I talk to you in the kitchen?" Reynolds said as he motioned the man in that direction.

Once in the kitchen with the door closed, Reynolds asked, "Okay, can we start with you telling me your name?"

"Bruce," the man replied.

Suppressing a smile at the thought of how often this name is associated with homosexual men, Reynolds asked, "Okay, Bruce, can you tell me what caused you to be so upset today?"

Bruce took several deep breaths, then sighed and began. "Well, my boyfriend James and I decided to go down to The Pirate's Cove on Broadway for lunch. James saw a guy there that he knew and invited him to have lunch with us. James spent the entire time we were there engrossed in an animated conversation with this guy and virtually ignored me. I finally got so angry that I just got up and left. He showed up here a little while ago, and I asked him to leave, and he refused to go."

"I see," Reynolds replied. "Who is the legal resident in this apartment?"

"We're both on the lease," Bruce answered.

"Well, we can't make James leave the apartment unless we have grounds to arrest him," Reynolds responded. "Has he physically threatened or harmed you?"

"No, he has just been sitting on that damn couch and refusing to talk," Bruce replied.

"Do you mind if we return to the living room and try to talk with him?" Reynolds asked. Bruce shrugged and followed Reynolds back into the room. Reynolds glanced over at Donnelly, who just gave him a raised eyebrow look, stating, "Mr. Burton says he has nothing to say or apologize for."

"Bruce tells me your name is James," Reynolds said. "Do you mind if I call you James?"

"No," came the response.

"Well, to start with, can we all sit down? Oftentimes, just sitting down to talk can greatly reduce the temperature in an argument," Reynolds said as he pointed Bruce toward the chair next to the couch. Reynolds sat down on a chair adjacent to Bruce's, and Donnelly sat on the couch with James.

"First of all, have either of you ever heard of the concept of an 'I statement'?" Reynolds asked. Both Bruce and James shook their heads in the negative.

"Well, an 'I statement' is just a way to express your feelings in a non-threatening, non-accusatory, very objective way," Reynolds added. "Let me walk you through the process."

"First, Bruce, I would like you to tell James specifically what he did today that made you upset," Reynolds continued. "Try to do it in a calm and dispassionate manner, without blaming or shaming."

"Well, when we went to lunch today, you spent the entire time we were there talking to your friend and ignoring me," Bruce said.

"Okay, now can you tell James exactly how that made you feel and why, starting with an 'I'?" Reynolds asked. "Try to be as specific as possible in regard to what you were thinking and feeling. This is where you take responsibility for your own thoughts and feelings."

"I felt angry and hurt because I thought you were flirting with your friend and rejecting me."

"Good job," Reynolds said. "Now, can you tell James what you would like him to do in the future to avoid such situations?"

Bruce thought for a minute, then responded, "In the future, I would like you to include me in your conversations with others and not ignore me."

"Very good," Reynolds said. "Now, James, can you tell Bruce in your own words exactly what you heard him say?"

James looked Bruce in the eye for several seconds, then said, "Bruce, it sounds like you were very angry and hurt when I got involved in a conversation with my friend and didn't include you. I understand that you may have felt rejected and thought I was coming on to him and that you don't want the situation to repeat itself in the future."

"Now, James, can you tell Bruce how you felt at the time, why you acted as you did, and what you are willing to do in the future to avoid a repeat of the situation?" Reynolds asked. "You must be completely honest in this response, even if it might be hurtful to the other person."

James continued looking Bruce in the eyes as he responded. "Bruce, I realize now that I was completely insensitive to your feelings and how hurtful that must have been given how committed our relationship has been. I just feel so comfortable in our relationship that I did not consider your feelings and got carried away in talking to my friend, who I had not seen in a long time. Now that I am aware of how you feel, I promise that in the future, I will not let that happen again."

Reynolds saw tears well up in Bruce's eyes as he reached across and offered his hand to James. "Are we all right here?" Reynolds asked. "Is there anything else that either of you would like us to do?"

Both looked at Reynolds and shook their heads. "Okay, we'll let ourselves out," Reynolds said as he and Donnelly stood up and headed for the door. Reynolds looked back as he left and observed that Bruce was sitting next to James on the loveseat, together, hand-in-hand.

"Wow, partner, that was pretty impressive," Donnelly said as they got into the car. "Did you take counseling when you were in college, too?"

"Actually, it was part of my addiction studies minor," Reynolds responded, "along with relationship skills."

"Have you ever seen such a flaming queen in your life?" Donnelly asked, shaking his head.

"Well, he was pretty over the top," Reynolds responded. "But I think he was just being himself. Nothing wrong with that."

"Are you suggesting that gays are born that way and that it is not a choice?" Donnelly asked.

"I am," Reynolds responded. "Homosexuality has been part of human behavior and some animal behavior from the beginning of our existence. Medical science has not determined specifically what genes or biological processes might cause homosexuality, but there is strong evidence that it is genetic in nature and, therefore, hereditary. My mother has had several gay relatives in her family, including one of my cousins. He swears that he knew by the time he was six years old that he was different than other boys and came out as gay when he was still in junior high school. So, no, I don't think it's a choice, with the possible exception of some deviant personalities in a prison environment who use it as a power and control technique or are just seeking personal gratification."

"Well, that would certainly disappoint some of my Catholic friends," Donnelly responded. "They swear that it is chosen behavior and a sin against God that must be condemned. I've taken the implicit bias training through the Department and have to admit that my upbringing has made me a little homophobic, even though intellectually, I agree that LGBTQ+ individuals deserve to be treated with the respect and dignity of any other person and be given the same rights as everyone else."

"If there actually is a God who is the ultimate creator of mankind, then I guess we're going to have to blame Him for the existence of homosexuality," Reynolds replied. "Personally, I think it is the people who judge others based on factors beyond their control that should be condemned."

"Well, I know who's going to take the lead in all the family beefs we get from now on," Donnelly said.

They finished out the day with routine calls, and Dan was soon on his bike, heading home to Tawnya. *Damn, I'm glad I didn't get those genes*, he thought as he entered his apartment and saw Tawnya's naked body poised in front of the door.

CHAPTER 13

TYRONE'S REGRET

Tyrone Banks sat in the rented Chevy Yukon in the parking lot of the Whole Foods grocery store on Capitol and Madison. It was approaching 9:00 p.m. on a rainy Wednesday evening. The vehicle was sporting the license plates that he had stolen from an apartment house parking lot earlier in the evening. The AK-47 that Benny Malone had given him, and that he had spent the last week at the gun range practicing shooting, was lying on the seat next to him. He had just dropped Benny, Duke Robinson, and Slick Jackson off at the front entrance to the store and had driven to a position from which he could see inside, with a clear shot at any police car approaching the store from either side.

As he sat in the driver's seat with the engine running, watching the raindrops running down his windshield, his thoughts returned to a theme that had recurringly haunted him recently: *How did I ever get to this point in my life?* He thought about the consequences if he were to be arrested again and the very real possibility that he could be killed in a shootout with the police. All for a possible payout of $5000–6000.

He wondered if there had ever been a time in his life when he could have made different choices and had a different outcome. By the time he had started school, his mom was heavily addicted to drugs, was turning tricks, and was hardly ever around, so he and his older brothers were left to fend for themselves and take care of his four younger siblings. From the time he joined that gang when he was ten years old and began his criminal career, the gang had become his only real family.

Banks was a natural athlete but had only played organized sports while locked up in juvenile detention. There were times in lockup when he would lie in bed at night and envision a different future for himself. He saw himself staying in school, getting a scholarship to play basketball in college, and then going on to the NBA. But then he would get out and hook back up with other gang members who were burglarizing houses and selling drugs and allow himself to get talked into joining them to make a little money for groceries and to help pay the rent.

Then he got into the habit of snorting a little of his mom's meth before hitting a house because it made him feel ten feet tall and bulletproof. Pretty soon, the occasional snort had become a daily habit, and he had had to up the ante on his criminal activities to supply his own shit.

He graduated from daylight residential burglaries to night-time commercial burglaries as well as the occasional stick-up of a convenience store. His luck eventually ran out, and he wound up doing three to five years at the Monroe Reformatory, which had led to where he was today.

But what if he had followed that wishful childhood dream? Where would he be today? He might be playing big-time ball in the pros and making buckets of money. He could be living in a grand home on the other side of the lake with hot-and-cold-running bitches instead of sitting in this car in the rain, waiting for his homies to pull off a grocery store heist.

His reverie was interrupted when he saw his accomplices running out the front entrance of the store carrying a small duffle bag. He threw the Chevy into drive and pulled up to the front of the store, tires squealing. Benny, Duke, and Slick piled into the car, and they sped out of the parking lot.

"Slow down, bro," Benny Malone told him. "We don't want to attract attention from any police cars responding to the store. Use the side streets."

They worked their way back to Benny's apartment in West Seattle, where they divvied up the take from the store and celebrated another successful heist by Benny passing around a framed mirror with a dozen parallel lines of coke stretching across its surface. Each of them rolled up a C-note from their take and took turns snorting the coke. Benny put some loud hip-hop music on the stereo, and they spent the next hour spouting their own praises as the baddest stick-up team ever, who might someday be the subject of a rap song.

Banks eventually decided it was time to go check on his girls, so he made his way down to the car that they had rented under a stolen ID, put the legitimate plates back on, and headed back to the CD. As he crossed the West Seattle Bridge, he chucked the stolen plates out the window into the Duwamish Waterway. He made his way back to 14th and Yesler and was pleasantly surprised to see both of his girls standing in the rain, actively soliciting passing cars. "Not a bad night," he thought to himself as he pulled to the curb a block away to watch them for a while. He had made ten grand in these first two heists, and there were a whole lot more grocery stores out there ripe for the picking. He knew he didn't want to do this forever, though. Their luck would surely run out at some point. So, he had put out some feelers and gotten a line on a sex trafficker who was bringing in migrant girls from Mexico and Central and South America. For $5000–6000 each, he could have a pretty young Latina girl delivered to his door. Another couple of scores and he would have enough to bring in three or four girls who could satisfy both his monetary and physical needs for many years to come.

But he still could not shake the disturbing thought that he could have had a much more comfortable life without the constant worry about getting caught and going to prison if he had just used his natural athletic ability in a more productive way. What if he had had a father who had actually been there as a positive role model for him, encouraging him to put in the work to be successful? What if he had had a real mother who had been there to love and support him? What if he hadn't had to take care of his four younger brothers and sisters while his mother was out turning tricks? Maybe life could have been different. Maybe he could have graduated high school and gone on to college. Maybe he could have played pro ball. He briefly allowed himself to consider what it might be like to be a father himself someday. *I'd be a real father*, he vowed to himself before succumbing to the fear of the very real possibility that he would either be dead or in prison by the time he was thirty. His mind flashed on the lyrics of a George Strait song he had once heard after having been coerced by a girl into going to a cowboy bar: "I ain't here for a long time, I'm here for a good time." He allayed his negative feelings with another quote that he had once heard: "You don't choose your life; it chooses you." With this thought, he fired up the Chevy and headed back to his apartment. *Fuck it*, he thought, *I'm just going to go home, get loaded on smack, and be thankful for the life I have today. To hell with tomorrow.*

CHAPTER 14

THE FIX

Reynolds awoke Saturday morning to the sound of rain on his bedroom window. He and Tawnya engaged in what had now become their morning ritual—peeing, lovemaking, coffee, exercising, showering, having breakfast, and then Reynolds heading out the door to work.

Again, the shift started out relatively quietly, and they spent their time slowly patrolling their district. Then, the radio came to life. "Two-George-Three," the dispatcher intoned, "we have a report of a possible 220 at 516 East Magnolia Street. White male in his twenties apparently hearing voices."

"Two-George-Three, responding," Donnelly replied as he kicked the vehicle up to speed, and Reynolds made notes on the steno pad.

"What's a 220?" Reynolds asked.

"A psycho," Donnelly responded. "In the old days, they used to pay cops $2.20 for each nut case they brought into the hospital, hence the 220 designation."

They pulled up in front of a large, two-story colonial-style home overlooking the bluff paralleling Lake Washington. "Nice home," Donnelly commented as they made their way to the front door and took up positions on either side. Donnelly knocked, and a woman immediately opened up with a panicked expression on her face.

"What seems to be the problem, ma'am?" Donnelly asked.

"It's my son," she responded. "He seems to be having a psychotic episode. He's been diagnosed with schizophrenia and apparently hasn't been taking his medication. He started yelling at the voices in his head and throwing some of my ornaments in the front room at the wall."

"What's his name?" Donnelly asked.

"Trevor," she responded.

The woman led the officers into the living room, where they observed her husband sitting on an ottoman with his hands clasped, staring into the corner of the room. They followed his gaze to a young man who was lying on the floor in a fetal position, with his arms clasped over his head. He kept sobbing. "Go away. Leave me alone."

Donnelly placed his hand on the husband's shoulder and motioned for him to come. He led the man and his wife out of the living room, whispering to Reynolds as they left, "He's all yours, counselor." Reynolds moved the ottoman to a position about fifteen feet from the young man and took a seat. He just sat there for several moments without talking, letting the man become aware of his presence. Finally, in a soft, low voice, he asked, "Trevor, what seems to be the matter?"

The young man initially did not respond, then looked up and stared at Reynolds. "Who are you?" he asked.

"I'm a police officer," Reynolds responded. "I'm here to help you. Can you tell me what is bothering you?"

"They won't leave me alone," Trevor responded. "They keep telling me to kill myself."

"Who's telling you to kill yourself?" Reynolds queried.

"These voices in my head," Trevor responded.

"Do you want to kill yourself?" Reynolds asked.

"No, I just want them to leave me alone," the young man replied.

"I think I know some people who can help make them go away," Reynolds said. "Would you like to come with us, and I'll take you to them?"

"No, I'm not going to let them lock me up in the nuthouse," Trevor answered vehemently.

Reynolds spent the next twenty minutes asking the young man about the voices, how long he had been experiencing them, what else they had told him to do, and what could he do to help. Trevor expressed, hopelessly, that he did not know what anyone could do to help him. Finally, Reynolds asked him again, "Would you come with us so we can take you to see a doctor who can help you?"

The young man did not say anything for several moments, then looked up. "Okay."

Reynolds motioned to Donnely to join him, and they slowly approached the man from either side. They gently helped him to his feet and, each lightly taking an arm, started leading him out of the house. "We're going to take him to the Harborview Medical Center emergency room for evaluation," Donnelly said to the parents on their way out. "Can you meet us there?"

The parents nodded in the affirmative, and Donnelly and Reynolds escorted Trevor to the squad car, where they placed him in the back seat. Reynolds got in the driver's-side rear door and sat beside him. Donnelly drove slowly and cautiously to the hospital emergency room and parked just outside the front entrance in the space reserved for police cars.

They led the young man into the waiting area, which Reynolds was surprised to find was filled to overflowing with people waiting to be seen. They proceeded to a far corner of the room, as far from the other people as possible, and Donnelly said to Reynolds, "You wait here with Trevor while I check him in."

Donnelly went up to the admissions window and explained to the young lady behind the glass why they were there. She typed the necessary information into her computer and then said to Donnelly, "We're really backed up. It may be a while. Can you have a seat in the waiting area?"

"What seat?" Donnelly replied.

The girl just smiled sympathetically. "I'm sorry."

Donnelly returned to where Reynolds and Trevor were standing. "It looks like we might be here for a while," he said. Donnelly knew that hospital policy was that police officers had to stay with psychiatric patients until they were seen, evaluated, and a decision was made on whether to admit them or not.

"It's going to be alright, Trevor," Reynolds told the young man. "Someone will be with you soon to help you with those voices."

Trevor sank down to the floor and sat with his legs crossed and his face in his hands, his body visibly shaking. His parents soon arrived and joined them in the waiting room. It was two hours before a nurse approached them and led them down a long hall to an examination room. They waited there for another hour before there was a light tap on the door, and a young, boyish looking intern came into the room. Donnelly took him aside and briefly explained what had transpired with Trevor. The intern then asked the officers and the parents to step out into the hall while he conducted a brief psychiatric evaluation of Trevor.

The intern soon joined them in the hallway. "I'm sorry, but your son does not meet our criteria for an involuntary admission, and he does not want to admit himself. He is of age and, therefore, has the right to make that decision. We will give him some medication that will help with the voices, and then I suggest you contact your personal psychiatrist and get him in to see them as soon as possible."

Trevor's parents nodded in understanding, but each had a very disappointed and anxious look on their face.

"Would you like us to transport him home?" Donnelly asked.

"No, we'll take him with us," the father responded.

A nurse soon appeared and administered a large dose of Thorazine to Trevor, then gave his parents the remainder of the prescription. Donnelly and Reynolds waited with Trevor and his parents until it started to take effect. The parents then led Trevor out to their car, and Donnelly and Reynolds left with them.

Once back in the squad car, Reynolds said, "I was scared shitless that kid was going to go off on us the whole time we were with him. Does it always take that long for a patient to be seen here?"

"I hear you," Donnelly replied. "And yeah, I've heard of people waiting five to ten hours to be seen in this place. You need to remember, this is the only public hospital in the area, and a lot of people without health insurance or on Medicaid use it as their primary care provider because it can't refuse them service. It's our only option for people with psychosis issues."

After this almost four-hour ordeal with a mentally unstable individual, Donnelly and Reynolds were ready for a break. "How does a burger and a cup of coffee sound?" Donnelly asked.

"Sounds perfect," Reynolds replied.

Donnelly cruised down to their favorite drive-in and put them out for lunch. After leisurely consuming their burgers and while sipping their second cup of coffee, Reynolds asked, "How often do you get calls involving mental health crises?"

"They're virtually a daily occurrence somewhere in the precinct," Donnelly responded.

"We had to take classes in crisis intervention in the academy," Reynolds said, "and we do have crisis intervention teams available, right?"

"We do, but they're overwhelmed. If Trevor hadn't agreed to go with us to the hospital, I would have called them," Donnelly answered. "Fortunately, with the resources we have available, it is not as bad as it was back in the '60s and '70s when they initially started closing down mental health institutions and kicking people out on the street. But even today, we have way too many people living on the streets because they can't work due to mental illness or drug or alcohol addiction, which often stems from their desire to self-medicate their mental problems. Then we have the issue of our jails and prisons becoming de facto mental health facilities because we don't have enough dedicated facilities to care for the severely mentally ill. Now, since they've passed laws where you can't even charge someone with a crime who has a mental illness, we don't even have that option to get potentially dangerous people off the street."

Reynolds noticed a sudden smile cross Donnelly's face. "What's funny about that?" he asked.

"Oh, I just happened to think about a situation I had about a year ago," Donnelly replied. "I was working the night shift, and my regular trainee had called in sick, so they stuck me with a fresh-faced young recruit who obviously had lived a rather sheltered life. We were out patrolling at about three in the morning when we saw a middle-aged white woman walking down the sidewalk in a predominately Black part of town. She was gesticulating wildly and talking loudly to herself.

"As it turned out, I had handled this woman before, so I kind of knew what to expect. I pulled to the curb, and my partner rolled down his window to ask the woman if she was alright. She immediately came over to the car and said she was lost and couldn't find her way home. My partner asked if she knew where she lived, and surprisingly, she was able to give us an address on East Mercer Street. So, my partner looked at me and asked if we could take her home, and I agreed, even though it was out of our district. Long story short, we get to her apartment building and start to escort her to the front entrance when she suddenly falls to the ground and complains that she can't get up. She says, 'You'll have to carry me to my apartment.' Like I said, I had dealt with her before, so I told my partner to take her legs while I picked her up under her arms. We got in the front entrance and started carrying her up the stairs to the second floor when she reached down and managed to hike her skirt up above her waist. As I expected, she wasn't wearing any underwear. I looked up to see my partner's mouth drop open and a look of total astonishment in his eyes when he found himself staring at her hairy beaver. I almost burst out laughing but managed to contain myself.

"Fortunately, she had a key to her apartment in a small purse she was carrying, and we were able to get her inside and lay her on her bed. Her apartment was a total disaster. Dirty clothes were spread all over the floor, the sink was piled high with dirty dishes, and the refrigerator only had a container of sour milk and two pieces of moldy pizza in it. I knew from my previous encounter with her that she had been released from a mental health group home and was living alone on a small disability check, with no family in the area. We had taken her to Harborview for a mental health evaluation and were told, like Trevor, that she did not meet their criteria for involuntary admission, so we had taken her back home, and she'd done the same exact thing—but I'd made the mistake of taking her legs." Donnelly chuckled loudly as that image again popped into his mind.

"What did you do with her?" Reynolds asked.

"Well, to cover ourselves, we called Medic 1 to come evaluate her for any medical issues. While we were waiting for them, my partner and I washed up her dirty dishes and cleaned up her apartment a little bit. Then, the next day, we contacted a relief organization and arranged to have some food delivered to her apartment once a week so they could do a welfare check on her. Apparently, that's no longer happening."

"What do you suppose she was doing out that late at night in a strange area of town?" Reynolds asked.

"Probably a combination of things," Donnelly answered. "Loneliness, anxiety, inability to sleep, maybe voices in her head. Maybe she was just out trolling. She probably hadn't been taking her medication regularly. At any rate, she was a good example of what is happening to a lot of mentally ill people with limited resources in this country. Trevor is lucky that he has two parents who care about him and have the means to provide him with ongoing treatment. A lot of folks don't."

Suddenly, Donnelly looked at his watch. "Shit, time got away from us. It's time to head for the barn."

When Dan got home, Tawnya was waiting for him at the door—completely nude, as usual. He wasted no time in snatching her in his arms and carrying her to the bedroom, where he ravaged her for over an hour. After, as they lay in each other's arms, Tawnya asked, "Hey, remember when I told you that my graduation ceremony is going to be next weekend and that my folks are flying in from Phoenix to attend? Have you checked on getting some time off?"

Dan felt an instant sense of guilt when he realized he had spaced it out. He gazed at the concerned look on her face for several seconds before replying. "No, but I promise I will do it first thing in the morning. Do your folks want to stay with us?"

"No, they've booked a hotel room downtown. They want to attend my dance recital on Friday night and then probably hit the jazz club downtown after the graduation ceremony on Saturday," Tawnya responded.

"I'd love that," Dan replied. "I'll put in a vacation request in the morning. I'm sure it won't be a problem." With that, they drifted off to sleep.

CHAPTER 15

THE PARENTS

Reynolds checked in with his patrol sergeant as soon as he got to the precinct the next morning. Luckily, they had plenty of relief help available on the weekend, and he was able to get Friday and Saturday off. When he told Donnelly that he would be abandoning him for the weekend, Donnelly immediately retorted, "Bullshit, I don't want to have to work with another rookie. Maybe I'll take the weekend off myself and join you at the jazz club Saturday night if you wouldn't mind."

Reynolds felt a pang of doubt about having Donnelly join them on his first encounter with Tawnya's parents, but then thought that his partner probably rarely got out in the evening, other than hanging at the Greeks, and he apparently shared Reynolds' love of jazz. Besides, it might be nice to have someone else to help carry the conversation. "That would be great," Reynolds replied. "Would you like to go to Tawnya's graduation as well? We'd love to have you."

"No, I'll let you enjoy that with the parents, but I definitely would like to take in the jazz club. I heard that Herbie Hancock is playing."

Herbie Hancock, the jazz legend, was one of Reynolds' favorite musicians, and his dad had had many of his recordings. He couldn't wait to hear him play "Watermelon Man" in person.

"Okay, we'll get your ticket," Reynolds responded. "You can buy me dinner next week."

"You got it," Donnelly replied.

It turned out to be a relatively quiet Sunday. They hung out in front of the AME church for a while, listening to the gospel music, then responded to a domestic disturbance call in which a wife was angry with her husband for eating at a drive-in restaurant on his way home and not bringing her anything. She wanted him arrested. They gently told her that they did not have sufficient grounds to arrest him but did convince the husband that it might be best if he left for a while until she cooled down and to maybe bring her something to eat when he returned home.

Then they got a call of a residential burglary. The homeowners came back after a weekend of camping and found their home had been broken into and their TV and stereo taken, along with some jewelry and prescription drugs. While writing up the report over coffee and lunch at their local Burger King, Reynolds mentioned to Donnelly how these items seemed to be at the top of thieves' wish lists. "Sure, they're the easiest things to fence, pawn, or sell," Donnelly had replied.

They finished the shift after a couple more routine calls for service and called it a night. When they got to the station, Reynolds went with Donnelly to check with the sergeant about both getting Friday and Saturday off. "Tell you what," the sergeant said, "you guys are scheduled for Tuesday and Wednesday off this week. How about you work those days and then take a four-day weekend? I'll find someone to switch with you."

"Sounds good to me," Donnelly replied. "How about you, Dan?"

Reynolds nodded affirmatively, and they headed for the locker room. When Reynolds got home, he managed to hold Tawnya off for a few minutes while he got online and ordered tickets for the show at the Jazz Alley.

The rest of the week passed quickly. Reynolds and Donnelly kept busy chasing radio calls and had little time for any real police work. Neither was particularly disappointed, as they were looking forward to the weekend off.

Before Reynolds knew it, it was Friday morning. He had to admit to himself that he was experiencing a degree of trepidation over meeting Tawnya's parents. He wasn't sure how they were taking the news that their precious daughter and only child was living with a white cop who she had just met. Much too soon for Dan, he and Tawyna were on their way to the airport to pick up the parents.

Dan spotted them as soon as they came through the exit door from the arrival terminal. The mother was a tall, slender blonde who still carried herself like a prima ballerina. Dad was an imposing figure himself. He stood probably 6'5" tall with a lean but muscular build and a complexion slightly darker than Tawnya's. He still looked like he could suit up for the Seahawks, even though his hair and goatee were starting to show a little gray.

Tawnya introduced them to Dan as Clarence and Marie Fitzgerald. Dan was taken off-guard when Clarence immediately embraced him in a hug and said, "It's just Fitz to you, Dan. If you ever call me Clarence, I'll kick your ass." Then, as Fitz held him at arm's length, he added, "Damn, boy, I think I could make a tight end out of you. Ever thought about playing some pro ball?"

"No, I'm more of an individual sport guy, myself," Dan replied, "but thanks for the compliment."

Marie was considerably more reserved toward Dan and said little on the drive into town. They had made early dinner reservations at Trader Vic's in downtown Seattle, so after checking the parents into their hotel and giving them time to freshen up a bit, they walked together down to Fourth Avenue and entered the lounge area of the restaurant. Fitz ordered a double Glenlivet single-malt scotch, neat, and Marie got one of Trader Vic's signature Mai Tais, while Dan and Tawnya each had their usual club soda and lime. While sipping their drinks, they looked over Trader Vic's famous hors d'oeuvre menu and wound up ordering a combination plate of the Polynesian specialties.

While Marie grilled Tawnya on her dance recital and how she did on her final exams, Fitz regaled Dan with war stories about his football career. Dan found Fitz extremely easy to talk with, and Marie was polite and cordial but still a little distant.

They got Tawnya to the auditorium where the dance recital was to be held barely in time for her to get dressed for her performance. Her dance team was performing *Giselle*, with Tawnya in the lead role as the young peasant girl who dies of a broken heart after finding out her lover is engaged to another woman. Dan, who had never been an aficionado of the finer arts, found himself enthralled by the grace, beauty, and athleticism of the dancers, particularly Tawnya. Even if he had not been totally captivated by her prior to seeing her dance, he certainly was by the time the curtain went down on her performance. He could not wait to get her home.

The next morning, after going through an abbreviated version of their morning routine, Dan and Tawnya drove her Honda SUV back into the city to meet Fitz and Marie for breakfast at their hotel. Marie had made reservations for her and Tawnya at the spa in the hotel, so immediately after breakfast, they made their way downstairs to begin what had always been one of their favorite activities together.

The first stop was the sauna, and surprisingly, they were the only ones there when they first arrived, which greatly pleased Marie since she had been dying to get Tawnya alone to talk. "All right, young lady," she began, "tell me what could have possessed you to move in with a boy that you have only known for less than a month."

Tawnya and Marie had always been more like sisters or best friends from the time Tawnya had reached puberty and had always been up-front and frank with each other—so Tawnya, with a slight smirk on her face, replied, "Oh, I suppose the same thing that possessed the only child of two college professors to get knocked up by the star wide receiver on the football team in her senior year of college, having to walk across the stage to get her diploma with a baby bump."

Marie winced at that reminder of her past but vividly remembered how overwhelming an intense physical attraction can be. "So, where do you see this relationship going, and how do you think it's going to affect your dance career?" she asked.

Tawnya had to acknowledge to herself that she did not know the answer to either question. "I really don't know, Mom," she replied. "After working my butt off for four years in school and after putting so much time and effort into my dancing—to the exclusion of any real social life—I guess I just felt like I deserved a reward. These last three weeks have been one of the happiest times in my life. Dan and I seem to connect on every level—intellectual, emotional, spiritual, and physical. Especially physical. Believe me, I'm having the best sex of my life."

"You can't live on just great sex, honey," Marie responded. "Your dad and I have been more than happy to pay for your schooling and help you get to a position where you can achieve your dreams, but now it's time for you to take responsibility for your own life. You've got a great start, being accepted into the dance company, but it's going to take real dedication and commitment to reach the level you've always aspired to."

"I know, Mom," Tawnya replied, "and I fully intend to continue pursuing a career in dance, but can't I have both a dance career and a great relationship? You seem to have managed it nicely."

"You can do it, dear, but it takes a great deal of time and effort, which I know you are capable of," Marie answered. "You just have to want it bad enough."

"I do, Mom, I really do," Tawnya replied.

Meanwhile, Dan took Fitz on a walking tour around Seattle's Pioneer Square, where he and his teammates would often go after games. Unfortunately, many of his old haunts were no longer in business, but Fitz wanted to stop at the old Central Saloon on 1st Avenue, where—surprisingly for Dan—Fitz was recognized by several of the regulars, and he met a few of his old teammates, now long since retired, drinking beer at a corner table. Dan thoroughly enjoyed listening to their reminiscences, especially Fitz talking about playing with Hall of Famers Curt Warner and Steve Largent in their last year with the Seahawks and how he had been instrumental in recruiting some of the players who finally brought a Super Bowl win to Seattle in 2013 against Peyton Manning and the Denver Broncos. Before he knew it, it was time to pick up Tawnya and Marie and head for the Hec Edmundson Pavilion at the University of Washington for the graduation ceremony.

There were a lot of graduates from many different colleges, and the ceremony seemed to drag on forever. But finally, Tawnya's group stood up and lined up to take their turn. Dan found himself swelling with pride and adoration as Tawnya crossed the stage to receive her diploma. He found it amazing that he had developed such a deep connection to this person after only knowing her for a few weeks.

When the ceremony was over, the three of them met Tawnya in front of the pavilion, from where they drove down to Dan and Tawnya's favorite diner on Lake Union. After dinner, they proceeded back downtown and made their way to the intimate little jazz club in the alley off 6th Avenue. They found that Donnelly was already there and had reserved a table for them. While Dan had primarily invited Donnelly to join them as a courtesy after having told his partner why he was taking the weekend off, as he had guessed, Donnelly was a big jazz fan who rarely went out to clubs because he didn't like going alone. The chance to see Herbie Hancock in the company of Fitz Fitzgerald, who Donnelly had watched play throughout his career, was an opportunity he could not pass up. After Reynolds made introductions all around, they ordered drinks and settled back for the night's entertainment.

They soon found themselves immersed in the music, and no one felt any urge to talk for the remainder of the evening except for the frequent grunts and exclamations from Fitz as he was moved by the music. Herbie started off with some of his earliest work from the '60s, including "Watermelon Man," "Driftin'," and "Empty Pockets," then graduated to songs from his *Head Hunters* album before going on to some of his jazz-funk work in *Man-Child* and *Secrets*. The highlight of the show, however, was when he unexpectedly brought Joni Mitchell up from the audience, and they did several selections from his *River: The Joni Letters* album, including "Tea Leaf Prophecy," "River," and "Sweet Bird." When all too soon the show was over, they walked in a euphoric state to the hotel lounge, where, over several drinks, they relived their favorite moments from the performance. Marie warmed up to Dan considerably as they talked and gave him a big hug when they left the bar and she and Fitz were ready to head up to their room.

Dan and Tawnya picked up Fitz and Marie at their hotel late the next morning and took them back down to the diner on Lake Union for breakfast. The parents were booked to fly out of Sea-Tac Airport that afternoon, and it was soon time to head for the terminal. As Dan bid them goodbye at Departures, he felt an unexpected sense of loss. Somehow, over the course of two days, he had developed a bond with these two people and found himself wishing they could be a more constant part of their life. As they walked away from the terminal, Dan found himself looking forward to an enduring relationship with Fitz, Marie, and their daughter.

On the drive home, as he considered the events of the weekend, Dan said, "I was kind of surprised that your parents seemed to accept me as readily as they did."

"Why should that surprise you?" Tawnya replied.

"Well, I wasn't sure how they would feel about a white boy dating their daughter," Reynolds answered.

"It would be pretty hypocritical of them to object, given that they are a multi-racial couple themselves," Tawnya replied. "Besides, they are probably the most inclusive people I have ever known. Growing up, my dad, the consummate extrovert, constantly had teammates, coaches, and team execs over to the house for parties, and they were of every color and background imaginable. He got along with all of them, and so did I. My mother, in order to have someone to talk to, would invite her friends and fellow dancers from the dance company, and again, they were of many nationalities, races, colors, genders, and sexual orientations. I was able to get to know and interact with all of these people and it taught me that people are basically the same. I learned we all have the same basic human needs, the same emotions, and the same fundamental values and goals. Race, color, nationality, language, religion, sexual preference, and cultural traditions are really superficial differences that have nothing to do with the essential worth and dignity of the individual person. I'm sure my parents feel the same way."

"Well, that's certainly been my experience as well. The military gave me an opportunity to travel extensively, and, except for those superficial differences like language and culture and religion, I found that I was always able to find common ground with and mutual respect for almost everyone I met," Reynolds replied. "It's a relief to know your parents don't see the color of our skin as an issue."

"I can assure you, my dear, that both I and my parents like you just the way you are and wouldn't change a thing. We just need to make sure that we don't allow other people who may not be so enlightened to jeopardize our relationship," Tawnya answered.

Dan reached over and clasped her hand. "Never going to happen with me," he replied.

CHAPTER 16

THE ALIENS

Monday morning came quickly for Reynolds. Too soon, he found himself walking into the Crime Analysis Unit, where Donnelly was just finishing going through the police reports.

"Hey, you must have got here early," Reynolds said.

"Yeah, nothing better to do this morning," Donnelly replied. "I wanted to have plenty of time to make the rounds of the dicks this morning. Curious if they've got any leads on that group taking down grocery stores."

They soon found themselves in the office of the detective sergeant in the Robbery/Homicide Unit.

"What's up, Bob?" Donnelly said as they entered his office. "You got any new scoop on that stick-up gang?

"None, other than they hit again on Friday evening at an Albertson's on Empire Way. Sounds like the same four guys. Three entered the store wearing ski masks and packing AR-type assault rifles, and the fourth was driving the getaway car, but no one got a good look at it or got a license number. We did see a black SUV leaving the area on the store's outside security cam, but can't be sure if that's the one."

"All right, we'll keep an eye out for it," Donnelly responded, "and we'll check in with our informant today to see if he's heard anything. Anything else shaking?"

"Yeah, we're planning on staking out some area grocery stores this Friday," the sergeant replied. "You and your partner interested in a little overtime?"

Donnelly looked at Reynolds and got an immediate thumbs-up before replying. "Damn straight, what time do we meet up?"

"We're going to meet in the patrol assembly area at 6:00 p.m.," the sergeant responded. "You'll have to arrange to get off shift a little early."

"Shouldn't be a problem," Donnelly said. "Anything else?"

Well, one of our informants told us there's a rumor that Tyrone Banks is bringing in some migrant girls and is planning on turning them out. Sounds like it might be a sex trafficking situation since the girls are supposed to all be teenagers. No word on where he may be keeping them, though. Doesn't he live up in your district?"

"Yeah, he does. We'll keep our ears to the ground. Thanks for the info," Donnelly said as he and Reynolds left to prepare for another day on the street.

As soon as they cleared "In Service" with Dispatch, they were assigned to a commercial burglary call at a little bodega-type store off Empire Way. Someone had broken in the back door, apparently on Sunday night, and made off with a small safe in the office that contained the weekends' cash receipts. Unfortunately, the store only had fake security cameras and no alarm system, so there wasn't much to go on. Donnelly contacted the Commercial Burglary Unit but, knowing Donnelly's experience and quality of work, they advised him simply to dust for prints and take pictures.

They finished up the report over a cup of coffee at the local Burger King, then headed down to the Blackbird to see if they could hook up with Dixie. He wasn't there, so they tried Snookers, where they found him shooting pool.

"Good shot, partner," Donnelly said as he casually walked past the pool table, glancing only momentarily at Dixie. Dixie gave him a sullen stare and then started lining up his next shot. After finishing their sweep of the pool hall, Donnelly and Reynolds headed back to the patrol car.

After cruising around for a while, they made their way to the underground parking garage and soon saw Dixie slipping into the garage entrance.

"You got anything for me?" Donnelly asked as soon as Dixie had crawled into the back seat.

"Maybe," Dixie replied. "Word is that Tyrone Banks just brought in some new girls from Mexico over the weekend and is stashing them in the apartment next to his. Apparently, he has come into some money recently and had the cash to buy these girls from some cartel trafficker. They say he's going to run the girls out of the apartment cause he can't trust 'em on the street yet."

"He still living up off 25th Avenue?" Donnelly asked.

"Yep, in that three-story unit on the corner of 25th and Walnut," Dixie answered.

Donnelly walked around to let Dixie out of the back seat and then reached in and took a small packet from his attaché case. He walked away with Dixie, then turned and shook his hand before returning to the squad car.

"Sounds like something we might want to bring the Vice Squad in on," Donnelly said as he started up the car. "We'll check in with them in the morning."

. . . .

The next morning, Donnelly and Reynolds did their usual due diligence in Crime Analysis and then headed up to the Vice Squad's office, where they met with Sergeant McBride, the day-shift duty officer.

"Got something you might be interested in," Donnelly said as they entered the office.

He filled McBride in on what they had and told him they would like to be in on the bust if the Vice Squad wanted to take him down.

"So, if these girls are working out of an apartment, how do we get an undercover in to bust them?" McBride asked.

"Banks hangs out at the little coffee shop on the corner of 14th and Yesler during the day," Donnelly replied. "Have a white guy go in there during the afternoon, and Banks will probably contact him. Needs to be somebody who doesn't look like a cop, though."

"Well, that leaves you two out," McBride said. "I'll see if I can get someone out of the academy. I'll let you know when I can set something up."

It was a little after 3:00 p.m. when Donnelly's cell phone rang.

"This is Sergeant McBride in Vice," the voice on the phone said. "I've got a guy who I think will work for us. Can you do some drive-bys at the coffee shop and let me know when Banks is there? We'll keep our undercover on standby here until you contact us."

"Copy that," Donnelly replied. "I'll call you on your cell." Donnelly pulled over and opened the little file box containing his mug shots. He pulled out a photograph of a good-looking Black man in his twenties with a well-trimmed mustache and goatee.

"You remember this guy from The Blackbird a while back?" Donnelly asked Reynolds.

"I do," Reynolds responded. "He was there with those three other dudes."

"Okay, I'm going to make a slow pass in front of the coffee shop, and you check if you can see him inside. He usually sits at a table in the corner," Donnelly said.

They drove by the coffee shop, sending the girls out front scurrying inside upon seeing the patrol car.

"Didn't see him," Reynolds responded.

"Me either," Donnelly replied.

They continued for three blocks, then took a right, circling back around to take up a position two blocks away with a view of the front of the coffee shop. Donnelly pulled his binoculars from his briefcase and handed them to Reynolds.

"You've probably got better eyesight than I do," he said. "Let me know if you see him go in."

Sure enough, twenty minutes later, Reynolds observed a tall Black man with a mustache and goatee strutting down the street toward the coffee shop. He was wearing green satin slacks, a bright-yellow, silky-looking shirt unbuttoned to below his nipple line, and two heavy gold chains around his neck. A bright green fedora sat upon his neatly coiffed hair. He cheerily smiled at the girls on the sidewalk and flashed them the victory gang sign as he entered the coffee shop.

"He just went in," Reynolds said.

"Yeah, he's pretty hard to miss, isn't he?" Donnelly responded.

Donnelly got on the phone with Sergeant McBride and was told that they would send their undercover out immediately and have a team of Vice cops in the area. He asked Donnelly to stay close to the area of the coffee shop in the event that the undercover was able to make a connection. They wanted to arrest Banks for procuring, if possible, but first needed to confirm the girls were tricking.

Donnelly called Dispatch on his cell phone, advised them of the situation, and requested they hold their calls until the situation resolved itself. They then began slowly cruising the side streets in the area. A half-hour later, Donnelly again received a call from the Vice sergeant. "He just went in," the sergeant advised. Donnelly cruised back to his spot a couple of blocks from the coffee shop. Fifteen minutes later, they saw Banks emerge with a pudgy-looking white guy wearing glasses in tow.

"Looks like Banks is going to introduce this guy to the girls personally," Donnelly said as he got on the tactical channel with the Vice dicks and intoned cryptically into the mike, "Looks like the subject's on his way, and our man is with him." He received a couple of mike clicks in reply.

Donnelly started slowly cruising back toward the area of Banks' apartment, keeping enough distance to avoid running into him. They parked a few blocks away and waited to see what would go down. Twenty minutes later, the Vice team came back on the tactical channel. "Two-George-Three, just heard the undercover make an arrest on the girl, we're moving in. Meet us at the apartment." Donnelly pulled out into traffic and headed for the apartment building, pulling up on the side street, out of view of the front of the apartment. The detectives pulled in behind, and they moved quickly to the front entrance of the apartment. One detective motioned Donnelly and Reynolds to a position at the front of Banks' apartment while they took up a similar position at the adjacent apartment. Reynolds noticed there was a hasp and padlock on the outside of the girls' apartment door. A detective yelled, "Police, open the door!" The undercover yelled from inside, "I can't, the door is locked from the outside." The two detectives immediately stuffed the door and burst inside. Almost simultaneously, Reynolds heard movement inside Banks' apartment, and he and Donnelly applied their boots to the door. It tore loose from the jamb, and they jumped, guns drawn, through the opening to either side of the door. They saw Banks running toward the sliding glass door leading to the lanai.

Donnelly shouted, "Stop right there, Banks, you don't want to die over a misdemeanor!" Banks immediately pulled up and put up his hands. Reynolds put him against the wall, patted him down, and cuffed him. He sat him down on a chair in the living room and read him his rights while Donnelly went next door to see if they needed help. "We're Code 4," he yelled back to Reynolds moments later. Reynolds pulled Banks up and escorted him out of the apartment just as the detectives led three young Latina females out in cuffs, followed by the undercover officer. Donnelly called for another patrol unit to provide transport for the girls, and after notifying the apartment manager that he had a couple of doors that needed repair, he met Reynolds and Banks at the squad car.

The detectives advised Donnelly to book Banks on charges of suspicion of unlawful imprisonment and suspicion of trafficking—both felonies—in addition to the procuring charge. They advised the Patrol Unit to take the girls up to the holding cells in the detective division, put them in separate cells, and wait with them until the detectives arrived.

Banks did not say a word on the way to Headquarters other than, "I want my lawyer." Donnelly advised him he would get a phone call after he was booked. After completing the booking process, Donnelly and Reynolds went down to the detective division to see what the Vice dicks had gotten from the girls. All three girls, after being advised they were under arrest for prostitution and read their Miranda Rights, immediately began spilling their guts. It turned out they were all from Venezuela, that all were underage, and that they had paid a cartel coyote $6000 each to guide them through the Darien Gap between Columbia and Panama and across Mexico to the US border. There, the coyote wanted an additional $5000 to help them cross into the US and get them to Houston, where they had relatives. They did not have the extra money, so the coyote had sold them to a sex trafficker, who put out the word through an underground network that he had girls for sale. Tyrone Banks had agreed to pay $5000 each for the girls to be brought to Seattle, and he had kept them locked in the apartment since they had arrived the previous Saturday. Banks had told them they would have to pay him back $15,000 each if they wanted to be set free and that they had to earn the money by turning tricks.

"So, what are you going to do with the girls?" Donnelly asked.

"We're going to charge them with misdemeanor prostitution," Sergeant McBride said, "but then we will work with the prosecutor to dismiss their charges if they agree to testify against Banks and give the feds information on this smuggling operation."

By the time they had finished their reports and statements, it was the end of the shift, so they turned in their gear and headed for the locker room.

"So, how long do you think it's going to be until Banks bonds out?" Reynolds asked Donnelly.

"Well, he can't get bail while he's under a suspicion charge," Donnelly responded, "but we can only hold him three days before he has to be either formally charged or released. I would guess that Vice will be submitting their report to the prosecutor tomorrow, and it will probably take the prosecutor a day or so to file charges. Chances are he'll be out on bail by the weekend. You did see that wad of flash money he was carrying, didn't you?"

"Yeah, we should all be packing around a couple of Gs with us, just in case we need some incidentals," Reynolds said.

"I think that bust deserves a drink," Donnelly said. "Want to join me at the Greeks?"

Tawnya had arranged to go out with some of the members of her school dance team that night to celebrate the end of the dance season, and Reynolds didn't expect her to get home until around midnight. "Hell yeah, I'll join you for a drink."

They took seats at a table in a corner of the bar. Donnelly ordered a double Dalwhinnie single-malt scotch straight up and a club soda for Reynolds. "I feel like splurging tonight," he explained as the drinks arrived.

"So, what do you think about those girls' story?" Reynolds asked.

"I think it's probably all too true," Donnelly responded. "The immigration crisis at the southern border has gotten out of hand, and the cartels are making bank exploiting these poor people who are just trying to make a better life for themselves and their families. But we can't continue to just let them pour into our country at the rate they are. They're overwhelming our entire immigration system."

"Like you say, though," Reynolds responded, "you can't blame them for trying to escape the poverty and violence they're experiencing in their own countries. Maslow's Hierarchy of Needs tells us that the two greatest human drives are survival and security, and that is just what's motivating most of these people. It's only through an accident of nature that you and I were born in this country and can take advantage of all it has to offer in terms of economic opportunity and freedom from exploitation. If we were in their situation, I have no doubt that we'd do the same thing."

"You're probably right," Donnelly replied, "but we still can't be letting people stream across our borders without going through any type of vetting process. Obama is basically putting out the welcome sign and encouraging them to come on over."

"I don't know if I would agree with that," Reynolds replied. "The Obama administration has been deporting record numbers of people. But you're right. They are overwhelming the resources we have in place."

"Maybe the right-wingers are right," Donnelly said. "Maybe we need to deploy the military down to the border and completely shut it down. Let Mexico deal with them since they don't do much to keep them from traversing their country. What do you think?"

"Well, I agree that the military, at least the National Guard, should have a role in dealing with the problem, but I think we need to start with diplomacy and economic aid to the Central and South American countries that these people are fleeing from. The conditions in those countries are the root of the problem, and the long-term solution lies in trying to change the conditions that are driving these people to flee in the first place."

"Easier said than done," Donnelly responded. "Most of those countries are so riddled with corruption that effecting any kind of real change is almost impossible."

"That may be true," Reynolds responded, "but the US bears a great deal of responsibility for the conditions in these countries. Going back to the 1950s, in the name of fighting communism, the CIA supported coups ousting democratically elected leaders and replacing them with right-wing dictators and military juntas backed by the US government.

"The result was destabilizing these countries and creating many of the economic and social conditions that are now driving their citizens to leave. That persisted throughout the 1960s, '70s, and '80s in Guatemala, Honduras, and El Salvador, causing thousands of ordinary people to flee their homes and migrate to the US, where some of their children had to form street gangs to protect themselves from other local gangs. That's how Trump's favorite whipping boy, MS13, originated in Los Angeles and then was exported back to El Salvador when a number of them were deported or returned voluntarily after the end of the civil war in that country.

"Now, they have evolved into highly organized criminal enterprises shipping drugs into this country, engaging in human and sex trafficking, and inflicting physical and economic violence on their own people. Hell, our own border enforcement actions have created a market for the drug cartels to charge exorbitant fees to smuggle drugs and people into the US. There is no doubt the US helped create the conditions driving these people to our border, and we need to take the lead in trying to ameliorate the problem."

"But what do we do at this point without bankrupting the country and destroying our way of life?" Donnelly asked.

Reynolds replied, "Well, like I said, I would start with trying to impact the root of the problem, the political, economic, and social conditions that are driving people to flee their homes in the first place. The US can exert considerable diplomatic and economic pressure, along with potential economic assistance, to give them some incentive to change. It would be a long-term process, though, and we would need to take other measures in the interim."

"What do you suggest?" Donnelly responded.

"Well, I would start with Mexico," Reynolds replied. "As you said, Mexico is doing very little to keep these people from traveling through their country on the way to the US. We trade a lot of goods with Mexico. I would have the US threaten to boycott business with Mexico until they agreed to work with us to set up humanitarian refugee camps at both Mexico's northern and southern borders. This is where I think the US National Guard and the Mexican Army could come into play. The military has the resources and expertise to set up large encampments complete with air-conditioned tents, dining and medical facilities, showers and latrines, as well as providing both internal and external security.

"We could work with the Central and South American authorities to identify residents wishing to migrate to the US and with the Mexican authorities to intercept any migrants crossing their southern border. Together, we could provide transportation to one of these refugee camps, where they would stay until they had completed the legal immigration process. We would need to greatly expand our Immigration Court system and locate the courts in the refugee camps to be able to process the migrants quickly and either approve entry into the US or deport them back to their home countries or some other country that would accept them."

"So, what do we do with all these migrants once they get to the US?" Donnelly asked. "We already have over 11 million undocumented workers in this country. In many places, particularly in rural communities, they are taking over the local culture."

"Well, I wouldn't say that," Reynolds responded. "Hell, we're a nation of immigrants. The only true Americans are the Native Americans, and even they migrated from East Asia. Every new wave of migrants coming to this country has brought with it both positive and negative effects on the country. Trump likes to rail against Mexico, sending us drug dealers and murderers and rapists, but every influx of migrants over the last two hundred years has brought with it a criminal element. Think about the Italian, Irish, Jewish, Eastern European, and Russian mafias, and the Sicilian La Cosa Nostra. But most of these immigrants have assimilated into American life and become an overall positive addition to our society. Nobody is forcing anyone to change their customs and traditions or language, but we can be respectful of other people's cultures and traditions as well. And you are right. There are over 11 million undocumented workers in the country, and most have been here for a long time. I've read that over half have been in this country for over a decade and 80 percent for over five years, which generally means they have found work to support themselves and have become integrated into the community."

"But we're having to subsidize them," Donnelly responded. "We educate their kids, provide medical care for them when they're sick, and a lot of them are on public assistance."

"I don't think that's entirely true," Reynolds replied. "A truly undocumented worker does not qualify for any federal assistance programs. Granted, there are many categories of so-called 'qualified' migrants who are eligible for federal assistance, and undocumented workers can access dedicated programs at the state and local level, including the provision of education for their children. But, for the most part, at least in my experience, these migrants just want a chance to work and take care of their families. I went to school with some when I lived in Idaho, and their parents were some of the hardest-working people I knew.

"Besides, these people do pay taxes, just like you and me. Unfortunately, many of them are working under the table or using fake social security numbers and other forged documents, so they don't get credit for the money withheld from their paychecks. I think this is a serious problem that needs to be addressed. We need to bring these people out of the shadows and provide some type of legal work visas for them."

"How do you propose we do that?" Donnelly asked.

"Well, to start with, I would pass a federal law requiring every resident of this country to have and carry in their possession some form of certified identification. Think about what it would do in our profession if everyone had to have a valid ID on their person. We wouldn't have to accept anyone's word for who they are and could detain people who could not provide ID."

"Sounds like a lot more work for us," Donnelly responded. "But I agree, it would make us a lot more effective in our jobs. What do you mean when you say 'certified identification'?"

"I mean they would have to provide valid documentation to prove they are who they say they are—either a certified birth certificate, a passport, or some other incontrovertible proof of identity. A certified identification card could include a state driver's license, state identification card, social security card, a military ID, a medical identification card, et cetera. Each ID card would have to have a picture along with some form of biometric marker with which to validate your identity. The goal obviously is to make it as difficult as possible to forge identification instruments and to ensure people can validate their identity when they get stopped by the police, go to vote, or apply for a job."

"One of the major reasons liberals put forward against requiring mandatory identification is that some people can't afford it, or they are not physically able to go where they need to go to obtain it," Donnelly said. "How are you going to deal with that?"

"If the federal government is going to require it," Reynolds responded, "then the federal government should pay for it. It should also provide outreach programs to allow federal or state workers to go to people's houses, nursing homes, et cetera, if necessary, to process the ID cards. The burden should be on the government to ensure everyone is able to obtain an ID card."

"Okay, so everyone now has to have a valid identification," Donnelly responded. "How does that solve our undocumented worker problem?"

"Well, we also pass a federal law that requires every employer in the country to recertify that every one of their employees is either a US citizen or lawful resident by requiring them all to submit their certified identification," Reynold replied. "Obviously, we would need to provide sufficient time for workers to obtain a certified identification if they did not have one—say, one year from the day the law went into effect. At that point, employers would have to terminate anyone who was unable to provide a certified ID."

"Okay, so now you have 11 million unemployed workers who then become a burden on society," Donnelly retorted. "What do you do with them now?"

"We provide a mechanism in the law that allows employers to retain their undocumented workers if they can establish that they are unable to fill the vacant positions with US citizens or permanent residents. The undocumented workers would be required to register with the federal government as guest workers and be given a guest worker visa. They would be allowed to stay in the country as long as they had confirmed employment and paid all taxes required of any other worker. As guest workers, they would be issued a guest worker identification card and a tax identification number that would allow them to file income taxes and get refunds under their true identity. They could be exempted from contributing to social security until they became legal permanent residents or received citizenship under existing rules, but they would not be eligible for federal assistance programs until then, except for medical care under a universal system."

"Okay, then how about the thousands of new immigrants coming into the country as economic refugees or claiming asylum—what are you going to do with them?" Donnelly asked.

"Well, as part of the guest worker program, the federal government could establish a database of all employment opportunities that are available to guest workers in the country. Businesses would submit periodic reports to the government detailing available jobs that they were unable to fill using local residents, along with the qualifications for these jobs. As part of the processing in the refugee camps, asylum-seekers and economic refugees would be able to choose a job they wished to pursue and submit an application. Businesses could accept or reject them, and if accepted, the business would pay for transportation to the location of the job and for sixty days' living expenses for the worker and their family, if applicable. Some would-be immigrants might already have family in the States who could provide for them for a period of time, but regardless, they would still need to secure employment before being allowed into the country and would have to maintain employment for as long as they are here."

"How about farmers looking for seasonal farm workers?" Donnelly asked.

"Same process, basically," Reynolds replied. "Farmers would submit their requirements to the government, which would include these jobs in the database. The farmer would be required to pay transportation costs and provide housing and subsistence to the workers for as long as they were employed by him. If the season ran out for one farmer, workers would be allowed to move on to other areas if they could obtain employment within a reasonable timeframe. Once the agricultural season was over, they would be required to return to their home country unless they could claim asylum status. They would remain in the seasonal worker database, and farmers, or other seasonal employers, could request the same workers back year after year."

"Got an answer for everything, don't you?" Donnelly chuckled. "I swear you need to run for office."

"I've thought about it," Reynolds replied, "but I need a little more real-world experience before I give it serious thought. Speaking of the real world, I better pedal my ass home. Tawnya should be home soon."

Reynolds was mesmerized by the lights reflecting off Lake Union as he rode home on his bike. Luckily, he got there before Tawnya returned, and, for once, was able to meet her at the door—naked as a jaybird.

CHAPTER 17

DEATH WITHOUT DIGNITY

They had no sooner put themselves "In Service" the next day when Dispatch came back with, "Two-George-Three, handle a welfare check at the residence, 2609 East Springfield Street. Complainant reports her neighbor has been ill and has not been seen in a couple of days. Her newspapers are piling up on her porch."

"Two-George-Three, copy," Reynolds replied. "Do we have a name and address for the complainant?"

"Two-George-Three, complainant is a Mrs. Anderson who lives next door at 2613 East Springfield Street," Dispatch responded.

"Two-George-Three, roger that," Reynolds replied.

Upon arriving, Donnelly and Reynolds approached the door, and Donnelly knocked loudly while announcing, "Seattle Police." No one answered. Donnelly knocked and announced again, and still, no one answered. They could see three newspapers lying on the porch in front of the door, and the mailbox was full.

"I'll go right, and you go left," Donnelly said. "Let's check out what we can see inside."

Reynolds made his way around the corner of the house, looking in windows as he went. All he could see were stacks of boxes and piles of sacks strewn all over the floor in each of the rooms he looked into. He reached a bedroom window on the back-left side of the house and peeked in. He was able to see a bed on the opposite side of the room with what appeared to be a human form under the covers. He knocked on the window, but the form did not move. He quickly went around the corner of the house and met Donnelly at the back door.

"It looks like there is a person in the back bedroom under the covers," Reynolds advised, "but they're not moving when I knock."

Donnelly took out his aluminum flashlight and broke out a lower pane in the window of the back door, then reached in and unlocked it. The back door opened onto the kitchen, which was also piled high with boxes and bags of various kinds of merchandise. There was a path through the detritus leading to the sink, stove, and kitchen table, with a branch going out into the hallway and into the master bedroom. Donnelly and Reynolds followed the path. Once inside the bedroom, they were confronted with a gruesome sight. Lying in the bed with the covers pulled up to her chin was the body of a woman of indeterminate age. Her face was bloated, and a foamy, red substance leaked from her nose and mouth. The smell of death permeated the room. Donnelly pulled his ever-present cigar from his shirt pocket and lit it to mask the smell. Reynolds, even while knowing it was a futile effort, checked her carotid artery for a pulse and listened for the sounds of breathing. "She's gone," he said.

"No shit," Donnelly replied.

Donnelly got on his portable radio and informed Dispatch they had a DOA—presumably from natural causes—and asked them to notify the Homicide detectives and the coroner's office. He and Reynolds then did a sweep of the house to see if there were any signs of forced entry or a struggle. They had to navigate through piles of junk in every room but found no sign of either.

Donnelly asked Reynolds to go next door and talk to the complainant to see what she knew about the woman. Reynolds returned shortly and informed him that the neighbor did not know the woman well but had said that she had been taken by ambulance to the hospital a month or so previously and that she apparently had been ill for some time.

A few minutes later, a Homicide detective called to see what they had. Donnelly informed him of what they had determined so far and stated that death appeared to be by natural causes and, based on the stage of decomposition, that she had been dead for three or four days. The detective asked if the coroner had been notified, and Donnelly confirmed they had. "We'll let them handle it," the detective said. "My name's McArthur. Have them call me if they find anything suspicious."

It took forty-five minutes for the coroner's crew to arrive. In the meantime, Donnelly and Reynolds looked around the house for any identifying information on the deceased or next-of-kin. The mailbox was full of mail addressed to Mrs. Dorothy Cunningham. Reynolds found a cell phone that he was able to unlock by holding it over the deceased's face, activating the facial recognition software. In her contacts was the name of William Cunningham in Boston, Massachusetts. He called the phone number.

In response to a male voice on the other end of the line, Reynolds stated, "Hello, this is Officer Dan Reynolds with the Seattle Police Department. We were called to do a welfare check at a house at 2609 East Springfield Street in Seattle and found the deceased body of a woman in the bed. We believe her name is Dorothy Cunningham. Is this William Cunningham, and are you related to Mrs. Cunningham?"

"That's my mother," the man said, "and yes, I am William Cunningham."

"My deepest condolences, Mr. Cunningham," Reynolds replied. "I'm sorry to have to be the bearer of such news."

"That's all right," Mr. Cunningham replied. "I've been expecting this call for some time."

"Can you tell me if your mother had been ill lately or anything about her physical condition? We understand she was taken by ambulance to the hospital a few weeks ago," Reynolds asked.

"My mother was diagnosed with liver cancer about a year ago," Mr. Cunningham answered. "They operated on her and removed a portion of her liver, but because she didn't have insurance, they didn't do any follow-up treatment. About a month ago, she became violently ill and was taken to the hospital. Apparently, the cancer had metastasized and spread throughout her body. They only gave her a few weeks to live."

"Does she have any next-of-kin or a caregiver in this area?" Reynolds asked.

"No, all our family live in the Boston area," Cunningham replied. "We tried to get her to come live with us, but she refused to leave her home in Seattle. My father died a couple of years ago, and she had no one else there. Unfortunately, due to family issues, I wasn't able to go out there to take care of her, and she didn't want any strangers taking care of her, so she refused hospice care. She said she just wanted to die in her own home."

"Well, the coroner's office will be taking custody of her remains, sir, so you can contact them with whatever arrangements you wish to make. Again, I'm so sorry for your loss," Reynolds stated.

A two-person team from the coroner's office arrived a few minutes later and took custody of the body. They then had the unenviable job of inventorying the contents of the home of an obvious hoarder and securing the premises.

Back on the street, Donnelly and Reynolds headed to Pinky's to write their report over coffee and lunch. Reynolds put the finishing touches on the report and handed it to Donnelly to review.

"Fuck, that was a pathetic situation," Reynolds said. "That poor woman probably put off getting medical attention for months or years because she didn't have any health insurance, and by the time she did, it was too late. Our health care and health insurance systems in this country really need a major overhaul. Personally, I agree with Bernie Sanders—it's time for a universal, government-run, single-payer health insurance program that provides affordable, accessible, and appropriate medical care to every legal resident of this country, regardless of their ability to pay," Reynolds said. "There is no justification for people dying prematurely because they can't afford medical care."

"You know, I think you really are a socialist at heart," Donnelly responded. "How is that working in Canada and the UK? I understand that people there often wait months for elective and even some necessary procedures, and many Canadians wind up coming to the US for treatment, even though they must pay out-of-pocket. Typical of government programs, their facilities are underfunded, and consequently, they're short-staffed and lack resources. I've heard a lot of their doctors have moved to the US to make better pay. I don't think getting the government more involved in our health care is the answer. Look at the issues they are having with veterans' hospitals and clinics.

"Why can't we just allow health insurance companies to sell across state lines and create more free-market competition? As it is now, many states only have a handful of companies to choose from, and with the so-called non-profit Blue Cross/Blue Shield companies getting preferential tax breaks, it makes it hard for any private, for-profit insurance company to compete."

Reynolds responded, "I've heard those same arguments and there is probably validity to some of them. As far as free-market solutions go, I think that is a fallacious argument. Years ago, Congress passed a law that made insurance companies subject to state laws and regulations. Consequently, you have a hodgepodge of different requirements in individual states that insurance companies must comply with to be licensed to do business in that state.

"By allowing insurance companies to sell across state lines, you would see large insurance companies locating in states with minimal insurance requirements and then offering low-cost plans that provide limited coverage to a relatively healthy population while making more comprehensive plans for people with higher levels of needs essentially unaffordable due to the reduced risk pool. One of the best parts of the Affordable Care Act was that it required minimum benefit standards and precluded basing premiums on a person's age or denying coverage because of pre-existing conditions. That allowed it to substantially increase the risk pool and spread out the cost of the program among more people.

"Also, even if you had a multiplicity of insurance companies operating in a state, each would have to comply with that states' regulations and would still have to negotiate with the medical providers in that state to determine their compensation rates for services and to establish preferred-provider networks. I've read that that is the biggest hurdle companies would face if allowed to sell insurance in other states. The Affordable Care Act apparently has a provision that allows states to set up coalitions that allow interstate sales. Of the six states that have enacted such laws, none has had a single new insurer enter its market.

"Granted, it may allow large, multi-state companies to increase the size of their total risk pool, but they still would have to negotiate with providers in individual states. The large nonprofits would still have a competitive advantage because the for-profits would only have so much room to negotiate rates and still make a reasonable return. I don't see that allowing more interstate competition would greatly reduce the cost of insurance or increase its availability, especially for low-income or chronically sick people who essentially would be shut out of the market.

Also, I think if you asked most Canadians, they would not trade their system for ours. Besides, I am not advocating for a completely socialized medical care system, only a single-payer health insurance system that would ensure that every citizen and permanent resident has access to essential health care. Given that, I do think we need to expand our public health system as well in order to provide greater accessibility.

"As to what role government should have in providing health care or health insurance, ask yourself, 'What is the role of government in any area?' To my mind, government exists primarily to provide those essential services that its citizens need or want but cannot reasonably afford to provide for themselves, and that are not appropriate for private-sector profiteering. National defense is a prime example at the federal level, and police and fire services are examples at the local level.

"Given the high cost of health care today, it certainly meets those criteria. Only the wealthiest of Americans could afford to pay out-of-pocket for the horrendously high costs of even routine medical care in this country, but almost every person, at some point in their lives, will need major medical services. Compare this to the relative few who will ever need to call for police assistance or have the fire department respond to a fire. When you think about it, no other factor contributes more to a country's vitality and productivity or to individual quality of life than good health.

"Hell, it's even in the US Constitution. One of the major roles of government is to provide for the general welfare. There is nothing more central to a person's welfare than health care. You do not hear cries of 'socialism' when governments operate taxpayer-funded law enforcement agencies or fire departments because most of us recognize these are essential services necessary for the common good and which any of us may need to use at some point in our lives. How would you like it if someone was breaking into your house, or it was on fire, and you called 911 only to hear the operator respond,

'We'd be happy to send someone. How would you like to pay for that, cash, check, or credit card'? Yet that is exactly the first question you are asked when you call to make a doctor's appointment, 'What kind of medical insurance do you have?' Besides, is it really appropriate to profit from other people's personal tragedies? Health issues create more personal tragedy than virtually any other cause."

"So, how do you propose we do that without increasing taxes?" Donnelly asked.

"Well, first, I think it's time to scrap employer-based health insurance," Reynolds replied. "It made sense back in World War II, when wages were frozen, and the only way businesses could attract workers was through benefits like health insurance. After the war, during the '50s and '60s, most workers expected to work their entire careers with one company. Unions were alive and well and had considerable power in negotiating for workers' benefits. The costs of health care were relatively low, and companies could provide such benefits and maintain profitability. None of those factors are true today. Most people will have several employers during their working lives. Unions are no longer an effective tool for ensuring appropriate compensation and benefits. Companies can no longer afford the ever-escalating costs of health insurance and still be competitive in a global market.

"Besides, it was never the responsibility of businesses to provide for their employees' health and welfare, as much as they benefit from having a healthy workforce. The goal of a business is to produce goods and services in order to make a profit for their owners and shareholders. They hire the workers they need to produce those goods and services at the lowest price they can in a competitive global market. With the cost of health care in this country comprising over 17 percent of GDP and going up every year faster than GDP, businesses are having to scramble to continue providing health insurance. They wind up expending considerable resources to solicit and evaluate bids for insurance, and then to administer the programs once in place. Many are having to increase employees' contributions or decrease benefits to continue providing insurance, and more and more companies are discontinuing the provision of health insurance altogether.

"Then consider the effects on workers who rely on employer-provided health insurance. With businesses renegotiating these contracts every year or two, employees are never sure who their insurance provider will be and how their coverage and costs will be affected. Prior to Obamacare's restrictions against using pre-existing conditions as a pretext to deny insurance, employees often felt bound to a particular employer to keep their health insurance, even though they would have preferred to leave for other opportunities. A government-run, single-payer health insurance system would alleviate all those issues."

"Do you really think a government-run insurance system would operate more efficiently and effectively than private insurance?" Donnelly asked.

"Absolutely," Reynolds responded. "First, go back to that concept of risk pool. A universal, single-payer system, even if it offered some options for insurance, would still have the largest possible risk pool and the largest possible number of insured paying premiums, which would spread the costs to the greatest number of people. Then, consider the costs incurred by medical providers when dealing with multiple private insurance companies. They must hire staff to deal with all those claims, submit multiple forms to multiple companies with different requirements, and then track reimbursements from these companies.

"Add to that the administrative costs of the insurance companies, who have to process each of those claims, determine its eligibility for coverage, and then process payment. Then, you have to add advertising and other marketing expenses. I've heard that by going to a single-payer government system such as Medicare—whose administrative costs run less than 2 percent, by the way—we could save up to 30 percent of our healthcare costs from the reduction in administrative costs alone. Then, when you take away the profit margin private companies expect, the savings would be considerably greater. Bernie Sanders estimated the US could save over $500 billion a year with a single-payer system.

"Imagine if every eligible person in the United States was issued a medical identification card, encoded with biometric markers to preclude forgeries and containing a computer chip with a person's entire medical history. Now imagine that every medical provider in the country used the same electronic medical records system and updated your medical records at every visit. Then, when you went to see a doctor anyplace in the country, all you would have to do is present your medical ID. No more filling out medical history forms or other insurance or consent forms. The doctors would have your entire medical history at their fingertips, as well as immunizations and pharmaceuticals you have used or are using. The doctor would be able to submit his bill directly through the electronic system and receive payment through the same system. You can't get much more efficient than that."

"I've heard estimates that going to a Medicare-for-all system would cost over $40 trillion over ten years. How are you going to pay for that without raising taxes astronomically?" Donnelly asked.

"Well, consider what we are paying now. Total spending for health care in this country is running over $3 trillion a year right now. That averages out to over $10,000 a year for every man, woman, and child in the country. Healthcare spending is projected to continue increasing at around 5 percent a year for the foreseeable future, which would add up to well over $40 trillion in ten years under the current system.

"Right now, the average cost for an employer-sponsored individual policy is over $6000, and for a family policy, it's over $18,000. Private insurance for individuals is considerably higher. As I said earlier, businesses are starting to pass a lot more of those costs onto the employee, so in many cases, employees are paying $100–

$300 a month out-of-pocket for health insurance. If you consider that employers' costs for all types of benefits are part of your overall compensation package, then all money paid by employers for health insurance is coming directly out of your paycheck.

"Then consider if we had a single-payer system that covered everyone in the country. We could eliminate Medicaid, Medicare, the VA medical system, and most of the indigent care accounts that many states and counties have. Plus, we would eliminate the extra costs that hospitals add to the bills of the insured to cover the cost of providing indigent care in the hospital, which is estimated to cost about $1000 a year for every insured American. That, combined with the $400–500 billion we would save on administrative and overhead costs for private insurers, would probably amount to well over $1 trillion a year." Reynolds sighed.

"So, assuming you *could* save a trillion a year, if you subtract that from the $3 trillion we're spending now, that still leaves a couple of trillion dollars. Allocated among 318 million people in the US, that is still a shitload of money. Where's that money going to come from?" Donnelly responded.

"Well, like I said, we're paying over $10,000 a year per capita now, which includes what we're paying for health insurance. With single-payer, we would actually be saving money. As to how we pay for it, consider that every wage earner and their employer currently pay a payroll tax of 1.45 percent each toward the cost of Medicare. Under the Affordable Care Act, people who make money from investments and sources other than wages such as being self-employed, pay a surtax on their income. We would basically fund the single-payer insurance system the same way, except I would have employers paying a lower percentage than individuals. I figure that since it is basically an individual insurance plan that goes with the employee if he leaves a company, the individual should pay the lion's share of the cost. I would say three-quarters for the individual and one-quarter for the employer, who undoubtedly benefits from a healthy workforce. The employees' increased costs would be made up with the extra money in their paycheck that is not going toward the employers' share of the cost of health insurance and the reduction of co-pays and deductibles. We could adjust the actual percentages of the tax annually to ensure that we cover the cost of the program, which would avoid the problems the Medicare system currently has of not generating enough money to cover expenditures."

"How about the people who don't work or who barely make enough money to live on?" Donnelly asked. "How are they going to be covered?"

"Obviously, people who have no income and don't file taxes would not be able to pay at all. As far as low-income folks go, I would use something like the federal poverty line we currently have. We calculate the average amount of money an individual or family would have to make to supply the basic necessities of life—housing, food, transportation, utilities, et cetera. We could do this on a regional basis to account for varying costs of living in different areas. Anyone making below that amount would not pay into the health insurance system but would still have access to it.

"We could then set the percentage basis of payroll tax a person would pay based on how much above the subsistence level a person's or household's income was. Say the payroll tax for a family making the median income for an area—say, $70,000—was 10 percent, and we calculated that a family of four would require a minimum of $40,000 per year just to subsist. Then, any household making below $40,000 a year would pay nothing. For every $10,000 in income above $40,000, we would add 2.5 percent to their payroll tax until they got to 10 percent, which would be the tax for all income above that level. Again, these percentages could be adjusted every year depending on actual expenditures. We also might want to think about putting a cap on income so that extremely high-income people were not paying an inordinate amount."

"So, you want to do away with private health insurers in the country altogether?" Donnelly asked. "How about all the thousands of people who work for these companies? What happens to them?"

"Well, we wouldn't necessarily have to eliminate all private insurers. The way I envision it, the single-payer system, like Medicare currently, would pay 80 percent of the cost of medical care for those paying the highest-percentage tax. For those below the poverty line, it would pay 100 percent, and that would decrease in 5-percent increments as a person's tax level increased up to the 10-percent limit.

"Also, I think that a person, if financially able, should have some skin in the game to avoid abuses of the system—but not to the point that we discourage people from getting appropriate care. So, most people would have to pay a small co-insurance payment out-of-pocket. For those who can afford it, private insurers could offer supplemental policies to help cover this co-insurance cost, like Medicare Advantage plans now, but there would be no government subsidies for these plans. I would also envision a yearly cap on out-of-pocket costs for everyone under the single-payer program.

"As far as workers being displaced from current private insurance companies—that will undoubtedly occur. However, the skill sets these workers have in administrative and clerical duties should be readily transferrable to virtually any business or government agency in the country. Plus, many could probably go to work for the expanded agency running the single-payer system. The rest, I'm sure, would be quickly absorbed into the general economy.

"The bottom line is, we do not owe private insurance companies anything. There are many other areas where these companies can and do provide a valuable service in protecting people against unexpected loss, which is what insurance is all about. Health care costs, which virtually all of us will incur throughout our lives, do not have to be one of those areas."

"So, are you proposing a one-size-fits-all policy that everyone must buy regardless of their individual needs, like Obamacare?" Donnelly asked. "And what about routine preventive care? Who pays for that?"

"I think preventive care needs to be the cornerstone of a revamped health care system in this country and, as such, should be fully covered by the single-payer system. When you consider the number of people who are obese in this country—over 40 percent of the population—and those who are suffering from chronic health conditions that could have been prevented through appropriate lifestyle choices and early treatment, just reducing those populations could significantly reduce our health care costs in this country.

"Covering the costs of regular preventive care is certainly part of the answer, but it needs to be part of a multi-faceted approach. Like I said before, I think we need to be teaching our kids, from the time they enter school, the importance of proper nutrition, regular physical activity, avoiding drugs and alcohol, and managing stress. We can't mandate what individuals do to their bodies, but I think, as a society, we have an obligation to at least educate people about the effects of negative lifestyle choices and how to avoid making them.

"Also, like I've said before, I think employers have a role in maintaining a healthy population. Making businesses have mandatory drug- and alcohol-testing programs to identify people suffering from addiction would be helpful if we have best-practice programs available in the community to help them overcome their addictions. These, along with other mental health treatments, should be fully covered by health insurance. Being able to retain their job is probably the greatest incentive many people have to actively work to overcome an addiction problem or deal with mental health issues.

"Also, businesses could provide financial incentives for people to maintain a healthy lifestyle, such as paying bonuses for maintaining a healthy weight or engaging in a regular exercise program, et cetera. These programs would probably more than pay for themselves through increased productivity and more positive employee attitudes at work, as well as decreasing absence and attrition rates.

"Finally, we need to make sure that every person in America has access to and uses a primary care health provider, who would act as a gatekeeper to a broader network of specialists. A major deficit in our current healthcare system is the lack of primary-care providers, especially in low-income and rural areas. The providers we do have are struggling to survive, partly due to the meager reimbursement rates they get from Medicare and Medicaid patients. Consequently, they tend to congregate in large urban areas or in highly affluent suburbs."

"So, how is your single-payer system going to get more primary-care providers in these areas?" Donnelly inquired.

"Well, first, we need to take a broader look at the problem. One of the issues we face is that we don't have enough medical education programs in the country to supply the number of doctors we need. This is an area that federal and state governments could impact by providing direct subsidies to colleges and universities to develop and implement more programs.

"Then, if we had an educational system, as I described earlier, that identified kids early on who had the aptitude and ability to become doctors and nurses, and we encouraged and incentivized them to pursue medicine as a career—to include partially or wholly subsidizing their education—we could undoubtedly produce enough doctors to meet our needs. Another benefit of subsidizing their education is that we could require, as a condition of doing so, that they work in an underserved area for a period of years after completing their training. This would help alleviate our doctor shortage in these areas."

"But who's going to provide the clinics and facilities for these doctors?" Donnelly asked. "Surely you would not expect them to build their own clinics?"

"No, this is where a government-run public health system would come into play," Reynolds replied. "Obviously, this is not an area the private sector is going to jump into on its own because there is no real profit potential. So, it would be up to the federal government to step in to construct clinics and other necessary facilities, or to contract with private entities to meet the needs of a specific geographical area based on population density and the demographics of the area. These would be staffed with either government workers or contracted employees, including the doctors, nurses, and other medical providers working there as part of their educational contracts, and other staff hired from the local community when possible.

"The local primary-care doctor or nurse practitioner would be part of a broader network of specialists located at the nearest full-service hospital, who would be available for consultation when needed or to whom patients could be referred when required. These specialists would be available through telemedicine facilities for consultations and by ground or air ambulances in emergencies. If no private full-service hospital was available within a reasonable distance, a public health hospital would be built and staffed by the government. Converted VA facilities could fill part of this need."

"But how about insurance options for individuals?" Donnelly asked. "I see no reason why I should have to pay for gynecological or obstetric services when I'm a single male and have no intention of having any more children. And why should a young, healthy guy like you pay the same as an old fart like me or someone with a large family?"

"As far as choice of insurance plans is concerned," Reynolds added. "There is no reason that a government-run, single-payer health insurance program could not offer options for coverage.

Older people, families, and those with chronic conditions requiring ongoing care should have more comprehensive plans and, based on their ability, should pay more than a young, healthy person or a single male or couple who don't intend to have kids. However, that would have to be balanced with the need to spread the overall cost as widely as possible in order to keep individual costs down.

"To me, it would be a matter of offering a limited choice of plans that fit most people's circumstances and then adjusting the payroll tax for these plans accordingly. We could have annual open-enrollment periods like Medicare offers in which individuals could choose a plan for that year. People could adjust their plans yearly as their circumstances changed. We would need to ensure that every plan covered the types of major accidental injuries and catastrophic illnesses that can occur to anyone at any time."

"Okay, so you've got everyone covered by insurance and have built facilities to provide medical care in underserved areas, but what about the consolidation we're seeing in the private healthcare sector, and how are private hospitals going to compete with your public health facilities?" Donnelly asked.

"I agree that consolidation is an issue," Reynolds responded. "It seems that these large health care systems are trying to outdo each other in building new, elaborate facilities, each of which must have the latest in technological equipment and offer the full variety of medical services. They're also buying up as many private practices and facilities as they can to increase their market share and, subsequently, their profits.

"Whereas Canada has a shortage of medical facilities due to the government trying to minimize costs, in the US, we have a dichotomy—not enough facilities in low-income and rural areas, and a redundancy of facilities in large cities and wealthy areas. The problem is that each new facility must have all the latest expensive medical technology, which often is not being utilized to capacity.

Consequently, the patients using this equipment are being charged excessive amounts in order to cover the costs.

"To my mind, a better system would be to divide up geographical areas based on the projected medical needs of the population of the area, then put out for bid a medical contract for that area. If a private provider were to submit a bid, they would have to agree to provide all the facilities, equipment, medical specialists, and other personnel required in that area and would essentially have a monopoly on those services. They would also have to agree to accept the reimbursement rates for services that were negotiated for that area. If no private provider bid on a particular area, then the government would establish public health facilities there. The goal would be to ensure that every person in the country had medical facilities and medical personnel available within a reasonable proximity to deal with any type of medical need they may have. That would not preclude the establishment of specialty facilities like burn centers or cancer centers throughout the country for dealing with specific issues."

"So, you would negotiate reimbursement rates?" Donnelly countered. "How is that going to work?"

"Let's assume that this single-payer program is administered by the Centers for Medicare and Medicaid Services, as Medicare is now," Reynolds replied. "At the inception of the program, they would bring together all the stakeholders involved in the provision of medical care, to include representatives of health care systems, doctors, nurses, and other health practitioners, as well as accountants, statisticians, and other experts. They would analyze the best-practice treatment protocols for all significant medical issues and determine, to the best of their ability, what the actual costs to providers are to administer these protocols. They would then factor in what fair compensation would be for the medical professionals involved, taking into consideration the education, knowledge, and experience required to perform the protocols as well as the social value of the work they do. Based on the best data available, they would agree to a fair and reasonable reimbursement rate for each procedure or protocol, which would ensure fair compensation for health care professionals and a reasonable profit for private providers. They could revisit this process as needed based on current cost data. The goal would be to ensure that providers were able to make a sufficient profit to stay in business, that medical professionals were fairly compensated, and that costs were kept to a reasonable level. Again, payroll taxes would be adjusted annually to make sure they covered the projected cost of the program."

"Sounds like you've got it all figured out," Donnelly said. "When do you have time to think about all this shit?"

"I spend many hours every week out running or bicycling or hiking and have nothing better to do than think about social issues. I guess it has become something of an obsession," Reynolds responded.

CHAPTER 18

MAN WITH A GUN

On Friday evening, Donnelly and Reynolds, dressed in street clothes, showed up at 6:00 p.m. in the Patrol assembly area along with about forty other officers drawn from Patrol, Special Squad, and the detective units. They were briefed on the operation, which involved two-man teams staking out all the major grocery stores in the Central and Rainier Valley areas—and included the admonition to not hesitate to use deadly force if necessary to apprehend these stick-up men.

After the briefing, Donnelly and Reynolds checked out a shotgun and AR-15 from the armory, and portable radios from the property room, then drove Donnelly's car to their assigned store in Rainier Valley. Donnelly, armed with the AR-15, took a position in the second-floor office area in the rear, which had a large opening in the front wall allowing a full view of the interior of the store. Reynolds, armed with the shotgun, set up in a rear storage room on the main floor that provided a clear view of the front entrance. Each tried to stay out of sight as much as possible while still having a view of the front entrance.

Two hours dragged by with no suspicious activity. Then, shortly after 10:00 p.m., Reynolds saw a slender Black male in his twenties, wearing dark clothing, enter the store. He lingered just inside the front entrance and visually scanned the entire building. Reynolds got on his cell phone and alerted Donnelly, who responded that it looked like Slick Jackson. Donnelly then put out a call to the mobile units that they had a suspicious person in the store.

Reynolds already had a round in the chamber of the shotgun. He checked to make sure the safety was on and mentally reviewed what he would do if the robbers entered the store. There was a waist-high cold storage unit between him and the front entrance that would provide cover while still allowing him a clear shot. He would need to take them before they got to the checkout counters. He informed Donnelly of his plan and confirmed Donnelly had a clear shot of the entire front entrance. Reynolds told him he would move to the cold storage unit as soon as Jackson left the store and would announce their presence when the robbers entered.

Donnelly agreed—and then said, "We're probably going to have to take them out."

"Roger that," Reynolds responded. "I'll start on the left and you take the right."

Slick Jackson scanned the store for a couple more minutes. Reynolds could see that the checkout clerks had noticed him and were fidgeting nervously. Finally, Jackson went back out the front entrance, and Reynolds moved stealthily to a position behind the cold storage unit. He felt the adrenaline surging as he waited. Five minutes passed, then ten, with nothing happening. Then he heard a radio broadcast in his earpiece from one of the mobile units. "All units, we see no sign of a suspicious vehicle around the Albertson's store. We will maintain surveillance."

Reynolds stayed in position for another twenty minutes until it became evident that the robbers had apparently been scared off. He returned to the storage room and contacted Donnelly to advise him. "Stay alert," Donnelly responded, "They may come back."

The store closed at midnight and Donnelly and Reynolds stayed in position until the doors were locked and the day's receipts were deposited in the safe, after which they drove back to Headquarters and returned to the assembly room for the debriefing.

"I thought we were going to get lucky tonight, guys," the Robbery/Homicide lieutenant said, "but something must have alerted them. Thanks to all of you for your work tonight, and hopefully, we can do this again."

"You want a ride home?" Donnelly asked Reynolds after they had turned in their radios and weapons.

"No, I think I need the bike ride home to decompress," Reynolds replied. "But thanks. I'll see you tomorrow."

....

Saturday morning dawned to a beautiful, clear, sunny day. Dan and Tawnya slept in a little later than usual because they had not gotten to sleep until after 2:00 a.m. As they rolled over into each other's arms, Tawnya asked, "Do you want to skip our usual start to the day and just get our run in?"

"Hell no, there is nothing more important than a little loving in the morning," Dan replied, reflecting his newfound philosophy.

After a leisurely coital experience, they managed to get in an abbreviated run and light breakfast before Dan had to get ready for work. Tawnya's dance company had an evening performance, and although she would not be dancing yet, she was needed to help with the set and costumes, so wouldn't be home until late.

The shift began rather slowly. They responded to a minor noise complaint in which a man was playing his music too loudly for his neighbor's taste. They were able to resolve the situation amicably and left with both neighbors happy. Then came a call of a suspicious vehicle parked in the middle of an alley, blocking through traffic. When they got there, the vehicle turned out to be stolen, so they had to call for an impound and write up a vehicle recovery report.

Then, at 3:10 p.m., Dispatch came on the radio. "All units, we have a report of a man with a gun in the residence at 2516 South Valhalla. Complainant is a female at that residence who states her boyfriend is threatening to shoot her and is armed with a handgun. Units responding?"

"Two-George-Three, responding from 23rd and Cherry," Donnelly intoned into the mike.

They heard two other Central District cars say they were responding, along with a Rainier Valley car.

"Two-George-Three will take the northeast corner of the residence," Donnelly said into the mike. They heard Two-George-Five say they would take the southeast corner, and the other two units said they would take the back. Within five minutes, Donnelly had pulled up in front of the residence. The other cars were only moments behind, and all announced they were in position.

Donnelly had positioned the patrol car at an angle in front of the residence, and after getting the shotgun from its rack in the car and the AR-15 from the trunk, he and Reynolds took up positions behind the front quarter panel and the driver's-side door of the car. After observing the residence for a minute or two and not seeing any activity, Donnelly switched the radio to loudspeaker and intoned into the mike, "Attention in the residence, this is the Seattle Police. Come out with your hands on top of your head." There was no response, so Donnelly repeated the order. Almost immediately, a shot rang out from inside the house, shattering the front window of the residence and striking the front right quarter panel of their squad car. "Fuck you, cop. Come in and get me!" came a voice from inside the house.

"Looks like this just got serious," Donnelly said as he got back on the radio. "Dispatch, this is Two-George-Three. Shots fired at this location. No known injuries. We will need a sergeant and notify SWAT we may need their assistance."

"Copy," Dispatch responded. "Do I have a sergeant available to respond to 2516 South Valhalla? Shots fired."

The George-sector sergeant immediately came on the air and advised he was en route. Within minutes, he pulled up and parked a half-block away on a side street. "Cover me," he yelled into the mike before running in a crouch to join Donnelly and Reynolds. Donnelly briefed the sergeant on what had occurred and that they suspected that a female was being held hostage in the residence. The sergeant immediately got on the radio and confirmed that they would need SWAT to respond and to also dispatch a hostage negotiator. Then he added, "All units at 2516 South Valhalla, stand by at your current locations; SWAT and a negotiator are en route."

"Can we take a shot if we get a clean look at him?" Donnelly asked.

"No, let's give the hostage negotiator a chance first. Then we'll use SWAT if we need to breach." The sergeant got back on the radio and so advised the other units.

They stayed in position for a half-hour with no activity visible inside the house. Finally, the negotiator showed up. After being briefed by the sergeant, he got on his cell phone and called the phone number they had for the complainant. It rang several times before a man's voice came on the other end. "What the fuck do you want?" the voice said.

"This is Lieutenant Jarbridge from the Seattle Police Department, and I'd like you to stay on the line with me and see if we can resolve this situation without anyone getting hurt. First, I need to know if your girlfriend is okay."

"She's fine," the man replied, "other than she shit her damn pants."

"Can you put her on the line so I can verify she's alright?" the lieutenant asked.

The man hesitated for a minute, then handed the phone to his girlfriend. "Tell them you're okay," he demanded.

The woman came on the line and said in a quavering voice, "I'm not hurt, officers, thank you—" The phone had apparently been ripped from her hand before she could finish speaking.

"You satisfied?" the man yelled into the phone.

"Yes, thank you," the lieutenant replied. "Now, what seems to be the problem today, and how can we help you fix it?"

"You can help me by getting the fuck out of here and leaving us alone. We can handle our own damn problems," the man yelled.

"You know we can't do that until we're sure that everyone is going to be alright," the lieutenant responded. "Why don't you just throw the gun out the front door and then come out with your hands on your head? I promise that no one will hurt you, and we will try to help you deal with this situation with your girlfriend."

"I ain't comin' out," the man yelled into the phone, "and if you try coming in, I'll blow her shit away, then I'll shoot you."

"Just tell me what has gotten you so upset today," the lieutenant responded. "Maybe we can help."

"The bitch has been fuckin' around on me," the man replied, "and I ain't takin' it no more."

About that time, the SWAT team rolled up in their armored transport vehicle and parked a block away. Several officers, decked out in full protective gear and carrying assault rifles, spread out and took up positions around the house. The remaining entry team drove the armored vehicle up behind Donnelly's squad car and took up positions behind the vehicle. The team leader gave the negotiator a thumbs-up and yelled, "We're ready when you need us."

The negotiator got back on the phone and spent the next thirty minutes commiserating with the man about having to deal with infidelity. He asked about his family and whether he had children and found out he had three kids. After discussing the joys of having a family, he began relating how devastated the man's children would be if they didn't have a father around and reassuring the man about how much he had to live for. The negotiator was apparently very convincing because they began to hear the man sobbing on the other end of the line.

"Just throw the gun out and come out," the lieutenant again enjoined the man. "We can work this out."

They heard the man end the call, and then, after several minutes, the front door opened slightly, and an arm emerged with the gun in hand. The man threw the revolver out onto the lawn, opened the door fully, and came out with his hands on top of his head. The SWAT team immediately converged on him, took him to a prone position, cuffed him, and then patted him down to make sure he did not have any other weapons. Donnelly and Reynolds approached and escorted the man to their patrol car and placed him in the back seat. Meanwhile, the SWAT officers cleared the house and found the girlfriend prostrate on her bedroom floor, crying hysterically and reeking of fresh excrement.

After she was allowed to clean herself up, one of the other units was assigned to transport the woman to the station for a statement, while Donnelly and Reynolds transported the man to the city jail for booking. After completing their reports and statements, it was again time to call it a day.

"I think I'm going to need another scotch tonight," Donnelly said as they walked to the locker room. "Want to join me?"

"Not tonight, Mick," Reynolds responded. "I need some fresh air tonight. But hey, we're off tomorrow—why don't you come over for dinner tomorrow night? We'll throw some steaks on the grill."

"Sounds good, but you better check with the better half to make sure it's alright," Donnelly responded. "Give me a call tomorrow to confirm."

Reynolds took a circuitous route on the way home, riding around the east side of Lake Union and then along Portage Bay and the Lake Washington Cut to the Montlake Bridge near the Arboretum, then meandered north through the University District to 50th Street. By the time he got home, he felt relaxed but somewhat enervated as the adrenaline rush he had experienced that afternoon had worn off. He fixed himself a cup of green tea, pulled up his "Jazz Favorites" playlist on his iPod, then stretched out on his recliner to allow the cool sounds of Sonny Rollins, Miles Davis, Stanley Turrentine, and Charlie Parker re-energize his body.

Tawnya stepped through the front door of the apartment a little after midnight. The first thing she saw was Dan stretched out on the recliner in front of the fireplace—totally naked and sound asleep. The music was still emanating from the speakers. Tawnya slipped out of her clothes, knelt next to the recliner, and began gently fondling Dan's flaccid cock. It soon began to come to life as Dan groggily opened his eyes, looked at her, and smiled. Tawnya took the engorging penis in her mouth and soon had it fully erect. She stood up and, straddling Dan in the chair, slowly inserted the swollen member into her now wet vagina. The next twenty minutes were an escalating, exquisite sensation for each of them until they both climaxed almost simultaneously. They lay spent in each other's arms for several minutes, listening to Miles Davis and John Coltrane play their version of "Round Midnight." Finally, Tawnya stood and pulled Dan to his feet. "I'm exhausted," she said, "let's go to bed." Dan let her lead him into the bedroom, where they collapsed into bed and immediately snuggled against each other. Within seconds, they both were sound asleep.

Tawnya was good with Donnelly coming over for dinner, so after sleeping in again on Sunday morning and engaging in some extended wake-up activity, they called him to confirm dinner, then headed down to their Lake Union diner for breakfast, after which they hit up a liquor store for a bottle of Donnelly's favorite Dalwhinnie scotch. Dan was taken aback by the price, but told Tawnya that it was well worth the experience of working with Donnelly. They picked up some genuine Idaho russet potatoes and fresh asparagus from the Pike Street Farmer's Market, then stopped by the meat market in Ballard for some New York steaks before topping off the propane tank and heading back to the apartment to prepare for Donnelly's arrival.

After a delicious dinner of grilled steak, baked potatoes, and asparagus cooked in olive oil and garlic, Dan, Tawnya, and their guest retired to the lanai to watch the sun go down. Dan found himself thinking back to the previous day's encounter and to the countless gun-related acts of violence that were being experienced all over the country.

"What do you think of the gun culture in this country?" he asked Donnelly.

"Well, guns have been a fact of life in this country since its inception," Donnelly replied, "from the very first colonists who needed guns for self-protection and hunting, to the early settlers moving west who used firearms to conquer the Native American tribes and take their land, to the Wild West where virtually everyone carried a firearm for self-protection, to the present day when people use guns for hunting, sport shooting, and to protect their homes. I guess guns have become an integral part of our culture, which is evidenced by the fact that we have way more guns in this country than we do people."

"Are you concerned about the ever-increasing number of school shootings and other mass-casualty events involving guns, as well as the number of individuals and kids who are killed every year by guns?"

"Of course I'm concerned," Donnelly said. "I think it's a damn shame that so many guns fall into the hands of people whose intent is to do harm to themselves or others or who don't know how to use them safely, but I also empathize with the countless law-abiding citizens who use and enjoy guns for completely legitimate purposes. I own several myself."

"What troubles me is the idolatry with which guns are viewed by so many people in this country. You and I carry a gun every day as a tool of our trade, but I'd like to think that we don't consider it an object of worship," Reynolds replied. "Scarily, a lot of people do—even a lot of cops. Do you really think that the Founding Fathers wrote the Second Amendment with the idea that every Tom, Dick, and Mary would be packing heat everywhere they went? Think of how that complicates our job as police officers when we roll into a scene and there are civilians standing around with guns in their hands, and we don't know who the good guys are and who are the bad."

"I hear what you're saying. I think it's pretty apparent the Founders' intent was to ensure that regulated militia members, who we initially relied on for the country's defense, had access to firearms. They would shit their knickers if they could see what we're dealing with now. I've heard that we have about 15 million AR-15-type assault rifles in this country. Who in the hell needs an assault rifle unless their goal is to kill people? They aren't worth a shit for hunting (if you're concerned about preserving the meat), and there are lots of other less lethal choices for sport shooting. It seems they've become a status symbol for every would-be 'patriot' who thinks they are going to save the country from some imagined conspiracy," Donnelly responded. "But what are we going to do about it at this point? With over 400 million guns in the hands of private owners in this county, and with gun manufacturers pumping out and selling firearms as fast as they can make them, how are we ever going to keep them from getting into the wrong hands?"

"It seems that we're the only major country in the world that is experiencing this level of gun violence," Reynolds replied. "Other countries seem to be dealing effectively with firearms. In Germany, you must be a licensed Jaeger or belong to a licensed gun club to own a weapon. Getting a Jaeger license is extremely difficult, and less than half a percent of the population is licensed to hunt. Most other European countries have strict gun laws that ban most civilians from owning guns. Look at what Australia did after a series of mass shootings in that country. They passed laws restricting gun ownership and started a gun buyback program that took about a third of privately owned guns off the street. There are things that can be done to reduce gun violence if you have the political will to do it."

"Therein lies the problem," Donnelly retorted. "When our politicians are more concerned about not pissing off the National Rifle Association (NRA) and jeopardizing their re-election than saving people's lives, what the fuck do you do?"

"Well, obviously, we have to get politicians in place who are willing to do something, which is a whole different discussion, *but* if we were able to do that, I'd start with the short-term actions we could take, such as implementing a National Gun Registry law requiring all gun owners to register their firearms with the federal government. That information could be fed into a large database like the National Crime Information Center (NCIC) and be accessible to all law enforcement officers. That way, if we encounter someone packing a gun in the course of our duties or discover firearms in a residence or other location pursuant to a lawful search, we can immediately verify the weapons' legal owner. If a person is in possession of firearms that cannot be identified as registered to them, we should be able to legally confiscate the weapons and require the owner to provide proof of ownership and valid registration before releasing them. That would greatly assist law enforcement in taking stolen and illegal guns off the street.

"Second, as part of that law," Reynolds continued, "we should require all gun dealers and other sellers of firearms in public settings, such as gun shows, to verify the identity of every buyer—which brings into play that mandatory certified ID law we discussed before—and then report every gun sale to the feds. Buyers should be required to register their weapons within a specified timeframe. In addition, licensed gun dealers and anyone selling firearms at gun shows or other public events should have to get a background check on the buyer before making the sale. Anyone acquiring a weapon from a friend or relative should have to get a certificate of transfer and register the gun within a specified timeframe, which also should require a background check."

"Whenever we hear politicians talk about this, they bring up mental health issues as the primary driver of mass violence, not the guns themselves," Donnelly responded. "Wouldn't that be the best place to start, given the difficulty in taking any significant number of guns off the street?"

"Well, it is damn sure true that is what most Republican politicians bring up," Reynolds replied, "but that's because they don't want to piss off the NRA and the gun manufacturers, who are major donors to their campaigns.

"That said, according to research by the Violence Project, mental health issues are a factor in perhaps 20 percent of mass shootings. Most are driven by domestic disputes, employment issues, and interpersonal conflicts. That is not to say that we don't need to deal with mental health issues.

"However, do you notice that Republicans never take any action to actually do something to improve mental health treatment in this country? To my mind, in addition to training on recognizing behavioral issues, we need to train all health care professionals, mental health practitioners, teachers, law enforcement officers, counselors, case managers, and other professionals who engage with the public to recognize the signs and symptoms of mental health problems, or people they suspect represent a danger to themselves or others, and couple that with a national Red Flag law that mandates they report these individuals to a responsible authority. It should also preclude a person, whether a professional or even an average citizen, who reports someone from any civil or criminal liability. The person reported should be mandated to undergo an in-depth psychological/psychiatric evaluation at government expense. If a competent assessment team deems that person a threat to themselves or others, they should be placed in a national Red Flag database and prohibited from buying, owning, or possessing a firearm or other dangerous weapon. This would be another great tool for law enforcement. If we find someone who is in the database in possession of a weapon, it will give us authority to confiscate their weapons."

"You do realize that most states do have laws regarding what they call 'mandatory reporters,' which require that doctors, nurses, teachers, et cetera report what they consider dangerous behavior?" Donnelly replied.

"Yeah, I realize that, but they are obviously not being stringently enforced. We need to put some emphasis and teeth into those laws that hold people accountable for actually doing it. These individuals need to be identified and referred for treatment, but that is going to require us to develop more mental health treatment facilities, both inpatient and outpatient, to provide that treatment, which means we need a lot more mental health professionals in the system. To me, that takes us back to some of the educational and healthcare solutions we have talked about before, such as promoting career tracks in our schools based on individual ability and interests and societal needs and developing a national system of primary-care clinics, both private and public, that provide both physical and mental health care and referrals."

"Well, I can certainly see what a master's degree in criminology gets you these days," Donnelly said, "but how in the hell are you going to get the politicians in this country to go along with it when the NRA, gun manufacturers, and so many gun owners who contribute to political campaigns oppose any restrictions on guns, and nobody wants to spend money on more mental health facilities, which frankly have had a lot of problems in the past?"

"Polls show that over half of the people in the country support reasonable gun laws," Reynolds responded. "Even the NRA says it supports more mental health treatment. It's past time when the majority in this country should let a deluded minority and a bought-and-paid-for political system dictate policy. Rational, intelligent people need to stand up and take this country back by voting those kowtowing politicians who oppose reasonable laws out of office."

Tawnya had been patiently listening to this discussion and had finally had enough. "As the only Black person here," she interjected, "let me tell you what I think about this issue. While I don't disagree with what you both have said, my primary concern is the disproportionate effect gun violence has on the Black community. You do know that even though Black people comprise only about 12 percent of the population, we are the victims of over 60 percent of all gun homicides, right? And the disparity is even worse among our young Black population, particularly males aged eighteen to twenty-four, who are almost twenty times more likely to die by gun violence than a white male in those ages. Hell, gun violence has been the leading cause of death of Black children for years. And that's not to mention the fact that Blacks are twice as likely to be killed by the police as white people."

"You're absolutely right," Donnelly responded. "What do you think is driving that and what can we do about it?"

"I think systemic racial inequality is probably the biggest factor," Tawnya replied. "Black people have been repressed for far too long in this country, particularly in terms of access to safe housing and educational and employment opportunities. We have kept Black people trapped in poverty and living in unsafe communities where crime is often the easiest or only means of survival, and the kids have to join gangs just to have some measure of security. Then there are the persistent racial stereotypes that portray Black people overall as lazy and stupid, and Black men as dangerous and evil, which drives how the police and public interact with them."

"That's all too true, babe," Dan responded. "Do you think things are getting any better?"

"Oh, I think there has been some incremental improvement since the civil rights movement in the '60s and '70s, but progress has been far too slow. Black leaders have started developing community violence intervention programs in Black and Brown communities to work on the causes of conflict and violence, and community policing programs are starting to improve relationships between the police and these communities, but we still have a long way to go. Like we've discussed in the past, a lot more resources have to be invested, both public and private, in these communities to have any appreciable effect."

"Amen to that," Donnelly responded. "Well guys, I think I've had about all the scotch I can handle and still drive home, so I'm going to bid you two goodnight. Thanks again for the wonderful dinner. Next time, it will be my treat."

CHAPTER 19

NARROWING THE GAP

The work week began relatively quietly for Donnelly and Reynolds, with lots of routine calls yet nothing to stimulate the nervous system. It did appear from studying the crime reports that there had been an increase in daylight burglaries in George sector. They decided to spend as much time as possible patrolling the residential streets and alleys, looking for suspicious activity.

Late on Wednesday afternoon, they got a call of a burglary at a residence on 17th Avenue. As they pulled up in front of the tiny, dilapidated wood-frame house, Reynolds was struck by how poor the entire neighborhood appeared. Most of the houses were desperately in need of paint, their roofs appeared worn and porous, and virtually all seemed in need of repairs—both major and minor.

As he and Donnelly walked across the wooden front porch, the boards underfoot creaked and sagged with their weight. The screen door had a long tear down the middle and the bottom hinge had been torn loose from the door jamb. They knocked and announced, "Seattle Police." An elderly Black woman quickly opened the door. Somewhat on the heavy side, she was wearing an ankle-length print-cotton dress, and a red bandana was tied around her hair, knotted at her forehead. The woman was obviously extremely agitated but seemed relieved to see the officers. "Oh my God," she said, "I'm so glad you're here. Someone broke into my house while I was at work today."

"I'm sorry to hear that," Donnelly responded. "Can you show us where they got in?"

The woman escorted them through the living room to the back door off the kitchen. Reynolds noticed that the furniture in the living room was very old and threadbare, but the room itself seemed clean and tidy. The kitchen was also clean and well-kept, even though the linoleum floor was well-worn, and the kitchen table and chairs showed their age and extensive use. Again, the perpetrators had broken out a pane of glass in the back door to gain entry and then had apparently gone straight to the living room and taken the large-screen TV, which was the only thing of apparent value in the whole house. None of the other rooms appeared to have been disturbed.

Donnelly dusted the broken glass and inside doorknob for prints while Reynolds sat down with the victim at the kitchen table and started gathering information for the report. She immediately began pouring out her entire life story. It turned out the woman, who identified herself as Martha Worthington, had just turned seventy and lived alone in the house, which had been passed down in her family for three generations. She worked as a housekeeper and cook for an affluent white family who lived on the rim overlooking Lake Washington, and walked the four-mile round trip to work five days a week. Her house had long since been paid for, but she did not own a car and had no insurance on the home or her belongings. Her only income was her job and a small Social Security check from her deceased husband, which barely covered her food, utilities, and the medicine she took daily for hypertension and diabetes. It had taken her a year to save enough to buy the TV, and now she was going to have to start all over again.

Reynolds commiserated with her situation and assured her they would do everything possible to get the TV back even while knowing that it undoubtedly had already been pawned or fenced, and the chances of getting it back were slim given the fact that she did not save the serial number or model and could only remember it was a Sony. He hoped they would be as fortunate as they had been in the first burglary he had been involved in, but in searching the area around the house, they were unable to locate anywhere it might have been stashed.

Donnelly cruised down to the local drive-in, where Reynolds finished writing the report over a cup of coffee. No sooner had they finished and cleared with Dispatch than they were given a call of a residential alarm having been activated, this time in the wealthy, predominately white area bordering Lake Washington.

As they pulled up in front of the house, Reynolds was struck by the dichotomy between this home and the one they had been to just previously. The lawn was lush and freshly trimmed, the landscaping was profuse and well-maintained, and the two-story colonial home with pillars in front appeared freshly painted and pristine. As they walked to the front door, Reynolds noted the sign on the front window— "Protected by ADT Security"—and the doorbell video camera on the wall next to the door. They rang it and were soon greeted by a distinguished-looking gentleman with greying hair and a well-trimmed mustache. He was wearing high-end grey flannel slacks and a dress shirt covered by a navy-blue cashmere cardigan.

The man introduced himself as Greg Baxter, the owner of the house, and advised the officers that he had just arrived home from work at a downtown law firm after being notified of an alarm at his residence, and found someone had kicked open the back door. This had set off the home's audible alarm, which apparently had frightened off the would-be burglars. Nothing in the house appeared to have been disturbed or missing, the man said, but he had captured the two suspects on his video camera system. The time stamp on the video was two hours previously.

Donnelly and Reynolds got the information they needed for their report, dusted quickly but unsuccessfully for prints, and downloaded the video onto a thumb drive, noting the description of the suspects. They put out the descriptions on the radio to notify other units and then began a patrol of the area west of the residence leading back into the Central District but were unable to locate any suspects.

Donnelly decided to go into the Headquarters precinct to write their report, and to show the video to the Burglary and Juvenile Detective Units to see if any of their detectives could recognize the suspects. No one could, but they assured Donnelly they would run the pictures on their facial recognition software and compare them to any mug shots they had on file.

By the time they had finished at Headquarters, only a couple of hours were left of the shift, and they realized they hadn't had dinner yet. "Let's do The Harbor," Donnelly suggested, and Reynolds immediately seconded that choice because he knew Tawnya was working that evening. It was approaching 6:00 p.m.—prime dinner hour at The Harbor—so Reynolds called ahead to see if their usual table was open. Fortunately, it was, and Tawnya assured him she would save it for them. Tawnya met them at the door, escorted them to their table, and took their order. She lightly brushed Dan's shoulder with her hand as she gayly sashayed back to the kitchen to drop off their order. It was a very busy evening, so she was kept running and was unable to stop and chat.

"Did anything strike you about those two burglary reports we just handled?" Reynold asked Donnelly as they sat drinking their coffee.

"Well, obviously, the difference in economic circumstances between a poor, elderly Black woman and a rich white couple," Donnelly responded. "That man and his wife, who is a pediatric physician, by the way, probably make a seven-figure salary between them. They live in a million-dollar home, drive luxury vehicles, and undoubtedly send their kids to private schools. They probably sock away a good chunk of change in the stock market and will pass on a healthy legacy to their children, who will carry on their affluent lifestyle."

"Yeah," Reynolds replied, "and that poor Mrs. Worthington told me that she has lived her entire life in that little dump of a house in which she can barely afford to keep the lights on. She has five kids—two girls and three boys—all in their forties and fifties. None of them graduated from high school, and all are surviving on minimum-wage jobs and public assistance. Between her five kids, she has eleven grandkids, who undoubtedly will follow in their parents' footsteps. It's a sad situation."

"But you have to ask yourself, does it really have to be that way?" Donnelly responded. "With all the government programs out there, you'd think that with a little effort, those people could pull themselves up by their bootstraps and make something of themselves. A lot of young Black kids have."

"Yeah, some kids are born with unusually resilient characters or with special talents that allow them to make it out of poverty," Reynolds replied, "but even then, they usually need some help in the form of a strong parent or mentor who exerts a positive influence in their lives. Most of these kids, however, are raised on the streets and indoctrinated from the time they can comprehend that there is little hope for them to make it in a white man's world without resorting to crime or accepting a life of menial work and a meager existence. Once those beliefs are formed as a child, they are hard to change.

"Then, if you consider the discrimination we have subjected Black Americans to since we supposedly freed the slaves, it is not hard to understand why so many of them have not been able to break the chains of poverty—look at the Jim Crow laws that effectively imposed racial segregation and marginalization of Black Americans up until the 1960s. Then you have the landmark legislation in the mid-twentieth century, such as the Federal Housing Act, the Social Security Act, and the GI Bill, that provided the foundation for a broad-based white middle class in this country. All those laws effectively excluded Blacks, who were, for the most part, denied the benefits. Only 2 percent of the housing built through the Federal

Housing Act was available to Blacks because of 'redlining' and other built-in obstacles. A lot of them were denied Social Security benefits because they did not cover agricultural and domestic workers, who were often Black. Even the GI Bill benefits for veterans of World War II were discriminatory in nature. Because of these and other—often subtle—systemic forms of discrimination, Blacks in this country, on average, have only one-eighth of the net worth of a median white household.

"The government started to correct some of these issues back in the '60s with Johnson's War on Poverty, but unfortunately, that effort has stalled in many areas, often due to adverse court rulings upholding the concept of reverse discrimination."

"Okay, I'll grant you that Blacks often start life with two strikes against them," Donnelly responded. "What do you suggest, more government programs? Or maybe you're one of those who want to give them lump-sum reparations. Where do you think that money would go? A bigger TV or a new Caddy, no doubt."

"Well, I think that response kind of exemplifies our racial stereotypes. But no, I agree that lump-sum reparations are not the answer," Reynolds replied. "You're right, people who have never had a significant amount of money would probably not manage it very effectively or make the kinds of investments in themselves that would lift them from poverty long term. Many lottery winners are a good example. But I do think that some of the things we've talked about—such as universal health insurance for everyone, early childhood education, and major investments in our public schools, to include tutors, after school programs, more guidance counselors, a track system for secondary education, and subsidized post-secondary education and training—would greatly benefit poor Black families and give their children a more equal shot at achieving a middle-class life."

"But what about those who choose not to take advantage of those opportunities?" Donnelly queried. "Do we just make the decision to support them with taxpayer money?"

"No, there has to be a role for personal responsibility and accountability for everyone, regardless of their race or ethnicity," Reynolds answered. "If someone chooses not to partake of the programs available, they must be left to their own devices and deal with the consequences. Granted, such choices may end up with the person in prison or homeless, in which case we will be supporting them with taxpayer or charitable money anyway, but hopefully, the numbers in those circumstances would be significantly reduced, and the greatly increased tax base in the new economy would allow us to provide the necessary assistance to keep people from starving and living on the street."

Donnelly finished the last bite of his steak and threw his napkin on the table. "We'd better get back on the road," he said, "this shift is almost over."

Reynolds was able to get a moment with Tawnya on the way out to see what time she would get off work. "I should be home about 10:00 p.m.," she said. "You going to be ready?"

"I'm always ready for you, babe," Reynolds responded. "I'll be waiting at the door."

CHAPTER 20

BUSTED

Reynolds arrived at the Crime Analysis Unit the next morning to find Donnelly poring over the residential burglary reports. He had printed off a map of their sector and was noting the location of each recent burglary with a circle containing a number. On a separate sheet of paper in his notebook, he was annotating next to that number the date of the burglary, the day of the week, the inclusive times the burglary occurred, the method of entry, and what items had been taken, along with suspect information, if there was any. When he was done, he sat there studying the finished product for a few minutes, then pushed the notebook to Reynolds.

"See any patterns there?" Donnelly said.

Reynolds focused on the location, the day of week, the times of occurrence, and the method of entry as he read through each annotated incident.

"Looks like most of these burglaries occur on weekdays between 1:00 and 3:00 p.m. They always enter by breaking a window or forcing the back door. And most are happening in a corridor between 29th Avenue and Lake Washington Boulevard, which is a mostly white area."

"Yeah, and they mostly steal electronics—TVs, computer equipment, and stereo components—which means they must be using some type of vehicle to transport the take. They probably park nearby, sneak down the alley to the house, gain entry, stack up the booty by the back door, then go get the car and load it up," Donnelly added. "Let's see if the sergeant will let us go out plainclothes for a couple of days and do an intensive patrol of that area."

The sergeant said that he had some extra bodies for the next couple of days and agreed to let them go out plainclothes. Donnelly and Reynolds changed into street clothes and then checked out an older Buick sedan from the motor pool, a couple of hand radios, and a shotgun from the equipment room. They were soon patrolling, as inconspicuously as possible, the residential streets in the area they had identified.

"Pay particular attention to any activity in the alleys," Donnelly said. "But I guess you knew that," he added after thinking about how obvious his statement had been.

The first day was a bust, and when Reynolds showed up at the Crime Analysis Unit the next morning, he found that there had not been any burglaries reported the previous day.

"Let's hope we have a little better luck today," he said as he and Donnelly cleared the gas pumps and headed for their sector.

At about 1:45 p.m., Donnelly suddenly pulled to the curb after just passing an alley. "There's a couple of Black males walking down the alley a block down," he said. "Jump out and watch where they go."

Reynolds hid behind some garbage cans in the alley and watched as the two males continued their slow walk for a minute, then stopped, looked around briefly, and disappeared into a backyard. Reynolds ran back to the car. "They just went into a backyard on the east side of the alley, about three-quarters of the block down."

Donnelly quickly drove around the block and pulled up on the side street just before the alley. "Alright, let's go on foot from here.

You stay on the right side of the alley, and I'll take the left. Try to stay out of sight as much as possible."

They worked their way up the alley to the third house from the corner. Reynolds could see the back of the house from his position behind a detached garage adjacent to the alley. He noticed that a windowpane had been broken out of the back door and that the door was slightly ajar. Reynolds motioned for Donnelly to join him and pointed out the door.

"We might be in luck," Donnelly said. He got on his portable radio. "Dispatch, this is Tactical Unit One. We have a possible burglary in progress in the 5400 block of 35th Avenue. We would like a two-man backup unit to meet us in the alley on the west side of 35th and Chesapeake, three houses up the alley. Have them come in quiet—and bring a shotgun."

"Okay, I'm going to work my way around to cover the front of the house. You wait here for the backup unit, then send one of them around to the front," Donnelly said, before starting to circle around the residence next door to take up a position at the front of the house.

The backup unit was there within three minutes. Reynolds instructed one of them to join Donnelly at the front of the house and the other, with the shotgun, to take a position behind a shed just down the alley. The officer had no sooner gotten into position than Reynolds saw a figure appear inside the back door of the house. He sat something down, then disappeared back into the house. Reynolds got on his portable radio's tactical channel and advised Donnelly and the other officers of what he had seen.

Not more than two minutes later, two male figures appeared at the back door carrying items. They set them down by the door, then one of the men emerged from the house and started down the steps. Reynolds signaled the other officer, and they simultaneously sprang from their cover positions, weapons at the ready. As the patrol officer cranked a round of 00 buck into the chamber of the shotgun, Reynolds shouted at the suspect, "Freeze! Seattle Police, put your hands on your head." At the sound of the forearm of the shotgun slamming forward, the young male in front immediately stopped in his tracks and clasped his hands to the top of his head. The other male, however, bolted from the door back into the interior of the house. "Got one coming out the front," Reynolds yelled in the radio. Within seconds, he heard the sound of crashing glass and a loud thump coming from the front of the house, followed immediately by Donnelly yelling, "Police! Don't move."

Reynolds and the patrol officer approached their suspect, and while the officer covered him, Reynolds patted him down and cuffed him, then read him his Miranda Rights. They led him around to the front of the house, where they found Donnelly standing over the cuffed, prostrate form of a young Black male groaning on the ground. Donnelly was in the process of calling for a Medic 1 unit to respond to the scene, as the second suspect, in his desperation to escape, had dove headfirst through a front-room window and slid to a stop, face down, just in front of the tree that Donnelly was hiding behind.

They proned out the other suspect next to his injured accomplice and had one of the patrol officers cover them while Donnelly, Reynolds, and the other officer shook down the house. They found a TV, desktop computer, stereo receiver, and several pairs of speakers stacked up just inside the back door. They proceeded to search the house, which was clear.

Donnelly called the Burglary Unit to advise what they had, and they agreed to send a detective along with a forensics team out to the house to process the scene. The Medic 1 unit arrived and treated the window-diving suspect for numerous cuts, then advised that they would need to take him to the hospital for x-rays and possible additional treatment. One of the patrol officers rode with the suspect in the ambulance while his partner agreed to stay behind and wait for the detectives.

Donnelly and Reynolds placed the other suspect in their car, where Donnelly began questioning him about the location of his vehicle. After several minutes of the suspect refusing to talk, Donnelly, in his most fatherly manner, finally told him, "Hey son, we've got you dead to rights. If you cooperate with us, you might get off with just probation on this thing. If you don't, it's likely you're going to be doing three to five at Monroe and will wind up somebody's punk. Take your pick, but you really don't want to have to do time."

The suspect, who had no ID but admitted he had just turned eighteen and didn't want to go to prison, pointed out an old white panel van parked a half-block down the street. While Reynolds stayed in the car with the suspect, Donnelly checked the vehicle, where he found a Sony flat-screen TV in the back that matched the description of Mrs. Worthington's. He called for an impound, and while they waited, Donnelly continued to question the young man. Reluctantly, he finally copped to him and his buddy having ripped off numerous houses over the last month, including that of Mrs. Worthington. He agreed to make a written statement if Donnelly would promise him a good recommendation to the judge. Donnelly said he would tell the prosecutor about his cooperation and make sure the judge was aware as well.

It was past 8:00 p.m. when Donnelly and Reynolds finished booking the TV into Evidence, taking the suspect's statement, booking him into jail, and writing their burglary report and individual statements.

"Good day's work," Donnelly said as they headed to the locker room. "Time for a scotch—want to join me?"

"Think I'll take a raincheck," Reynolds replied. "I'm beat and my brain feels like mush. I need a good bike ride to clear out the cobwebs. See you tomorrow."

It was after 9:00 p.m. when he got home, which left about an hour before he could expect Tawnya's return. He stripped off his bike togs and took a long, hot shower, then slipped a pair of cutoff sweatpants and a sleeveless sweatshirt over his naked body, put his "Jazz Favorites" playlist on the box, brewed a cup of green tea, and stretched out on his recliner.

When Tawnya got home, they cuddled up on the loveseat, and Reynolds gave her a detailed rundown of his day. She smiled compassionately at him, stood up, took him by the hand, and pulled him to his feet. "Come with me," she said, "I know exactly what you need."

CHAPTER 21

THE PLAN

On the Friday following Tyrone Banks' arrest, he was advised that he had been formally charged with unlawful imprisonment, trafficking, and procuring and was scheduled for an arraignment that afternoon. At the arraignment, the District Court judge advised Banks of the charges against him and his right to counsel. Banks said he could not afford an attorney and asked that one be appointed. The judge submitted a not-guilty plea on Banks' behalf, placed an order for a public defender, and scheduled a preliminary hearing on the charges for the following Wednesday.

Banks met with his court-appointed attorney on the morning of his preliminary hearing. He was extremely agitated by the fact that the attorney had not yet even read the police reports but agreed that the lawyer would enter a plea of 'not guilty' and push for as low a bail as possible. The judge found there was probable cause to support the charges, accepted his plea, and set a cash bail of $50,000.

Banks had no appreciable assets. He was even upside down on what he owed on his Escalade. He had spent all his available cash, other than the $2500 flash money he always carried with him, to pay off the cartel and bring the three girls up from Arizona. And that money was his cut from the grocery store heists they had pulled off previously. So, when he got back to the jail and was given a phone call, that call went to Bennie Malone.

Bennie agreed to front him the cash for his bond but told him that they would negotiate the terms of the loan once he got out. Bennie was waiting outside the entrance to the jail when Banks was released. They drove straight from the jail to Bennie's apartment in West Seattle, where Banks was surprised to find Duke Robinson and Slick Jackson waiting in the front room.

"What's up, homes?" Banks said as he entered the room.

"We gonna give you a chance to get square with me," Malone answered. "It looks like the cops are staking out grocery stores, so we decided that we're gonna make one more really big score and then split this town."

"Yeah, I'm thinkin' I need to do the same thing before they lock me up on these bullshit trafficking charges," Banks replied. "What you got in mind?"

"Slick's been checkin' out this bank up on East Magenta Way. Seems they get in a big cash shipment every other Friday when the shipyard workers get paid. We figure we can hit 'em right after the armored car leaves and before the ship workers get off shift. The place is usually pretty quiet 'round that time of the afternoon," Malone answered.

"What would my job be?" Banks asked.

"Just what you have been doin'. We need a wheelman and someone to provide cover for us from the outside," Malone responded. "We need you to set up in the parking lot across the street from the bank in case any cops show up and take the motherfuckas out. You been practicing with that AK I gave you, ain't you?"

Banks nodded his head as he ruminated on that for a minute or two, not sure if this was something he wanted to take on. Hitting a grocery store was one thing; robbing a bank was a whole different ball game. They'd probably have an armed guard in the bank who would have to be taken out, one way or another. Did he really want to get involved in a shootout with the police? Robbing a bank would also get the feds involved, which would greatly increase the risk of getting caught.

"What if they have an armed guard inside?" Banks asked.

"We're going to wear body armor," Malone responded, "and we'll all have assault rifles, which should discourage him from taking us on. Most of these guards they hire are just old men anyway."

"Yeah, but some of these banks are using off-duty cops," Banks retorted. "I really don't want to be involved in killing a cop."

After several moments of thought, Banks finally asked, "What do you think the take might be?"

"We're thinkin' at least $500,000," Malone responded. "That would be $125,000 each, or $75,000 for you after you pay me back the $50K I fronted you today."

Banks thought about that for a moment. It occurred to him that with $75,000 in cash, he could head down to Mexico and maybe hook up with the cartel down there. He knew his prospects if he stayed in Seattle would probably include at least ten to fifteen years in the joint, so he heard himself say, "Okay, I'm in, dude. When we gonna move?"

"The next cash drop is a week from Friday," Malone responded. "We gonna do it then."

....

It was late Saturday afternoon when Donnelly said that it was about time that they checked in with Dixie. They tried Snookers first, and sure enough, he was at his usual table playing pool. After a quick shake, Donnelly maneuvered his way back to the underground parking garage, where they waited for forty-five minutes before Dixie emerged from the side door.

"You got anything for me, bro?" Donnelly asked.

"Maybe," Dixie replied. "I hear Tyrone Banks has been tryin' to pawn off his girls to another pimp. Seems he may be thinkin' of skipping town before he goes to trial on them charges you hung on him. Plus, I saw him hanging out with Bennie Malone, Slick Jackson, and Duke Robinson at the Blackbird last night, and they seemed to be celebrating something, toastin' each other an' shit."

"Hmmm, wonder what they got going?" Donnelly said as he reached into his attaché case and pulled out a small packet in aluminum foil, which he then gave to Dixie. "Thanks, man. Let me know if you hear anything else."

As Dixie slinked away into the darkness of the garage, Reynolds had to confirm a lingering suspicion he had, "You giving that guy drugs for information?"

Donnelly looked him in the eye for several moments before responding, "Yeah, it's the coin of the realm with guys like that. I don't get any cash from the Department for CIs, so I have to do what I have to do."

"Where do you get the shit?" Reynolds asked.

"Some of it I get from shaking down dopers on the street, and then occasionally, I get in on a bust where we find a quantity of the shit. It doesn't hurt the case to siphon off a little before you book it into evidence. You think you can live with that?"

Reynolds considered that question for a minute before responding. "And that doesn't present an ethical dilemma for you?"

"It did at first," Donnelly replied, "but I justify it in my mind by thinking of what is in the best interest of the community. Both Dixie and LaTasha are long-time recreational drug users. If they don't get their shit from me, they get it from some other source. The information I've gotten from them over the years has allowed us to take some major dealers and other sundry assholes off the street, so I figure the ends justify the means. Besides, the drugs are only one reason they talk to me. I've bailed both of them out of some major shit shows. Dixie was heavily in debt to a ruthless drug dealer and couldn't pay, so he helped us take the guy and his crew down. LaTasha got the shit beat out of her by a savage, sadistic pimp, and we were able to get him put away, so she feels she owes me something. The puny amount of drugs I give them might get them off for a night, but it's not enough to contribute to their addiction. When they give up something really big, I'm usually able to get some money from the dicks to compensate them."

"But is it worth possibly forfeiting your job and your retirement if you get caught?" Reynolds responded.

"I take my chances," Donnelly replied. "I figure that with my overall record, the worst that could happen is being forced to retire. If I were to lose my pension, then you just might find me parked on that dirt road in the mountains with my gun in my mouth. But at least I would go out knowing I did everything I could to make the city safer."

Reynolds looked Donnelly in the eye for several moments before responding, "Mick, you know I have a tremendous amount of respect for you and the way you do your job, but you also know that I joined the police department to redeem my family name after my father's corrupt behavior and I don't want to do anything that would further tarnish it. So, I can't be part of essentially dealing drugs, even though it may be to accomplish a greater good."

"You saying you don't want to work with me any longer?" Donnelly asked.

Reynolds had to think about that for a minute. He finally decided to strike a compromise with Donnelly. "I definitely want to work with you, Mick, but I need your assurance that I won't be implicated if this ever results in a departmental investigation. You can be sure that I will never tell anyone, but you never know what people like Dixie and LaTasha might do if they get jammed up legally and need a bargaining chip. Can you give me that assurance?"

"Dan, I would never intentionally do anything to damage your reputation or cause you problems with the Department, you have my word on that," Donnelly replied. "If someone does roll over on me, I will take full responsibility and make sure you are not involved, okay?"

Reynolds could see in Donnelly's eyes the seriousness and sincerity of his statement. He and Donnelly bumped fists and gave each other an approving smile before heading back out onto the streets.

After riding several minutes in silence, Reynolds said, "You know, ever since we busted those burg suspects this week, I keep thinking about the disparities in lifestyles between the little old Black lady that got ripped off and the rich couple who avoided getting ripped off because they could afford a state-of-the-art security system. It just seems so unfair that we should have such a wealth gap between the richest and poorest in this country."

"There's always been rich and poor, Dan, from the beginning of human history," Donnelly responded. "The rich get rich generally because they're smarter, work harder, are more creative and innovative, and are willing to take more risks than us poor schmucks working for wages."

"That's probably true, at least for the initial accumulation of wealth," Reynolds replied, "but then you have the heirs of the wealthy who are rich because of inheritances and the inherent advantages that accrue to them because of their wealth, such as enhanced educational opportunities and living in a network of other wealthy people. Then you have the legal criminals who get wealthy by manipulating the system and taking advantage of the rest of us."

"So, what do you propose we do, Dan—let the government take over the means of production in the country and dole out just what they think people need to survive? Socialism hasn't worked well in the countries that tried it. Look at Russia and China. They've both forsaken their strict Communist ideology and embraced limited capitalism, which rewards hard work and innovation."

"No, I'm all for capitalism and entrepreneurship," Reynolds responded. "I just think those people who have been successful and acquired wealth should pay their fair share to pull the rest of the people up as well."

"Hell, Dan, the top 1 percent of earners in this country already pay over 40 percent of the income taxes collected in the country, while the bottom 50 percent only contribute 2–3 percent. How much more are you going to ask of them?"

"Well, it's like what Willie Sutton said when he was asked why he robbed banks," Reynolds replied, "'because that's where the money is.' If we want to equalize the opportunities for success for everyone in this country, we are going to have to invest substantial amounts of money in improving education funding and providing financial assistance to would-be entrepreneurs and innovators, and the only way we are going to get the money is by asking the rich to do more. Besides, who benefits most when you allow all people to reach their full potential and maximize their incomes and opportunities? The wealthy—who *do* control most of the means of production in the country. Their businesses and careers thrive when more people are doing well because a larger, more productive workforce has more money to spend on their goods and services. I'm sure you've heard the aphorism, 'A rising tide lifts all boats.' The government benefits because of a greatly expanded tax base, which allows it to spread the cost of these positive programs out to more people over time while at the same reducing the costs of negative expenditures such as dealing with crime and incarceration and public assistance programs."

"So, how do you propose we implement higher taxes on the wealthy?" Donnelly asked.

"Well, I would rule out a 'wealth tax' such as Elizabeth Warren suggests," Reynolds replied. "They tend to be extremely difficult to administer and enforce. And I would not focus solely on taxing businesses. I'm no economist, but it seems axiomatic to me that most businesses don't pay taxes, they just collect them. Taxes are just another cost of doing business that gets passed on to the consumer in the form of higher prices for the goods and services businesses provide. Then, there is the cost to businesses of hiring accountants and tax lawyers, which again inflates the price of their products. Businesses exist primarily to make a profit for their owners and shareholders, so I think we need to focus tax revenues on the profits distributed to those owners and shareholders, as well as the exorbitant salaries their executives make. I would do that by increasing the capital gains tax to the same level as taxes on ordinary income.

"In the same vein, many rich people get the bulk of their income from accumulated assets such as real estate and stocks and bonds. We should be taxing the capital gains on those assets the same as ordinary income, as well. Look at Mitt Romney. When he ran for president, he released his tax records, which showed he only paid an effective rate of 14.1 percent on over $13 million in investment income. That's a lower percentage than a lot of working stiffs in this country. Even if we just raised the capital gains tax to 30 percent from its current 15 percent, we could bring in more than enough revenue to finance most of the things we have talked about.

"The other area I would focus on is the step-up basis on inherited assets like stocks. Your parents may have held a share of stock or owned a house for decades, and the value of that stock or house may have increased 1000 percent, but if they pass that stock or house on to you and you decide to sell it, you only have to pay capital gains on any increase in value it gained while you actually owned the stock or house, which means that all that accumulated value under your parents is basically tax-free. Fixing that and increasing inheritance taxes generally could generate hundreds of billions of dollars without adversely affecting the economy."

"But the rich will tell you that if you tax them more, you will actually hurt the economy because there won't be as much investment in businesses, research and development, and new start-ups," Donnelly responded, "and what really concerns me is that if we give the federal government all that extra money, it is just going to be wasted on pork-barrel projects for politicians and ineffective programs. I don't think making Big Government even bigger is the answer."

"Well, I wouldn't buy that argument about a decrease in investment. That's how the wealthy got rich in the first place. If anything, it might mean they can't buy that next vacation home or upgrade their yacht quite as often. Also, I don't think Big Government is the problem," Reynolds responded. "I think the problem is inefficient and ineffective government, which mainly results from partisan politics, undue corporate influence and lobbying, and the big money going to politicians in our electoral process. Until we deal with those issues, you're right—more money just might mean more waste, fraud, and abuse.

"We need to find ways to make our political process more effective. If I were president, my first order of business would be to do a complete audit of all federal programs, looking for redundancies between federal, state, and local programs, inefficiencies within programs, and whether they were giving us a real return on investment based on a cost/benefit analysis. Then I would establish a system of objective metrics that would allow us to track their performance in real-time."

The conversation was cut short by the blare of the radio. "Two-George-Three, take a stolen vehicle report at 2016 East Maple Street, Suite 201."

"Two-George-Three, en route," Donnelly replied into the mike.

CHAPTER 22

THE PRELUDE

Reynolds met Donnelly the next morning just as he was leaving the Crime Analysis Unit.

"Nothing much new today," Donnelly said. "Let's go up and have a chat with the detectives."

They stopped first in the Vice Unit offices, where only a detective sergeant was on duty. They filled him in on what they had heard about Tyrone Banks.

The sergeant raised his eyebrows. "Hmmmm, that's unusual. Never heard of a pimp giving up his meal ticket before. Banks must be entering a new line of work, or he's planning on skipping town. I'll give the prosecutor a call and give her a heads-up."

Donnelly and Reynolds then proceeded to the Robbery/Homicide Unit and checked in with the sergeant there. They gave him the information they had on Banks, emphasizing that he had been hanging out with Benny Malone and his crew. The sergeant thought that was very interesting and said he might try to get the Special Squad to stake out Malone's place to see who was moving in and out.

Back in their sector, Reynolds, who was now being allowed to drive every other day, began patrolling the back streets of the district, half-hoping that they could spot someone speeding on one of the arterials they crossed so they could get their ticket for the day.

"We're obviously in the political campaign season," Donnelly said as he looked around at all the signs in people's yards. "It never ceases to amaze me that politicians spend good money on all these damn yard signs, bumper stickers, and billboards that basically are just a name, maybe a picture, their political affiliation, and the office they're running for. I'm sure there is some psychological research that supports it, but I can't imagine that any voter would be influenced by them."

"I think it's mainly just a name recognition thing," Reynolds replied. "There apparently are lots of voters who just cast their ballot based on a name they recognize or whether a person has an 'R' or a 'D' next to their name. There also may be some type of social connection thing going on, at least with yard signs and bumper stickers. If your neighbor or someone you know has a sign in their yard or a bumper sticker on their car, it may influence you to vote for that person—or not—depending on how you feel about the neighbor."

"I'd like to think people aren't that stupid," Donnelly said.

"Unfortunately, it appears that some are," Reynolds responded. "I'm afraid I don't have a lot of faith in the collective judgment of human beings. Look at how many millions of dollars candidates and their organizations spend on those ubiquitous thirty-second TV ads that are usually nothing but hyperbole, demagoguery, or outright lies about their opponents, or one-sentence position statements that offer no specifics on the viability, rationality, or short- and long-term consequences of their proposals, and are only intended to appeal to people's greed, self-interest, or preconceived ideas.

"Then there are the so-called TV debates that are not debates at all—merely Q-and-A sessions in which candidates dodge direct questions and manipulate every answer into simplistic, nonoffensive statements of their positions or unsupported attacks on their opponents' positions. There is little opportunity, with the time candidates are allowed, to offer specific data to support their position, rebut their opponent, or directly question each other. And seldom is there an opportunity for listeners to pose direct questions to the candidates in response to their answers.

"On top of that, we have the traditional whistle-stop campaign events in which candidates spend millions traveling their electoral districts wearing coveralls and cowboy hats, playing pianos and singing songs, and, of course, shaking hands, kissing babies, and delivering carefully scripted speeches designed to appeal to the specific constituency they are addressing. I'm sure this satisfies the public's desire to meet and greet their candidates, but any real benefit in terms of judging the best candidate is negligible compared to the costs involved."

To that, Donnelly responded, "You ever watch the old *Tonight* show on TV with Jay Leno? He had a segment called "Jaywalking," in which he would go out on the street and ask random people questions on politics and government. It was amazing how many people did not know who the current vice president was or how many branches of government we have in this country. Too many Americans are ignorant, ill-informed, or both. I blame a lot of that on the rise of political flamethrowers like Rush Limbaugh, Sean Hannity, Glenn Beck, and Tucker Carlson. Most of what they say is total bullshit, but people who are predisposed to conspiracy theories and hyper-partisanship eat it up."

"They say people get the government they deserve, and the US is certainly proof—an inefficient, ineffective, and totally partisan system," Reynolds replied. "The conservatives have instilled a mindset in their followers that government is inherently evil, but I don't think that's true. Government, like any organization, is made up of systems and people. If it isn't working, it is usually because we either have bad systems, or the wrong people, or both—and, to my mind, it is primarily our current governmental systems that are the main problem.

"Unfortunately, the people who created those systems are our elected officials and they are the ones who have the greatest stake in maintaining the status quo. We have allowed them to create an electoral process that gives them a virtual lock on re-election and a political system that practically guarantees mediocrity, cronyism, and special-interest favoritism.

"If we want to change the system, as a society, we have to put aside our biases, open our minds, and evaluate issues based on objective reality, empirical evidence, and reason. We must seek out the facts, critically analyze them, and make informed judgments based on what is going to provide the greatest good for the greatest number of people, not just those at the top. Then, we must demand candidates who are willing to do the same. We need statesmen in our government who put the needs of the country before their own self-interest and ego."

"Well, I wouldn't argue with that," Donnelly replied. "I'll readily admit that I don't spend as much time as I should learning about the issues facing the country. Like most people, I think, we just get so bogged down trying to do our own jobs and dealing with the day-to-day issues we face in our personal lives that we don't take the time to really think about or research these larger issues. When we do seek out information, it is usually from some source that tells us what it thinks we want to hear based on our political perspective. Then there is the feeling of futility many of us experience that nothing we do will make any difference anyway. Where do you start?"

"That's unfortunately very true," Reynolds responded. "Most people do not have the time or inclination to do the in-depth, personal research necessary to objectively evaluate candidates or their positions.

"The TV news, print media, and internet blogs could be an effective way to get to know candidates and the issues, but their coverage is too often superficial or slanted, and the voter never knows what to believe. Direct messages from candidates tend to be amorphous platitudes, and their opinion pieces often do not provide a thorough analysis of the issues or their proposed solutions. Did you ever watch the HBO show called *The Newsroom* with Jeff Daniels?"

"Yeah, I did," Donnelly replied. "I was really sorry when they took it off the air."

"That's my idea of how a TV news show should function," Reynolds responded. "Where the moderator is not afraid to really challenge politicians and their surrogates when they make outlandish statements, with the facts at their fingertips to back it up. Of course, if they actually did that, they would probably never get a politician to appear on their show."

"True, and then there's the fact that they never allocate enough time to really explore a topic," Donnelly replied. "They talk for two minutes and then break for commercials for another five. Got to pay the bills, you know."

"Which brings us back to the cost of the process," Reynolds responded. "Candidates for state office spend hundreds of thousands of dollars; candidates for national office spend millions trying to get elected. I've seen projections that estimate that this year's general election will cost $6.5 billion. Where does that money come from? A paltry amount comes from the average, small-dollar donor. The majority comes from special-interest Political Action Committees, large corporations, and wealthy individuals—each seeking a return on their investment in the form of favorable legislation, direct access to the decision-making process, or partisan political patronage. With elections commonly decided by who can raise the most money, we are indeed left with 'the best government money can buy.'"

"So, how do you suggest we go about changing that?" Donnelly asked.

"I would start with the first issue—that of the uninformed voter. There really is no excuse, in this age of electronic communication, for people not to get the information they need to effectively evaluate candidates. We have two virtually universal mediums that even the poorest voter has access to: radio and television. On top of that, most people have cell phones and access to the internet, which has become almost universally available.

"Imagine that instead of being able to mark a box on our tax return giving money to a political party, we were able to voluntarily designate a portion of our taxes to enable public radio and television stations to devote a dedicated channel to political candidates. We could provide free, virtually unlimited TV and radio time to candidates in which they could fully explain their positions and proposals and provide evidence to support them. They could also rebut their opponents' positions and, again, provide evidence to support their rebuttal. Voters could ask real-time questions to candidates through their phones or the internet—essentially providing a universal town hall experience. Nonpartisan analysts could provide detailed assessments of candidates and their positions, along with independent evaluations of their backgrounds and experience. Voters could access this information in their homes at their own convenience, and all without commercial interruption.

"We could effectively eliminate the necessity for all forms of paid political advertising, obviate the need for candidates to travel all over the state or country, and enable a truly informed electorate, which is really what most responsible voters care about. Perhaps we could then go to the polls thinking our votes actually counted and would not be subverted by an uninformed electorate voting for just a face, name, or political party."

"That sounds great," Donnelly replied, "but do you really think that would get the big money out of politics, stop the kinds of retail politics that we see today, or that people would actually tune in to those programs? Most would rather watch their favorite sitcom."

"Well, getting the big money out of politics is the next big hurdle we are going to have to cross. A good start would be passing federal legislation that limits the amount of money that any entity—whether individual, business, union, or political organization such as a PAC—could contribute to any one candidate during an election cycle, both state and federal. I think $2000 would be a good cap."

"But didn't the *Citizens United* court decision declare that violated people's First Amendment rights?" Donnelly replied.

"You're right, it did," Reynolds responded. "Unfortunately, a lot of the reforms that I envision would require amending the Constitution, which is never an easy task. But it's been done twenty-seven times and can be done again. Actually, I would be in favor of having a new Constitutional Convention to rework a lot of the antiquated provisions of the Constitution, that is, if we could guarantee that it would be done in a competent and comprehensive manner."

"I understand that there is currently a movement to allow the states to convene a Constitutional Convention and essentially bypass Congress. Apparently, they want to adopt a number of conservative ideas such as a balanced-budget amendment," Donnelly said.

"I would not support that, given the one-sided makeup of most of our state legislatures in the country," Reynolds replied. "If we were to do it, I think we need to have a general election in each state in which potential representatives to the new Constitutional Convention would be required to campaign for the position and be elected by a majority of the voters in that state. Hopefully, such an election would attract people who are genuinely interested in making the Constitution more relevant to our modern society and changing the things that have outlived their usefulness, such as the Electoral College and the provisions allowing congressmen to run for unlimited terms. We will have to exclude current politicians from running if we expect any meaningful change, however."

"So, you're in favor of term limits?" Donnelly replied. "What do you think would be appropriate?"

"Well, if we really want to get the big money out of politics and do away with career politicians, I think we need to restrict senators, representatives, and the president and vice president to one term. That would eliminate, or at least greatly reduce, their susceptibility to being swayed in their voting by large contributions to their campaigns by businesses and other special interests or supporting legislation just to appeal to their base or a faction of the electorate. It would also avoid the necessity of taking time away from their public duties to solicit donations or run for re-election. Running for public office should be considered a public service, not a career opportunity. I would pass a law that states you cannot run for a public office while you currently hold a public office. That way, a person who truly wanted to contribute to the public good could run again, but only after taking an election cycle off and returning to private life. I would, however, extend the terms of representatives to four years, senators to eight years, and the president and vice president to six years in order to give them more time to pass their agendas. Again, that is something that would require a constitutional amendment."

"Any other big ideas?" Donnelly said with a smirk.

"As a matter of fact, yeah," Reynolds replied. "I think our whole process of state-run primary elections for federal offices is a joke. Think of how it currently works. Each state is allowed to set up its own process for selecting candidates for representatives, senators, and the president and vice president. A few use partisan caucuses to select a candidate from each political party. Most use a primary election, which is paid for by the state. Many states close these primaries so that only registered voters of each party can vote in that party's primary, which effectively excludes independent voters from participating.

"States also set the dates when they hold these caucuses or primaries, which essentially sets up a winnowing process. Candidates focus their campaigns on the state with the next caucus or primary and spend most of their time and money in that state. Historically, these caucuses and primaries attract a very small percentage of voters, usually the most highly partisan. Typically, less than 20 percent of eligible voters actually participate in a primary election, and way fewer than that in a caucus. Unfortunately, because of the winnowing effect of this process, candidates for national office who lose in the early state primaries and caucuses often lose funding and support and wind up dropping out of the race. What that means is that fewer than 20 percent of a few states' voters can determine who the rest of the country has the opportunity to vote for.

"On top of that, because of the one-sided partisan makeup of the majority of states in the country, the winner of the general election is usually whoever wins the primary of the predominant political party in that state. And, when it comes to the president and vice president, since most states have a winner-takes-all rule when it comes to who the Electoral College electors select, whichever party nominee wins the popular vote in a state will receive all the Electoral College votes from that state. Say a candidate won 51 percent of the popular vote in a state. That means that 49 percent of the voters in that state have their votes for the president and vice president effectively nullified. I don't think that's fair."

"Okay, what would you do differently?" Donnelly asked.

"To start with, I would make each political party manage and finance its own nomination process, both for congressmen and for presidential and vice-presidential candidates. They could use a caucus system, an internal primary election, or a convention, but each would be responsible for selecting one candidate for each congressional office as well as for president and vice president. Anyone wishing to run for office on that party's ticket would have to be nominated and selected by their own party. This process could happen at the party's discretion but would need to be completed by January 1 of the current election year.

"Second, anyone who desired to run for political office as an independent would have to collect a qualifying number of signatures on a petition in a set number of states. So, say you wanted to run for president as an independent; you might start by going door-to-door in your local community, gathering signatures and soliciting donations. You then start having town hall meetings and urge people to attend during your door-to-door visits. At the town halls, you could state your case for election, answer questions from the attendees, and request donations. You could also start recruiting volunteers to work on your campaign. Over time, you could expand that process to other communities and neighboring states. A reciprocal agreement would be in place between states that provided that anyone who collected a sufficient number of signatures in a set number of states to qualify for their ballot would automatically be eligible for the ballot in every state.

"In my dream scenario," Reynolds went on, "the official election season would begin on January 1 of each national election year. Anyone who had qualified for the state's ballot by that time would be eligible for free airtime on the local public radio or television station. Airtime would be allocated in half-hour and hourly increments, depending on the candidate's preference, and each eligible candidate would be guaranteed the same amount of airtime.

"As I said earlier, candidates could use their airtime to fully explain their positions and agendas, provide evidence to support their positions, rebut their opponents' positions along with reasons why, and answer questions from the viewers. Candidates could do this from their local TV or radio station without having to spend any money for travel, accommodations, et cetera. Their presentations could be replayed periodically to reach as broad an audience as possible. People could listen to these broadcasts at their convenience or record them to listen to later.

"These stations could also schedule multiple 'real' debates between candidates, focusing on one or more issues at a time, and allow each candidate sufficient time to fully explicate their position on the issue and provide evidence supporting that position. Opponents could ask questions of each other and provide evidence refuting their opponent's positions. Viewers could call, text, or email questions to be answered in real-time. Independent analysts could critique each debate and provide objective data to support or refute candidates' statements. Hopefully this process would give every voter the opportunity to be truly informed when they went into the voting booth."

"Any other changes you would make to the process?" Donnelly asked.

"Maybe a couple more," Reynolds replied. "Going back to your statement about voters preferring to watch their favorite sitcom over watching a political program, I think voters who take the time to be truly informed—not only about the current issues and candidates but about our entire governmental process—should be rewarded at the ballot box. The way I see this playing out is that every eligible voter would have the option of voluntarily taking a civics test. This test would be developed each election cycle by a bipartisan team of objective academicians, educators, and political experts selected by an independent national organization and be subject to peer review and input. The test, like the citizenship test given to immigrants, would be designed to examine a person's knowledge of the functions and processes of government, as well as their knowledge about current issues and candidates. Those voters who scored 90 percent and above on the test would have their vote count triple. Those who scored 80–89 percent would have their vote doubled. This would apply to both the primary and the general elections in both state and federal elections.

"I would then mandate a national primary election to be held on the same date in every state, say, June 1 of the election year. This primary would be open, and all selected candidates from each party, along with independents, would run head-to-head on the same ballot.

"Voting would be by a weighted, ranked-choice system. That is, each voter would choose his first, second, and third choice for each position. First-place votes would receive three points, second-place votes would receive two points, and third-place votes one point. If the voter had taken the civics test and had their vote elevated, then each of their choices would receive the multiplier effect, so a 90-percent-and-above voter's first-place vote would receive nine points.

"The first- and second-place candidates, based on the total number of points received, would advance to the general election, regardless of their partisan affiliation, or lack thereof. The general election would be held in November, as usual, and the same voting procedure would be used. However, with just two candidates, obviously, you would not need to weight the votes, just apply the 'preferred voter' award. The candidate with the most total points would win outright. The Electoral College would no longer exist."

"Sounds complicated," Donnelly said. "It also seems like that would virtually eliminate the chances of any third-party or independent candidate getting to the general election."

"Well, that's probably true unless the third-party or independent candidate was able to garner widespread support, which they would have an equal opportunity to do," Reynolds replied. "But how many of those candidates win now? Usually, they just function as a spoiler, taking away votes from one or other of the major-party candidates, possibly allowing the less popular or less qualified candidate to win. As far as being complicated, with today's technology, it should not be all that difficult. Hopefully, the result would be a president/vice president and a Congress willing to take on the real issues facing our country and develop effective, long-term solutions to problems instead of just giving them lip service or putting in place half-measures to appease some portion of the electorate.

"Let's get real. Few of the issues facing the country are simple problems with simple solutions. Most are complex, with a multiplicity of contributing causes and influencing factors, which require a multi-faceted approach to solve. There are no silver bullets that will make them go away. Each will require thorough study, rational and objective analysis, and data-driven decision-making based not on subjective personal beliefs and ideology but on what realistically and practically will have the greatest impact on solving or mitigating the problem.

"Further, few of these problems will be solved strictly through governmental action at any level or by free-market solutions driven solely by the private sector. Each will require collaboration, coordination, and cooperation from all levels and branches of government, the business community, often foreign governments, and all other concerned stakeholders. Before any progress can be made in finding solutions, these entities will have to collectively agree on the outcomes they want to achieve. Each will need to subordinate their parochial views and interests and focus on what will provide the greatest good for the greatest number in this country and beyond.

"Effective problem-solving is not a quick or effortless process. It requires people of goodwill with open minds and innovative spirits. It requires intelligence—both intellectual and emotional. It requires knowledge and competence in the area of focus. It requires courage, honesty, integrity, and tenacity. In short, it requires the kinds of qualities we should be seeking in every candidate running for public office and every person we place in positions of power. Fortunately, we have a lot of really smart, competent, and well-meaning people in this country with access to virtually unlimited data. We just need to find them and use them.

"As Thomas Jefferson once said, 'An educated citizenry is a vital requisite for our survival as a free people.' He also said, 'An enlightened citizenry is indispensable for the proper functioning of a republic. Self-government is not possible unless the citizens are educated sufficiently to enable them to exercise oversight.' As citizens, regardless of our political affiliation, our first duty is to inform ourselves on the issues and the candidates, and then cast our ballots for those who have the necessary attributes and intention to contribute to a political environment committed to finding the best practical solutions to our nation's problems. Most importantly, we need every sane, rational, and objective adult citizen to stand up, suit up, and show up to vote so we can take this country back from the deluded minority that threatens our democracy."

"Wow, that was quite a speech," Donnelly responded. "Sounds like you've been taking lessons from Barack Obama."

"Yeah, I tend to get on my soapbox when I talk about politics, but it's an area that I'm passionate about, and I really worry about the direction in which this country is going. The hyper-partisanship and divisiveness in this country are reaching critical mass, and I'm afraid that it may lead to an outright civil war if we can't find a way to effectively deal with the problems we face. But I must tell you, it's really nice to be able to discuss issues like these in an open and civil manner, even when we might disagree. It's too bad our politicians can't do the same."

"Well, I can't argue with that," Donnelly replied. "I just can't see us actually being able to accomplish any of it, given the level of political dysfunction in this country. So, who are you going to vote for—Hillary or Trump?"

"Well, Hillary may have her flaws, as does any candidate, but she has the intelligence, experience, and temperament to do the job. I think she would be a good choice for the first female president of our country. On the other hand, Trump, in my opinion, is a vile, vicious, vindictive, and venal human being. I don't think he has the knowledge, wisdom, or moral character to be President of the United States. In fact, I think he is exactly the kind of person who would lead us into a civil war. So, who do you think I'm going to vote for? How about you? Who are you for?"

"Well," Donnelly replied, "my parents were Republicans, virtually all of my family are Republicans, and I have voted a straight Republican ticket my whole life, so I guess I'm going to have to vote for Trump, even though a lot of what he says, I think, is total bullshit. I do like the fact that he is a self-made businessman and not a career politician. Does that make me the enemy in your world?"

"No," Reynolds answered. "I try never to judge a person because of their political beliefs because I think we are basically hard-wired to lean toward one end or the other of the political spectrum. I've read research studies that suggest the brains of liberals and conservatives are structurally different. The gray matter in a part of the cortex that governs reasoning and decision-making tends to be larger in liberals, while conservatives tend to have a larger amygdala, which affects emotional memory, fear, and aggression.

"There has also been research that indicates that 30–60 percent of the variance in social and political attitudes is due to genetic influences, and other research shows that liberal and conservative brains process information differently. They've also found that social learning while growing up contributes to engrained attitudes and beliefs that affect how we interpret information. So, again, I don't judge people for their beliefs, but it does concern me that otherwise intelligent people cannot accept hard facts and objective empirical evidence in making judgments on political candidates or policy decisions.

"As to Trump being a self-made man. You do know that he was born into a wealthy family and was raised with a silver spoon in his mouth? His father paid to send him to the best private schools and colleges and then gave him a job in his real estate business, making

$200,000 a year. He gave Trump a million dollars and access to his network of business connections and eventually turned over his company to him. *The New York Times* has reported that over the decades, Trump has received over $400 million from his father, either directly or through loans or various tax scams. On top of that, his businesses have declared bankruptcy at least four times. Does that sound like a self-made man to you? With that kind of backing, even you and I could become billionaires."

"Hillary Clinton wasn't exactly born into a life of poverty either," Donnelly responded.

"True, her dad was a successful small businessman, and she had the advantage of a strong middle-class upbringing and was able to attend some prestigious colleges, but Hillary has demonstrated her intellect and competence from an early age. Everything she accomplished, she did pretty much on her own. You can't say the same for Trump. This is the guy who bragged about being able to touch women's genitals and get away with it and has been accused of sexual assault by at least a dozen women. He's been associated with the New York mob, had to pay a $25-million settlement over the Trump University scam, and has had one scandal after another for decades. On top of that, every other statement that comes out of his mouth is either an exaggeration or an outright lie. He has the maturity of a kindergartner, with all his belittling nicknames and petulant behavior, and he's obviously a classic narcissist, if not a psychopath, who doesn't give a damn about anyone but himself. Frankly, I think he's nothing but a charlatan, a grifter, and a thug—and this is a guy you would support for President of the United States?"

"Well, Hillary has not exactly been immune from scandal either," Donnelly replied. "How about Travelgate, the Whitewater affair, the Vince Foster suicide, Benghazi, and her latest email debacle?"

"Well, as I said earlier, Hillary may be a flawed candidate," Reynolds said, "but each of those situations was thoroughly investigated, and no criminal charges or administrative sanctions were ever levied against either Bill or Hillary in those situations. I think that she has exhibited some poor judgment over the years, but nothing compared to Trump."

"I suppose you think that a person would have to be stupid to vote for Trump," Donnelly retorted.

"Well, no offense—seriously—but if I did think that way, I would not be the first to attribute that label to conservatives," Reynolds replied. "The English philosopher John Stuart Mill, in a speech to Parliament back in the nineteenth century, when confronted over the allegation that he had called conservatives stupid, said, 'I never meant to say that the Conservatives are stupid. I meant to say that stupid people are generally Conservatives.' Then you have Bobby Jindal, the governor of Louisiana, stating back in 2013 at a meeting of the Republican conference, 'We must stop being the stupid party.' And then there's Jared Kushner, Trump's son-in-law, who admitted that Trump lies to his base because he thinks they're stupid. Trump himself, after the Nevada caucus last February, said, 'I love the poorly educated,' after receiving a majority of their votes. Unfortunately, the modern Republican Party, under Trump, seems to be driven by the lowest common denominator of its members and by an agenda centered around authoritarianism, isolationism, xenophobia, homophobia, misogyny, racism, evangelical religious belief, and white nationalism.

"For myself, as I observe the actions of conservative politicians in recent years, there are several other words and phrases that come to mind, such as narrow-minded, short-sighted, arrogant, vindictive, amoral, unethical, lacking integrity, resistant to change, governed by self-interest, and so secure in their blindered perspective of what is good for the people and the country that they totally disregard rational argument, empirical evidence, public opinion, historical fact, and demonstrated need. I'm sorry, but that is just my opinion, and it has no reflection on you. I have known some very good, salt-of-the-earth people in my life who are dyed-in-the-wool conservatives, yourself included."

"No offense taken," Donnelly replied. "I respect the fact you're not afraid to voice your opinion. I can't say I agree with everything you said, but you make a good case. It will give me something to think about."

The radio crackled. "Two-George-Three, we have a report of a nude couple walking down Capitol near East Union Street. Can you handle?"

"Two-George-Three, en route," Reynolds replied. Then, in an aside to Donnelly, "We don't have to rush to this call—there will probably be ten other cars that beat us there."

They made their way to Capitol Avenue and headed north. Sure enough, just as they approached Pine Street, they observed a young white male and female walking hand-in-hand, totally nude, down the sidewalk—and, surprisingly, they were the only car to have responded. Reynolds pulled to the curb beside the couple and Donnelly got out and directed them over to the squad car while Reynolds retrieved two blankets from the trunk. "Guess there is not much use in patting them down," Reynolds quipped as he wrapped each of them in a blanket and placed them in the rear seat of the patrol car.

"Okay," Donnelly said after getting back into the car, "do you mind telling us what occasioned this little bare-assed stroll today?"

The young man, who was probably in his early twenties, with long, stringy hair and a scraggly beard, replied, "We're just doing what John told us to do."

"And who is John, and what exactly did he tell you?" Donnelly responded.

"John Lennon," the boy replied. "He came to me in a dream last night and told me to meet him at the Mary Emmanuel Church today for a jam session."

"And was John there when you arrived today?" Reynolds asked.

"He was," the boy replied. "We jammed for a while on our guitars, and then he said we needed to cleanse our minds and bodies by walking naked down Broadway."

"Have either of you been taking any drugs today?" Donnelly queried.

"Only a couple of hits of LSD this morning," the boy responded. "Just enough to really get into the music."

"Okay," Donnelly said, "I'm afraid we're going to have to take you down to the station, kids. Are you both over eighteen?"

Both nodded their heads affirmatively.

"Are your clothes still at the church?" Donnelly added.

Again, they nodded, seemingly unperturbed by the fact that they were going to jail. They cuddled against each other, held hands, and seemed to blissfully enjoy the ride downtown.

Reynolds stopped by the church on the way and found their clothes and an old guitar on one of the back pews. He collected them and then continued to the jail. After having both checked by medical and obtaining a urine sample from each, they were booked for indecent exposure and for suspicion of being under the influence of an intoxicating drug.

Tawnya was highly amused that evening when Reynolds filled her in on his day's activities. "Your job never gets old, does it?" she said.

"Oh, it gets a little tedious at times," Reynolds replied, "but, fortunately, there are enough interesting and/or adrenaline-producing calls to keep you from getting bored."

CHAPTER 23

THE BEGINNING OF THE END

The following Friday morning dawned clear and warm. When Nancy's voice pierced the silence, Reynolds, almost automatically now, reached out to pull Tawnya close to him. She immediately rolled over and flung her arms around him. They engaged in a long, passionate kiss, which led, inevitably, to a heated bout of intercourse. When finished, they forced themselves to get up, put on their workout clothes, and go through their familiar routine of yoga and a morning run.

After a coed shower and breakfast, they sat at the kitchen table, drinking their third cup of coffee. "What do you have on your agenda today?" Dan asked.

"We have both an afternoon matinee performance and then an evening performance tonight," she responded. "I probably won't be home until midnight again."

"Okay, babe," Dan replied, "I'll try to keep myself entertained until you get home."

"Have a safe day, my dear," Tawnya said as she headed out the door.

"Break a leg," Dan replied.

It was a pleasant bike ride into the city, and Reynolds was in a chipper mood when he met Donnelly in the Crime Analysis Unit.

"It's going to be a great day, partner," Reynolds said as he greeted Donnelly.

"I hope you're right," Donnelly replied. "I woke up with a sense of dread in my bones this morning."

They hit the street after roll call and were immediately dispatched to take a runaway report. No sooner had they finished that than they were sent on a barking dog complaint.

"Looks like our day for chippy calls," Donnelly remarked.

It was approaching 3:00 p.m. when suddenly the radio blared, "Attention all units, robbery in progress at the Bank of America, 3212 East Magenta Way South. Units responding?"

Donnelly immediately got on the radio, "Two-George-Three, from 2000 block of Empire."

Donnelly flipped on the emergency lights but not the siren. Within five minutes, they were pulling up to the bank. Donnelly parked the squad car at an angle in the roadway just west of the front entrance to the building. "Two-George-Three, arrived," Donnelly calmly stated into the mike. "We'll take the west side front and back."

Donnelly unlocked the shotgun from its rack and told Reynolds to get the AR-15 from the trunk and cover the rear exit of the bank. Donnelly racked a round of 00 buck into the chamber and took a position behind the driver's door.

. . . .

A black Cadillac Escalade bearing stolen license plates sat parked in the lot of a warehouse facility two blocks from the Bank of America on East Magenta Way South. Inside, four men, each wearing black ballistics vests over black hooded sweatshirts, sat observing the bank as the Wells Fargo armored car pulled up in front. The driver of the Caddy, Tyrone Banks, looked at his imitation Rolex. The time was 2:30 p.m. As the guard in the armored car began unloading numerous bags of cash onto a four-wheeled cart, the man next to Banks in the passenger seat, Benny Malone, began to speak. "All right, let's go over the plan one more time. Ty, you're going to drop us at the back entrance and then drive across the street to the parking lot in front of the bank. Your job is to be the lookout and to stop any cops who might roll up. Are you up for it?"

Banks had given that question a lot of thought over the past week. He and some bros had taken out those two white dudes who had welched on their drug debt a few years ago, and he had justified that as necessary to maintain his street cred, which was the basis for his livelihood. The prospect of killing a cop, though, was a little more daunting for him. He had convinced himself that this bank job was critical to his future survival and that he had to do whatever it took to pull it off. He also had come up with a less selfish justification. *I'm doing this for every Black dude who has ever been unjustly killed by the po-lice*, he had thought to himself.

"I'm good," Banks answered.

"Okay, let's make sure that walkie-talkie is working," Malone said.

Banks turned on the little walkie-talkie unit and turned up the volume as Malone counted—one, two, three—into the one he was carrying.

"Duke, you're going to take out that cop they have working as a bank guard," Malone, who had cased the bank earlier in the day, continued. "He's a fat fuck who probably doesn't know which side he keeps his gun holstered, so you shouldn't have to kill him. We're going in fast and will probably catch him by surprise, so just disarm him and cuff him up with his own cuffs if you can.

"Slick, your job is to take the bank tellers and any customers who might be inside. Make sure those tellers don't have time to push any alarm buttons, get 'em all spread-eagled on the floor, and keep them covered.

"I will take the bank manager and make him open the safe, then load all the cash into these duffel bags. Ty, I'll give you a heads-up over the walkie-talkie when we're coming out. Get your ass in front of that bank fast, but we don't want to arouse suspicion driving away in case we pass any cops. Just four guys out for a leisurely drive, got it?"

Each of the other three individuals in the car nodded their heads. Banks took a small glass capsule out of his hoody pocket. "Anyone want a hit of coke?" he asked. He passed the capsule around, and each man poured a little on the back of his hand and snorted it.

"That's good shit," Slick commented as they observed the armored car pull out of the bank parking lot.

"Okay, let's roll," Malone exclaimed.

Banks wheeled the Caddy through the bank parking lot to the back entrance. Benny, Duke, and Slick pulled on the black ski masks they were carrying, grabbed the AK-47s by their sides, bailed quickly out of the car, and sprinted to the back door of the bank. Banks immediately drove around the bank and across the street to the parking lot in front of the building, where he parked with a view of vehicles approaching from either direction.

As he sat there with the engine running, nervously glancing up and down the street in front of him, his mind returned to another scenario he had been envisioning since they had begun planning this hit. He saw himself lying in a hammock in front of a white adobe casa overlooking a sandy beach and a broad expanse of water in front of him. Several small children, including a couple of his own, were running around in the yard playing tag while he lay there drinking a cold cerveza. A beautiful Mexican senorita would emerge from the casa periodically to see if he needed another beer, and he would grab her tight little ass as she walked away. *That's going to be my life*, he thought to himself.

Suddenly, out of the corner of his eye, he saw a white vehicle with red and blue flashing lights approaching from the north. "Fuck," he thought to himself, "the cops are here." He watched through the dark tinted windows of the Escalade as the squad car pulled up in the street in front of the bank, and two cops quickly emerged. He instantly recognized them as the two cops who had busted him two weeks earlier for prostitution, which aroused a strong feeling of anger and resentment inside him.

One cop grabbed an assault rifle from the trunk and ran toward the rear of the bank. The other, who he further recognized as the guy who had been shaking down the Blackbird and Snookers for years, pulled out a shotgun and set up behind the open driver's-side front door.

Another wave of emotion—this time fear mixed with anger and a strong sense of duty—swept over Banks. He grabbed the AK-47 from the seat next to him, cranked a round into the chamber, flicked off the safety, and then stood up through the open sunroof of the Caddie. He laid the forearm of the rifle across his left hand, which he rested on the roof of the vehicle, grasped the pistol grip with his right hand, and peered through the attached scope. He assumed the cop was wearing a bulletproof vest, so he moved the crosshairs of the scope up to where they centered on the back of his head. He inhaled and exhaled deeply, then squeezed the trigger.

. . . .

Reynolds grabbed the AR and ran in a crouch down the side of the bank to a position behind a dumpster in the rear. He cranked a round into the chamber and tried—unsuccessfully—to see into the bank through its mirrored rear windows. Within seconds, another patrol unit had pulled up in the alley behind the bank, and Reynolds motioned for them to set up on the east side of the building. Almost simultaneously, he heard the crack of a rifle at the front of the bank. He motioned to the other officers that he was going to the front and started running down the side of the building. He looked in the direction of his squad car but could not see Donnelly. Then, a black Cadillac Escalade roared out from the parking lot across the street and pulled up in front of the bank.

Reynolds ran to the corner of the building and quickly peeked around. Seeing only the black Caddy stopped at the curb, he moved in a crabwalk to his patrol car with the AR to his cheek and his aim directed toward the front of the bank. As he rounded the rear of the patrol car, he immediately saw Donnelly. He was sprawled on the ground, face down beside the car. Reynolds saw at once that the top of his head had been completely blown off and instantly realized there was nothing he could do to help Donnelly but take down his killers. Reynolds was now in full combat mode as his mind and body reverted to his days in Iraq and Afghanistan.

He moved to a position in front of the driver's-side front door, placed the bipod of the AR on the hood, trained his sights on the front of the bank, and waited. The Navy Seals' mantra, 'Slow is smooth, smooth is fast,' ran through his head as he cleared his mind and focused his attention on the front of the bank and the Escalade. At that moment, he saw a figure emerge from the front door of the bank. Instinctively, all the years of training in target identification and acquisition and his combat experience in insurgency operations crystalized in his brain. Everything seemed to be happening in slow motion. His optic nerve sent a message to his brain: *Large figure wearing a black ski mask and a ballistics vest carrying an assault rifle—definitely foe.* Almost simultaneously, he took a full breath, let out half, and held it as he centered his front sight just below the figure's left ear—and squeezed the trigger. The figure's head exploded. Immediately, his attention was drawn to two other similarly dressed figures coming out of the bank directly behind the first. Reynolds shifted his aim slightly to the second figure's head and squeezed off another round with the same result, then shifted his aim again and took out the third suspect.

A thought, *Disable the car*, shot through his head. He rotated slightly and fired three more rounds, taking out the driver's-side front tire and both rear tires of the Escalade. His attention then shifted to the driver, and he drew a bead on the front door opening. The door was suddenly flung open, followed immediately by the driver's left leg emerging from the vehicle. The driver began to swivel in his seat, and Reynolds saw the barrel of a rifle emerge and swing in his direction. Reynolds zeroed in on the largest area of body mass he could see and touched off a round. He could see the suspect's upper-right arm tear loose from the shoulder. His next thought was *Keep him from running*, so he shifted his aim to the exposed left leg and put a round into his left thigh, six inches above the knee. The driver reflexively lurched forward, grabbing his leg. The next thought to race through his mind was *That's the son of a bitch who killed my partner*. With that thought, Reynolds aimed at his left ear and fired one more shot. The .223 Remington bullet struck just above the ear and immediately began tumbling, creating an impact so powerful that it blew the upper-right side of Tyrone Bank's head completely away, splattering blood and brain matter all over the inside of the vehicle's door.

As this was happening, two additional patrol units had pulled up in front of the bank on the other side of the Escalade. Reynolds, recognizing that the situation was not yet completely neutralized, yelled, "Cover me!" as he sprinted in a low crouch over to the Caddy, rifle at the ready. He immediately confirmed the driver was dead and there was no one else in the car. He then motioned two of the patrol officers to move to the east-side front corner of the bank while he covered them.

The two officers reached the building and started moving toward the large windows at the front of the bank. When they peeked inside, a man in a business suit gave them a thumbs-up.

"Looks clear," one of them shouted.

Reynolds yelled, "Follow me in," and then proceeded in a low crouch, rifle at the ready, to the front door. One of the officers opened the door, and Reynolds and the other officer burst in, taking up positions on either side. Doing a quick scan of the bank, Reynolds saw two young Black females and a young white male behind the tellers' stations; four other people were spread-eagled on the floor, and a man in a grey suit was running towards them. Reynolds trained his weapon on the man and ordered him to get on his knees and put his hands behind his head.

"I'm the bank manager!" the man yelled.

Reynolds looked to the tellers behind the counter, and they all nodded affirmatively. "Is anyone hurt?" Reynolds yelled.

"No," the bank manager responded.

Reynolds keyed his portable radio and announced, "Bank of America is Code 4. We have four suspects down and apparently DOA. We will need Medic 1, the coroner, a forensics team, and the detectives to respond."

Reynolds exhaled deeply and stood up, still fired with adrenaline. He directed the two patrol officers to secure the scene and not let anyone in or out. He announced to the occupants of the bank, "Please stay put and do not discuss the situation with anyone until you are interviewed by the detectives." He then went outside and checked all four suspects. All had severe trauma to the head, and all—except for Banks—had obviously died instantly. By that time, several other patrol units and a patrol sergeant had arrived and were taking control of the scene.

Reynolds forced himself to walk back to his patrol car. As he walked around to the driver's side, the sight of Donnelly's body hit him like a sledgehammer. He instantly felt all the strength in his body flow out and he sank down to his knees beside the body.

Reflexively, he placed his hand on Donnelly's back and shook him, trying to revive him, even while knowing that it was way too late. Suddenly, all the pent-up emotion of years of loss—his mother and father dying, then so many of his friends and comrades-in-arms in the war being killed, and now his partner, who he had only known for a short time but with whom he had developed an indelible bond—burst inside him. He had never cried before when confronted with death, but now he could not help himself. He began sobbing uncontrollably, his body racked with spasms of grief.

After what seemed like hours but in reality, was only minutes, he regained some composure and grew quiet. He felt a hand on his shoulder and looked up to see his sergeant standing over him.

"Did *you* take them out?" the sergeant asked in a sensitive manner.

Reynolds nodded affirmatively.

"I'll need your weapon," the sergeant continued, taking the AR-15 from Reynolds' hands. "The detectives will want to talk with you."

The sergeant helped Reynolds to his feet, led him to the detectives' unmarked car, and placed him in the back seat. The next two hours passed in a blur. Two Robbery/Homicide detectives came back to the car and drove him to Headquarters, where they painstakingly took a video-recorded statement from him and then had him meet with the Department psychologist to determine his mental state. Reynolds vaguely remembered the chief of police coming up to him in the detectives' office, shaking his hand, and telling him that he was being placed on indefinite administrative leave with pay, pending the results of the investigation. The chief had looked him in the eyes and said, "I'm also putting you in for the Medal of Valor, son—you deserve it. Take all the time you need, and don't worry; your job will be here when you get back."

Eventually, the detectives released him and asked if he needed a ride home. Reynolds said no, that he needed the bike ride home to think. He started off slowly, maneuvering through downtown traffic, but when he hit the road around Lake Union, he opened up to full speed, trying to drive the feelings of emptiness and despair from his body. He got home and collapsed in his recliner. For the first time in his life, he felt like he would like a stiff drink, or maybe a dozen, to drown the emotions inside him. He settled for a cup of green tea and sat in silence in the dark, trying to erase the image of Donnelly's head from his mind.

The door burst open just before midnight, and Tawnya ran into the living room. She immediately threw herself on Reynolds' prostrate form in the recliner and pulled him to her.

"Oh, baby," she cried. "I just heard about what happened on the radio driving home. Were you involved? Who was killed?"

Reynolds nodded his head affirmatively and managed to utter in a choked voice, "It was Donnelly," then could not contain himself any longer. He started sobbing uncontrollably as he pressed his face into Tawnya's shoulder. They lay wrapped in each other's arms for many minutes, perhaps an hour, until Tawnya arose and, taking Reynolds by the hand, led him to the bedroom.

"We'll get through this together," she said as she stripped Reynolds of his clothes and laid him in the bed, then undressed herself and crawled in beside him. They entwined themselves in each other's arms and eventually drifted off, although it was a fitful night of sleep for each of them.

CHAPTER 24

THE RENEWAL

Reynolds woke early the next morning and lay spooning with Tawnya for over an hour, his mind racing, reliving the events of the previous day. Tawnya eventually stirred, stretched, and rolled over to face him, then spent several moments looking deep into his eyes.

Finally, she said, even while knowing the answer, "You've got something on your mind, my love. What is it?"

Dan hesitated for a moment before replying. "I've got to go to the mountains." He again hesitated before adding, "Alone."

"I understand," Tawnya said. "How soon will you be leaving?"

"Tomorrow morning," Dan replied.

Tawnya just nodded, then reached out and pulled Dan to her. They hugged each other tightly and lay that way for another half-hour. Finally, Dan disengaged and rolled out of bed.

"I've got to get ready," he said and walked to the bathroom to pee. It was the first morning since their first night together that they hadn't made love to start their day, but Tawnya understood that Dan was emotionally drained. She got up, showered and got dressed, then came out to find Dan drinking coffee on the lanai. She poured herself a cup and sat down beside him.

"I'm supposed to go in early today," she said. "We have an afternoon performance in Tacoma, and I have to help get all our costumes and props loaded. I'll probably be late getting home. That is unless you would like me to take the day off?"

Dan looked at her and nodded. "That's okay, babe. I need to get ready to go anyway."

After a quick breakfast of hot oatmeal and toast, Tawnya headed out the door, knowing in her heart that Dan needed this time alone. Dan began pulling his backpacking equipment out of the small storage locker on the lanai. He started checking things off his camping checklist and packing them in his old Kelty Expedition external frame pack. He checked the weather channel to see the forecast for the next week or so and was pleasantly surprised to find that it was supposed to be clear all week. He packed his rain gear anyway, just in case, and threw in a wool shirt and down vest for the cool mornings and evenings. The final item on his list was the Nikon DSLR camera with a zoom macro lens that he always took with him to the field.

Around 9:00 a.m., he headed down to Capitol Hill to the REI store to stock up on freeze-dried meals and to get the topographic maps he would need for the trip. He had been tentatively planning on doing a weeklong trip into the Goat Rocks area in the Cascades for his next vacation and figured now would be a good time to do it. There was a thirty-mile trail that connected a chain of high mountain lakes he had always wanted to fish.

Dan kept himself busy most of the afternoon, putting Sno-Seal on his hiking boots, tying some wet flies to replenish his little tackle box, and organizing and packing his backpack. By 5:00 p.m. he had his pack ready to go and stowed by the front door, and the clothes he was going to wear laid out on the couch. He was getting a little hungry, so he pulled the steak he had thawed out of the fridge and threw it on the grill while he cooked a baked potato in the microwave along with some frozen vegetables.

After eating and cleaning up, Dan retired to the living room, where he pulled up his "Blues Favorites" playlist on his iPod and plugged it into his receiver. He was definitely in the mood for some down-home blues and spent the evening sprawled out on his recliner in front of the electric fireplace listening to Walter Trout, the King boys—B.B., Albert, and Freddie—Josh White, Buddy Guy, and Big Mama Thornton, among others. At some point, he drifted off to sleep, only to be awakened by Tawnya when she rolled in a little after midnight. They were both exhausted and immediately headed to the bedroom. Within minutes they had stripped, crawled into bed, snuggled up, and fallen fast asleep.

Reynolds willed himself to wake up early the next morning. At 4:30 a.m. his eyes popped open. He glanced quickly at the digital clock next to the bed and then, carefully disengaging from Tawnya so as not to wake her, rolled out of bed. He dressed quickly in the living room, got the two cold liter bottles of water from the fridge, did a final rundown of his camping checklist to make sure he had everything, went quietly into the bedroom to give Tawnya a gentle kiss on the cheek, then threw the straps of the backpack over his shoulders and headed out the door.

He wanted to do a little carb-loading before hitting the trail, so his first stop was the 24-hour IHOP on University Drive. After a large breakfast of strawberry waffles, eggs, link sausage, and a couple of cups of coffee, he jumped in the Jeep and headed for Snoqualmie Pass. An hour and a half later, he pulled into the parking lot at the ski resort. He tightened up the laces on his hiking boots, checked the zippers and straps on his backpack to make sure they were closed and tight, donned the seventy-pound pack, and headed for the Pacific Crest Trailhead. It was just a little after 8:00 a.m.

It was fifteen miles to his first destination, a fairly large mountain lake at the bottom of the chain. The first ten miles required a lot of steep climbing over several ridges, but the last five pretty much paralleled a beautiful little creek running down the mountain. Dan stopped for a quick snack around 11:00 a.m. and decided, just for shits and giggles, to drop a dry fly in the creek to see what might happen. He tied an elk-hair caddis onto his leader and crept, low and slow, up to a small eddy at the base of a riffle. He gently tossed the fly into the riffle and let it float downstream. Almost instantly, he got a strike. He played the small fish for a few minutes and then reeled it to the bank. It was a nice little eight-inch rainbow. He didn't want to keep it, so he carefully removed the barbless hook and held the fish in the water for a moment before allowing it to swim away.

Dan stowed his fly rod and fishing tackle and headed back up the trail. From that point, it was a very pleasant hike on a wide pine-straw trail with only moderate elevation gain most of the way. The last half-mile into the lake involved some relatively steep switchbacks, but Dan soon found himself cresting a ridge and looking down at the pristine little lake. It was only three in the afternoon.

He found a nice flat area near the outlet to the creek, which already had a primitive firepit, to set up camp. He threw out a ground cloth and pitched his one-man Eureka tent as close to the creek as he could. He propped up his backpack with his hiking stick near the firepit and got out his fly rod. *Might as well try to catch a fish for dinner*, he thought.

He put together the four-piece fly rod, strung his line, and tied a pheasant-tail nymph onto his leader. Then he grabbed his fishing vest, tied his small fishing net onto the ring at the back, put the little aluminum tackle box in the back pocket, and headed out around the lake until he found the inlet. There were some large rocks near the shore by the inlet, so he mounted one and began casting into the deep pool that the inlet flowed into. He used a slow, slightly jerky retrieve, and on the third cast, he felt a fish hit his fly.

The fish immediately ran, and Dan raised his rod tip and let the slack line at his feet run between his forefinger and thumb as he tried to keep the line between the rod and the fish taut. The slack line soon ran out, and the fish began pulling against the drag. Occasionally, the fish would turn, and Dan would have to reel furiously to keep the line tight, then it would go on another run. On the third run, Dan saw that he was down to the backing on his reel. After about twenty minutes of this, the fish began to tire. Dan started cranking in the line on the reel. The fish would comply for a while and then go on another run. Dan kept the line taut and the tip up as he again began reeling the fish in when, unexpectedly, the fish came completely out of the water and did a somersault in the air. Dan could see the sun reflect off its silver sides. It was huge.

Finally, after another ten to fifteen minutes, Dan was able to bring the fish to the bank. He knelt on his rock perch and snatched the fish up in his net. It was a beautiful hybrid cutthroat trout, about twenty-four inches long, with a bright red patch on its gills. Dan recalled that Fish and Game had stocked this area years ago with these cutthroat and, apparently, they had been thriving. *This fish is too nice to keep unless you're going to mount it*, he said to himself as he removed the hook from its mouth and placed it back in the water, then watched it swim away.

Dan tried a few more casts and hooked into a fifteen-inch rainbow, which he placed in his creel. He headed back to his campsite, where he started a small Indian fire in the fire pit and then went down to the lake to clean his fish.

The fire had soon burned down to some white-hot coals, so Dan perched his aluminum grill on some rocks around the fire pit and placed the fish, wrapped in aluminum foil, onto the grill. He had already cooked up a pot of red beans and rice on his small camp stove and was soon enjoying a delicious fish dinner. After dining and cleaning up his dishes, he threw a couple more logs on the fire, brewed up a cup of tea, and sat back on his sitting pad to watch as the sun dipped below the ridge to the west of the lake. He breathed deeply of the fresh mountain air and let the quiet and solitude permeate his being. For the moment, he felt at peace with the world.

The peace didn't last. Around 9:00 p.m., Dan doused the fire, straightened up his camp, and retired to his tent. He crawled into the down mummy bag, donned his headlamp, and read a couple of chapters of *Thus Spoke Zarathustra* by Friedrich Nietzsche. It was pretty heavy reading, and he soon found his eyelids starting to droop and his concentration drifting. He put down the book and drifted off to sleep, only to awaken in a cold sweat a couple of hours later. He had a nightmare in which the half-headless figure of Mick Donnelly, along with a contingent of the soldiers, marines, and airmen he had seen die in the wars, had appeared at his apartment door and begun screaming at him for not having saved them.

He lay there for some time, wracking his brain for something more he could have done to save any of them, but he could not think of anything. He finally drifted back off to sleep, but it was a fitful night.

The next morning, he again grabbed his fly rod and headed back down to the inlet. Within thirty minutes, he had caught two nice twelve-inch rainbows and was soon smelling them grilling over his fire. He finished off the remains of the red beans and rice with his fish, then cleaned his dishes and decided to spend the day just kicking back and reading.

The next morning, he got up early and made a quick breakfast of oatmeal and a bagel, then began packing up his gear. Within an hour, he was shouldering the backpack and heading higher up the mountain. It was only a ten-mile hike to the next lake, and he was there by 1:00 p.m.

It was a beautiful afternoon, so, after setting up his camp, he decided to climb the rock outcropping overlooking the lake. It looked like it was only 200–300 feet high and that the route would be mainly boulder-hopping, with no technical climbing required. Going up was a piece of cake. He clawed his way up the steep rock face until he reached the relatively flat top. By this time, it was about two in the afternoon, and the sun was at its warmest. On a whim, he stripped off his clothes and lay naked and spread-eagled on the warm, flat rock, doing his best impression of Da Vinci's "Vitruvian Man," the symbol of man as the universe. He lay there for over an hour, just soaking up the warmth of the sun and breathing deeply while repeating his meditation mantra in his mind.

Eventually, he felt a slight chill as the sun started dipping below the western peaks. He dressed and carefully made his way down the rock face. It proved much more difficult than going up because, several times, he could not see the footholds and had to support his weight with his hands while he explored with his feet to find some purchase. He eventually made it down and got back to camp around 4:00 p.m.

He was feeling kind of fished out, so decided to just cook up one of the freeze-dried meals he had brought. He settled on the beef stew, boiled up some water, added it to the freeze-dried ingredients, and, within minutes, had a plate of hot beef stew.

After dinner, he figured he would try Nietzsche again, so he sat next to the fire on his sitting pad and read by the light of his headlamp until he could feel his eyelids drooping. He crawled into his sleeping bag and was soon fast asleep. Fortunately, he was able to sleep through the night without any frightful interruptions.

He spent the next day taking some short hikes to explore the area around the lake. He spent about an hour watching and photographing a mule deer doe and her fawn grazing in a small meadow not far from the lake. He went to bed early that evening and was up and at 'em by six the next morning.

The hike into the third lake in the chain was shorter but much steeper, and the trail was rocky and rough. Reynolds had to cross several slippery talus slopes and negotiate a number of very steep pitches to reach the lake, which was nestled in an amphitheater-like cirque that had been carved out by a glacier. The little five-acre lake was fed by snow melt from the surrounding mountaintop. There was an outlet on the north side that fed a small creek running down the mountain.

Reynolds found a nice little place to camp beside the babbling creek and set up his tent. He suspected that the lake might be barren but decided to give it a try anyway. He set up his fly rod and walked around the lake until he found a nice rock he could fish from. Then, he sat down with his back to another rock and just watched to see if he could see any fish rising. Sure enough, within minutes, he saw several fish breaking the water about thirty feet offshore. He mounted his rock and began casting. Thirty minutes later, he was walking back to his camp with a nice cutthroat. Apparently, they had stocked this lake as well.

Reynolds spent two and a half days at this lake, just fishing, reading, meditating, going through his yoga routine, and relaxing while soaking up the wonders of nature. By the end of the third day, he was beginning to feel whole again. The horrid emptiness had seemed to drain from his body. He decided he was ready to go home.

CHAPTER 25

TAWNYA'S MUSE

Tawnya awoke Monday morning to the sound of Nancy Wilson's rendition of "The Masquerade Is Over." Still half-asleep, she reflexively rolled over to put her arm around Dan, only to find he was not there. Her eyes popped open as she examined his side of the bed and found it empty. Then she remembered—*Dan has gone to the mountains*. She rolled onto her back and lay there for a few minutes while the recollection of last Friday's events flooded back into her consciousness. Her eyes welled with tears as she thought about Dan sobbing on her shoulder with a look of absolute despair in his eyes. She remembered her own slight feeling of rejection the next morning when he announced that he was going off by himself to the mountains, even though she understood that in his mind, this was something he had to process alone. As she thought of him lying by himself in his sleeping bag this morning, she could only hope that he was finding some peace, as much as she wished that he was lying next to her, where she could comfort him. A random thought jumped into her head: *I'm so glad he did not take his gun.*

Then suddenly, inexplicably, she felt a mild cramping in her lower abdomen and then an urgent need to pee. She got up and started toward the bathroom when a wave of nausea overcame her, and she barely made it to the toilet before throwing up. *Shit*, she said to herself, *I hope I'm not getting sick.*

Tawnya slipped on her robe and slippers and padded out to the kitchen, where the coffee maker was spitting out the last vestiges of freshly brewed coffee into the carafe. She poured herself a cup and headed for the lanai as the sun was casting its first warm rays onto the balcony.

As Tawnya stretched out on the chaise lounge and sipped the hot brew, she allowed her mind to retrace the extraordinary events of the last month and a half. She recalled that first afternoon at The Harbor when she had seen two cops enter the restaurant and had not been able to take her eyes off the tall, athletic-looking younger one in his neatly pressed blue uniform. She remembered bribing another server so she could wait their table and then the spark of attraction in his eyes when their gaze had first met. She had not been able to get him out of her mind for the next two days, and then, lo and behold, the two officers had come back. Never one to deny herself pleasure, she had felt compelled to initiate a connection and had passed him her phone number, not really expecting that he would call her at all, and certainly not the very next morning—and then to invite her to breakfast on their first date—but it had turned out wonderfully. He had seemed so interested in her life and interests and goals that she had felt truly validated as a person as she described her privileged childhood, her early introduction to dance, her goal of someday being a prima ballerina in a major dance troupe, and her year abroad studying dance in France. Although he had been a little more circumspect in talking about his own life, Tawnya had felt nothing but respect and admiration for the choices he had made and what he had experienced. She was truly sad that she had had to end their time together so soon that day, but then came the nightly phone calls and the easy banter as they discussed each other's day, and the more serious exchanges as they opined on current events in the country. She had been amazed at how closely aligned their social and political beliefs were.

Then came that fateful second date, ostensibly a lunch date, but that turned into a daylong hike in the mountains followed by pizza at his apartment and then kicking back listening to music in front of an artificial fire. She had never remotely considered sleeping with Dan that night, but the day had been so perfect, and she had felt such a strong physical attraction to him that she could not help herself when he had looked into her eyes with that expression of sincere and genuine affection.

Since then, their relationship had been a white-hot inferno that revolved around the best sex she had ever had, sex that she often initiated; but, as much as she enjoyed it, she could not deny the latent doubt in her mind, born of years of her Black ancestors' repression, that Dan, who could probably have any woman he wanted, could fall in love with a Black girl. Then, there had been the burgeoning concern that Dan only thought of her as a novel sex toy, a new experience that he would someday tire of and move on. She had to admit to herself that Dan had never been anything but loving and caring towards her, and that he had told her of the vow he had made to himself never to get involved in a relationship that was not based on real trust, respect, and true mutual affection, but there was still that lingering thought in her mind: *What does a young, virile, good-looking white guy want with a Black girl, other than sex?*

As she took another sip of her coffee, she again felt an urgent need to pee. *That's unusual*, she thought. Then, as she was heading back to the lanai, an even more disturbing thought crossed her mind. *My period is late—could I possibly be pregnant?*

She refilled her coffee cup and returned to the lanai. Immediately, thoughts about the ramifications of being pregnant raced through her head. Her lifelong dream of being a prima ballerina in a major international dance company would be dashed. She had long envisioned traveling the world, experiencing culture at its highest level, and interacting with the best and brightest of not only the dance world but society in general. And now, just as she was on the verge of perhaps bringing that dream to reality, it could all be gone. She could not imagine living that lifestyle while still being the kind of mother that she had had and would wish to be.

How the hell could this have happened? She had used a diaphragm and was usually very conscientious about using spermicide, but then it hit her. She had been so preoccupied with packing for the hike that she had not thought to bring her spermicide with her, not imagining in a million years that she would wind up in bed that first night together with Dan. How could she have been so careless? Why was that not on the list of the ten essentials?

She began to think about some of the other alternatives she had considered for her life. Her mother had managed to have a successful dance career with the local ballet company and still raised a child. It was certainly doable if you toned down your expectations and were able to achieve some balance between the two. Then, there was the option of starting her own ballet school and training young boys and girls to dance. That was something she could do out of her own home, and that would allow her to be a full-time mom to her kids while still having a positive impact on lots of other kids. She could foresee that as something that could be very rewarding.

A sense of anxiety and urgency suddenly overcame her. *I've got to find out*, Tawnya thought. She quickly showered and dressed and drove to the nearest pharmacy, where she purchased a packet of home pregnancy tests. She rushed home and went immediately to the bathroom, where she peed on the test strip and then waited anxiously for the results. Two minutes seemed like an hour, but gradually, she saw an image emerge in the window. Her heart sank as she observed a "+" sign and the word "Yes." *Maybe it's a false positive*, she thought as she tried to come to terms with this eventuality. She waited an hour and took another test, only to get the same result. *I need to get final confirmation*, she said to herself, so at 9:00 a.m., she was on the phone to her primary-care doctor's office to schedule an appointment for a pregnancy test. They could not get her in until the following Friday.

It was a long week. Fortunately, she was scheduled to work at The Harbor every evening and had dance rehearsals every afternoon through Thursday, so she was able to keep busy; but, in every quiet moment, her mind was deluged with a cacophony of thoughts and feelings that left her feeling totally overwhelmed. Finally, Friday morning came, and as she waited in the exam room for the doctor to return with the results of her test, she crossed her fingers, hoping it would come back negative.

The doctor returned to the room with a big smile on her face. "Congratulations, you're going to be a mom," she exclaimed. Tawnya's heart sank. The doctor, seeing the look of dejection in Tawnya's eyes, quickly added, "Oh, I'm sorry. Is that not good news?"

"Just not the news I was hoping to hear," Tawnya replied. "I'm not sure if the father and I are ready to be parents right now."

"I hear that a lot," the doctor responded. "Don't worry, most people are a little apprehensive with their first baby, but they eventually warm to the idea and seldom regret it in the long run."

"I hope you're right," Tawnya replied.

Tawnya got home from her evening dance performance around midnight, feeling totally exhausted. She slipped out of her clothes, put on a pair of flannel pajamas, and crawled into bed, only to lie awake, tossing and turning most of the night.

Finally, 6:00 a.m. came and she heard the stereo click on. She was not in the mood for noise this morning, so she got up, turned off the music, slipped on her robe and slippers, and headed to the kitchen for a cup of coffee.

She started toward the lanai but then glanced out the kitchen window to see that it was another gray, rainy Seattle morning, so she detoured to the living room and stretched out on the recliner.

How am I going to tell Dan? she thought to herself. *And how is he going to react? We're both just starting out on our long-term career paths, and this could totally upset our plans. And what about our houseboat? There's no way we can live on a houseboat with a toddler running around.* She felt a pang of guilt about this last thought, then her mind switched tracks to the idea that Dan might not even stick around or might want her to have an abortion. She wasn't sure she could do that.

Tawnya recognized that her thoughts were racing and that she was getting herself worked up to the point of panic. *I've got to calm down and think about this rationally*, she thought to herself. *What are my choices, and what are the logical consequences of each?*

Her mind went first to her lifelong dream of being a prima ballerina and traveling the world with a major dance company. How realistic was that? She knew that she was a good dancer and that she probably had the potential to one day be a principal dancer in a major company, but it would have to be the sole focus of her life. There would not be room for a committed relationship or for being a mother. No man, particularly Dan, would want to follow her around, holding her petticoats while she basked in the adoration of her admirers. And she certainly would not be able to care for a child. And how long would she be able to maintain such a career? What if she were to get injured and could no longer dance or just got too old?

If this were the direction in which she would choose to go, it would mean either getting an abortion or putting the child up for adoption. How would Dan feel about that? They had not even discussed the possibility of having children. And how would she feel about those choices? As a liberal, she had always supported the right of a woman to have autonomy over her own body and to be able to decide if she wanted to bring a child into the world. However, she was also in full agreement with Bill Clinton that abortion should be "safe, legal, and rare." She certainly did not think it should be used as a default method of birth control. Is that what she would be doing? And when it came to the reality of extinguishing a potential human life—a human life she had helped create—could she actually do that? And what about adoption? She knew there were lots of people in the world who were unable to have children but would give anything to be parents. She was sure she could find a suitable couple who could provide a wonderful life for her child, but how would she deal with that? Could she live every day of her life knowing that her child was out there somewhere and did not even know she existed—or, worse yet, thinking she might not want or be able to have any contact with her? She did not have answers to these questions.

Then, there was the option of following the same path as her mother. She could continue to dance with her local company—to still feel the exhilaration and joy of soaring across the stage to the sound of a symphony orchestra and of being the center of an audience's attention—while also being a wife and mother. It had worked well for her parents, and she had thrived as a child in that environment. She could have a nice home and a loving husband and still have a dance career. But was Dan the man she would want to do that with, and would he even want that? Again, she did not have the answers.

Finally, she could give up her dream of being a professional dancer and settle for being a wife and mother. Would she be happy with the life of a housewife? Sure, she could probably start her own dance school, and it might be very satisfying to teach young boys and girls to dance and experience the pleasure she felt on stage. She could even choreograph her own performances, something she had always wanted to do. She could almost see herself in that role—but, again, was Dan the person she would want to share that with, and would he be happy with that life?

The answers did not come and could not come until she had a chance to discuss it with Dan, and she did not even know when he would be home. Finally, she could no longer stand wallowing in her own musings, so she went to the bedroom and put on her jogging clothes. *Maybe a run will help clear my mind*, she thought.

After a six-mile run and thirty minutes of yoga, Tawnya felt better. She showered and dressed in her comfies, then fixed a breakfast of oatmeal and avocado toast. With a fresh cup of coffee in hand, she curled up on Dan's recliner and opened the Ann Rule true-crime story, *The Stranger Beside Me*, which she had bought at the school bookstore the previous week. She had been fascinated to learn that Ann Rule had also been a cop on the Seattle PD and had actually known Ted Bundy, the serial killer who ostensibly began his killing spree in the Seattle area. She spent the remainder of the day absorbed in the details of Ted Bundy's life, only taking a break long enough to grill up a hamburger for dinner. She finally closed the book at midnight, when she could no longer hold her eyes open.

As tired as she was, her sleep was interrupted a couple of hours later by a torturously realistic nightmare in which she actually felt someone pulling her by her feet from the bed and tearing off her pajamas. She let out a blood-curdling scream as she forced herself to wake up. As she lay there breathing heavily and soaked in sweat, she swore she would never again read about serial killers just before going to bed.

Tawnya finally drifted off to sleep and awoke to Nancy on the stereo. She was not ready to get up, so she shut off the stereo and tried to go back to sleep, but to no avail. Finally, she got up and fetched a cup of coffee, then returned to bed, raised the head, and turned on the TV. As luck would have it, the *Sunday Morning* TV show was just starting, which was one of Tawnya's favorites. Next, she watched a couple of Sunday morning news shows before getting up to fix some breakfast. She was famished and decided to indulge in a breakfast scramble. She cut up a potato into small chunks, put it into a frying pan with some crumbled sausage, added some diced onion and garlic, and finally poured the whites and yolks of two eggs over the top, frying everything up. After wolfing down this repast, she poured herself another cup of coffee and retired again to the recliner to finish reading her book.

It was early Sunday evening when she heard a vehicle pull into the apartment parking lot and looked out to see Dan's green Jeep come to a stop in front of the building.

. . . .

Dan arose early Sunday morning, had a quick breakfast of oatmeal with blueberry muffins, broke camp, and headed down the trail. There was a fork in the trail about two miles down from the lake, which would take him back to the trailhead in about twenty miles. He took the fork. His pace quickened as the image of Tawnya standing naked in the doorway of their apartment came to mind. He felt himself getting a slight boner at the thought, which he took as a good sign. The miles went faster going downhill, and by 5:00 p.m., Dan found himself at his car. By 7:00 p.m., he was pulling into a parking space in front of his apartment.

Tawnya was waiting by the door when he came in, but she was not naked. She gave Dan a rueful smile as she kissed him on the cheek. "I'm so glad you're home," she said. "We really need to talk."

"Let me wash this week of stink off my body first," Dan said as he gazed deeply into her eyes in an attempt to discern what might be the issue, "then we can talk all night."

Dan took a long, hot shower, shaved the week's growth of beard from his face, then slipped into an old pair of sweats and headed for the kitchen. He found Tawnya sitting at the kitchen table, drumming her fingers nervously.

He sat down on a chair across from her and, again, looked deeply into her eyes, trying to figure out what was wrong. "What's the matter, babe?" he asked. "You look worried."

Tawnya gazed into his eyes for several seconds before responding. "I'm pregnant, Dan. I had a positive home test on Monday and had it confirmed at the doctor on Friday."

The news hit Dan like the blast of an IED exploding. It was the last thing he had expected to hear. He sat processing this piece of information for a time as he continued trying to read Tawnya's face. Then, with a feigned look of concern, he said facetiously, "Damn babe, how the hell could that happen?"

He immediately saw the look of disappointment cross her face as she said, "I can get rid of it if you want."

Dan could not contain the huge smile that broke out on his face. "The hell you will. That's wonderful news, babe. I can't wait to hear the patter of little footsteps running around the house."

Tawnya continued looking into his eyes, trying to determine if he was serious or just attempting to assuage her feelings. But the happiness on his face seemed genuine. "Are you truly happy about it?" she asked.

"I'm overjoyed," Dan replied as he slipped off the chair and went down on one knee in front of Tawnya while taking the diamond ring that his uncle had left him off his finger and holding it out. "I've gone to sleep all week contemplating when and how I could ask you this question, but you just provided me the perfect opportunity. Tawnya, my love, will you do me the honor of being my wife and the mother of our children?"

She looked at him in amazement; this was not at all the response that she had expected from him.

"You don't have to do this," Tawnya replied. "I would understand if you threw me out on my ear."

"The only place I want to throw you is into bed," he said, "but I need an answer to my question first."

Tawnya looked earnestly into Dan's eyes for several long moments before responding. "I can't give you an answer right now." She saw the look of disappointment and hurt in Dan's eyes and reached out to stroke his face with her hand. "I'm sorry," she said, "but we really need to talk first."

Tawnya spent the next hour expressing to Dan all of the doubts and frustrations she had been having over the past week, concluding with, "We've only known each other for a few weeks. How do we know if these feelings we have for each other are real or if they will last? I feel like I've been caught up in a whirlwind that will one day dissipate and send me crashing back to earth. As much as I care about you, I'm just not sure that I'm ready to give up all my dreams to be a wife and a mother, and I'm concerned about your true feelings for me. I don't know what I want to do."

Dan did not respond for some time. He tried to understand what might be driving Tawnya's reluctance and doubt. He realized that he was a typical male who had been socialized from childhood to believe that men were supposed to be the provider and the protector in a relationship, and that they had to demonstrate dominance, toughness, and self-reliance and never show any vulnerability or express their emotions. He recalled reading a study by a psychology professor named Ronald F. Levant that discussed these issues. He remembered that the study also talked about the male norm of having a strong interest in sex and a disdain for anything feminine, which might be driving Tawnya's concern that he was only interested in her physically. He also had to admit to himself that he had latent tendencies to be chauvinistic and to objectify women, which also might be a contributing factor.

What was it that Levant recommended in dealing with relationship issues? Dan racked his brain for a moment before the answer came to mind. First, only let one person be upset at a time. He had to remain calm and not let Tawnya's obvious ambivalence drive his emotions. What else? *Oh, I need to use reflective communication and let her know I understand what she is feeling and why. Then, I need to let her know what I want in the situation.*

So, Dan took Tawnya's hands in his and looked deeply into her eyes. Finally, he said, "Babe, I know this has been sudden. I could not have imagined two months ago that I would meet both a man and a woman to whom I immediately felt so deeply connected. I do have to admit that my initial attraction to you was mostly physical. You're one of the most beautiful women I've ever met. But those feelings have evolved. I've come to care as much or more for Tawnya, the person, as I do for Tawnya, the gorgeous body.

"I've lost a lot of people I've cared about in my life, and then to have Mick taken so quickly and so tragically made me realize once again how capricious and tenuous life is and how important it is to grab onto and hold the really good people you encounter in life because you never know for how long you will have them. I hear that you have concerns about my feelings toward you, and I can understand what is driving them, but you need to know that as much as I value and enjoy our physical relationship, I cherish our emotional connection even more. I've given our relationship a great deal of thought this past week, and I've never been more sure of anything than that I want you in my life—forever.

"I appreciate that you're having doubts and that you feel that your dreams have been shattered," Dan continued. "Just know this: I want nothing but the best for you and for you to be happy. If that means you moving on with your life without me, I will understand and support you. But don't take my child from me. If you don't want the baby, give it to me. I will devote my life to being the best father I can be. If you want to keep it without me, then at least let me be part of its life. I would be devastated if you decided to have an abortion or give it up for adoption."

The tears welled up in both their eyes. Tawnya reached out and took Dan in her arms and held him tight as both began to sob. "Well, I have to admit that my initial attraction was mostly physical as well, but I really have come to love you deeply. Let's sleep on this tonight and talk about it again in the morning," she said as she stood, took Dan's hand, and led him to the bedroom.

Tawnya assumed her normal butt-in-the-belly sleeping position, and Dan held her in his arms, but they did not make love. Neither slept well. Tawnya's mind retraced all of the choices she had in front of her, and she again weighed the pros and cons of each. Finally, at 3:00 a.m., she reached a resolution and immediately drifted off to a contented sleep.

The stereo went off at usual at 6:00 a.m., with Nancy Wilson singing her version of "How Glad I Am." "My love has no beginning, my love has no end," the song began as Tawnya rolled over and looked Dan in the eyes. He was wide awake and had been for over an hour. He returned her gaze with a look of both concern and affection in his eyes. After several moments, with a blissful smile on her face, she said, "Dan, I have to apologize for ever doubting you and for putting you through such a difficult conversation last night. I only hope you will forgive me for being young and full of grandiose dreams that are difficult to give up. But after lying awake half the night, I came to realize that you and I have something special that I may never find again. I also decided that being the mother of your children would be the most rewarding experience I could ever hope for. So, if the offer is still open, I have an answer for you."

"Believe me," Dan replied, "the offer is not only open but doubly so."

"Then my answer is a resounding and heartfelt yes," Tawnya responded. "My love has no beginning, and it has no end, and I would like nothing more than to be your wife and the mother of your children, starting with this little blob that is growing inside me."

Dan took Tawnya in his arms and kissed her deeply and intensely, which inevitably led to their usual morning routine. As they lay in the afterglow of passion, Dan said, "We need to go downtown and find you a ring,"—to which Tawnya just smiled and nodded her head.

They spent most of the rest of the day in bed watching TV and making love, getting up only to eat and pee.

CHAPTER 26

THE END OF THE BEGINNING

The next morning, Dan awoke just before his stereo was set to begin playing Nancy. He shut it off and crawled back into bed beside Tawnya, who was still sleeping soundly. He dozed back off and did not awaken until he felt Tawnya stirring beside him.

"What time is it?" she asked while sitting up to look at the clock. "Damn, it's almost 8:00 a.m.," she exclaimed. "We never sleep this late!"

"It's a special day, babe," Dan replied, "and we deserve a little extra rest."

"Are we going for a run?" Tawnya asked.

"No, I thought we might engage in another form of physical activity for a while, then shower and go out for breakfast. Then we need to go out and find that engagement ring for you."

"Sounds good to me," Tawnya said as she fell back into his arms.

After forty-five minutes of gentle lovemaking, they finally rolled out of bed, jumped into the shower, dressed, and headed down to their Lake Union diner. After breakfast, as they sat at the outdoor patio table drinking coffee, Dan said, "I better call Headquarters and see what the status of the internal investigation is. And, by the way, have you heard anything about when Mick's funeral is going to be?"

"Oh, damn, I should have told you yesterday," Tawnya replied. "I read in the paper that it was going to be this Wednesday—that's tomorrow."

Dan made a call to the patrol commander to check on the investigation and was told it was still in progress but not to worry about anything. "Everyone I've talked to said this was the most righteous shoot we've ever had in the Department," the commander said. "By the way, we'd like you to say a few words at Mick's funeral tomorrow and to also be a pallbearer. I'll send you an email with all the particulars."

"I'd be honored," Dan replied. "Thanks, Captain."

"See you there," the commander replied.

At 10:00 a.m., Dan and Tawnya headed downtown to make the rounds of the jewelry stores. After three hours of shopping, Tawnya said, "Let's go back to that first store we were at. I think I like a set we saw there the best."

Ten minutes later, they were in the store sizing rings for each of them. They had lunch at a little French café while the rings were being adjusted to fit. Back at the store, Tawnya squirmed nervously as they waited for the jeweler to bring them out. Finally, he came out of the back room with two small felt boxes. He first showed Dan his ring, then handed Tawnya's jewel box to Dan, saying, "You can do the honors."

Dan carefully removed the engagement ring from the box. "To a forever marriage," he said as he slipped it onto Tawyna's extended ring finger. Tawnya threw her arms around Dan's neck and kissed him deeply. They spent the next several hours walking around the Arboretum and then the boat docks in Ballard before going to The Flame, the little steakhouse in the same neighborhood that was one of Dan's favorites. After a celebratory dinner of filet mignon and grilled shrimp, they returned to their little abode and sat on the lanai, sipping tea.

"Do you think this apartment is going to work for us once the baby comes?" Tawnya asked.

"Nope, I think the next thing on our to-do list is going to be house hunting," Dan replied. "Unfortunately, I don't think a houseboat on the lake is going to be in the cards with a baby on the way. We may have to save that until we retire."

Dan and Tawnya then retired to their bedroom, stripped off their clothes, raised the head of the adjustable bed, and turned on a movie. As the last scene came to a close and "The End" popped up on the screen, Tawnya said, "No, this is just the beginning," as she stroked Dan's rapidly hardening member.

....

Wednesday morning dawned clear but cool. Dan awoke full of nervous energy and needed a run to burn some of it off. After a light breakfast, Dan and Tawnya showered together and then got dressed for the funeral.

Dan put on the dress-blue uniform that he had purchased the day before. Fortunately, it fit perfectly. He turned to Tawnya, who was sitting at her small makeup table, and asked, "What do you think?"

"You look fabulous," Tawnya answered, "like a knight in shining armor."

"I wish I did have some shining armor," Dan replied. "I'm nervous about getting up and speaking."

"You'll do great, baby," Tawnya said. "You're one of the most articulate people I know."

They arrived at the large Catholic cathedral on Capitol Hill an hour before the ceremony was scheduled to begin. Dan was astonished to find that the large parking lot was already full of police cars from departments all over the state and the Pacific Northwest. Marked cars were also parked at the curb for three blocks in either direction. A sign directed them to another overflow parking lot two blocks away, where they were able to catch a shuttle that was ferrying people to the church.

The first two pews were reserved for family and close friends, and Dan and Tawnya were able to find a seat in the second pew from the front, just behind Mick's three ex-wives and all three of his children. Dan introduced himself to each of the ex-wives and offered his deepest condolences. "You're the one who took out his shooter, aren't you?" one of the wives asked. Dan nodded his head. "Oh, thank you, thank you, thank you," the woman responded. "I couldn't bear the thought of that asshole walking the face of the earth after what he did." Dan smiled sadly and put his hand on her shoulder before sitting back down.

The formal ceremony was quite impressive, full of the pomp and circumstance so characteristic of the Catholic Church. Finally, the priest ascended the pulpit and announced that several speakers would be making remarks. First, the chief of police came forward and praised Mick Donnelly's long and impressive record during twenty-five years of service on the Seattle PD. Then came the patrol commander, who gave a more detailed account of Mick's many accomplishments and outstanding arrest record. Finally, it was Dan's turn.

He stood at the pulpit and looked out at the crowd for several seconds before beginning.

"I only knew Mick Donnelly for less than two months," Dan began, "but it feels like he has been part of my life from the womb. I began to think of him as the father that I wished I had had, and I learned more from him in the past two months than I did studying criminal justice for six years in college. I have known some good men during my service in the military, but I never met a man with the courage and dedication that Mick Donnelly displayed every day that I worked with him. I can only hope that I can bring a tenth of the honor and accomplishment to the job as he did throughout his twenty-five years of service. He was a cop's cop, and I'm sure I speak for every one of the many officers who have worked with him over the years when I say that he will be sorely missed. However, if Mick were able to rise out of that casket and speak, I'm sure he would say, 'At least I died doing something I loved.'"

Dan then walked over to the closed casket, placed both hands on top, and bent over and kissed the top. "We loved you too, Mick," he said and walked slowly back to his seat.

The ceremony concluded, and Dan joined the other pallbearers as they hoisted Mick's casket to their shoulders, carried it slowly from the church, and placed it in the awaiting hearse. Dan and Tawnya joined the chief of police, patrol commander, and their wives in the stretch limo that was reserved for them, which fell in behind the family's limo as they followed the hearse out onto the road. It was a ten-mile drive to the Veterans' Memorial Cemetery in North Seattle. A line of police cars stretched out for miles behind Dan's limousine, and a cadre of motorcycle officers escorted the procession to the cemetery.

As a veteran, Mick Donnelly was buried with full military honors. The honor guard asked Dan to present a folded US flag to each of Mick's three ex-wives, which he did with pleasure. Each of them seemed genuinely touched by the gesture, and Dan could see the gleam of tears in each of their eyes. They each knew that they had lost someone special.

After the ceremony concluded, Dan spotted the patrol commander standing near the edge of the crowd and made his way over to him.

"I'm ready to go back to work," he said. "When do you expect the internal investigation to be done?"

"By the end of the week," the captain replied. "Why don't you plan on coming back next Monday if you don't hear something different from me in the meantime? There will still need to be a coroner's inquest, but it appears to be an open-and-shut case, and you will be fully exonerated of any wrongdoing. See me when you come in next week."

"Will do," Dan responded as he shook the captain's hand.

....

Dan and Tawnya sat on the lanai drinking coffee the next morning while discussing what kind of a house they would like to buy. Tawnya had come to terms with and now fully accepted that becoming a prima ballerina, at least with an international dance company, was not going to happen, and she was more than ready to start a new life as Mrs. Dan Reynolds. They both agreed that they would need a large two-story with at least five bedrooms because they planned to fill it up with kids. Dan had been thinking all the previous evening about where to buy and now decided it was time to share his thoughts with Tawnya. "Hey babe, I've been thinking that I would like to get a home in the Central District, preferably in my sector," he said. "I just think that if I want to have any credibility with the people I serve, I need to be a part of their community."

Tawnya looked at him with a troubled expression for several moments before replying, "Damn, honey, do you really want to raise our children in a low-income, high-crime area like the CD?"

"I know, that concerns me too," Dan responded, "but I feel like such a fraud riding onto their turf for eight hours a day on my big white stallion, pretending that I understand them and their issues and that I really care about them and want to protect them, and then going home after shift to my safe little abode in a lily-white area of town. I want the people in my district to feel like I'm invested in them and that we have common interests. I want to get involved with their community organizations and really contribute to improving the area. I think we could make a difference."

"I don't know," Tawnya replied. "I would constantly be concerned about not only our safety but our children's. And what about the schools? I want my kids to have the opportunity for a good education."

"We'll take precautions." Dan responded. "We'll install a security system with cameras and solid-core doors, and I'll buy you a gun and train you how to use it. Between the two of us, we can drop off and pick up the kids from school. We'll do whatever we need to do, but hopefully, by the time our kids are in school, we can accomplish the improvements to the area that I think are possible. Think about it. I can get involved in the community policing program and in the activity program for the kids, and maybe you could start a dance class. We could make a real difference in some of these kids' lives."

Tawnya ruminated on the idea for several minutes. She realized that she had always felt guilty for having been blessed with so much in her life while so many children of color lived in poverty and deprivation. Perhaps they could make a difference. Enabling even one child to escape from a dead-end existence would be a lifetime achievement. "Okay, I'm on board," she said finally. "Let's do this."

They spent the rest of that week looking at houses to either rent or buy. The price of homes in the Seattle area was astronomical, but they found that those in the CD were much more affordable. Dan still had the modest inheritance that his mother had left him, which he hoped would cover a down payment. Plus, he would be able to get a VA loan. After three days of looking with a real estate agent, they found an older two-story home in the CD that needed a lot of work but was structurally sound and had real possibilities. They decided to make a low-ball offer and see what happened. As it turned out, the owner was a retired army sergeant who had read about Reynolds in the newspapers and wanted to help out a fellow veteran.

The overjoyed real estate agent called them at 9:00 p.m. on Sunday evening to inform them the offer had been accepted. Dan and Tawnya celebrated in their usual fashion—naked in bed.

On Monday, Reynolds showed up at the Headquarters precinct at his usual time, an hour before his shift started. He was not sure where he would be assigned, so he spent time just perusing police reports from George sector and looking for major crime incidents. A half-hour before roll call, he walked to the patrol commander's office and found him sitting behind his desk. Reynolds knocked once on the outer door jamb and stood waiting at attention. The captain looked up and motioned for him to come in. Reverting to his military training, he walked briskly to the front of the captain's desk, stood at attention, and saluted. "Officer Reynolds reporting for duty, sir," he said.

"At ease," the captain replied, "have a seat."

The captain looked at him for several moments with a serious look on his face and then broke into a smile. "Welcome back, Officer Reynolds. We missed you. I want to personally commend you for your actions at the bank two weeks ago. You displayed an extraordinary degree of discipline and courage, not to mention outstanding marksmanship. As a small gesture of our gratitude and appreciation for your heroism that day, I would like to offer you Two-George-Three as your permanent district. You deserve it, and it's what Mick would have wanted."

"I'm honored," Reynolds replied, "but I'm still on probation. I didn't think probationers were allowed to have a permanent car assignment?"

"Considering your background and training, we're going to make an exception in your case. We'll pair you up with relief officers who are off probation until you decide who you would like as a permanent partner."

"Thank you, sir," Reynolds responded. "I promise I won't let you down."

With that, Reynolds stood to attention, saluted, did an about-face, and walked out of the office. The shift lieutenant called him over as Reynolds walked past his desk.

"Dan, I have something for you," he said as he walked to a cabinet in the corner of the office and pulled a large attaché case from its bowels. "Mick would have wanted you to have this." He handed the attaché case to Reynolds, who immediately recognized it as having belonged to his partner.

"Did you inventory its contents?" Reynolds asked cautiously as he took the case.

"Nope," the lieutenant replied, "we were afraid of what we might find."

Reynolds walked to the roll call room and took a seat at a desk. He shut his eyes, took a deep breath, exhaled slowly, and said to himself, *Welcome to the rest of your life, Dan Reynolds.*

THE END

Made in the USA
Columbia, SC
26 January 2025

23613134-ca97-4bee-aab4-54b4d8ec7210R01